Gulian Lansing

Egypt's Princes

A narrative of missionary labor in the Valley of the Nile

Gulian Lansing

Egypt's Princes
A narrative of missionary labor in the Valley of the Nile

ISBN/EAN: 9783337243999

Printed in Europe, USA, Canada, Australia, Japan

Cover: Foto ©ninafisch / pixelio.de

More available books at **www.hansebooks.com**

THE CONVENT OF OUR LADY DAMIANE.

EGYPT'S PRINCES.

A Narrative

OF

MISSIONARY LABOR IN THE VALLEY OF THE NILE.

BY

Rev. GULIAN LANSING,

MISSIONARY OF THE UNITED PRESBYTERIAN CHURCH IN EGYPT.

"Princes shall come out of Egypt."—Ps. lxviii. 31.

NEW YORK:

ROBERT CARTER AND BROTHERS,

No. 530 BROADWAY.

1865.

EDWARD O. JENKINS,
Printer and Stereotyper,
20 NORTH WILLIAM STREET.

CONTENTS.

(iii)

PREFACE.

THE Egyptian proverb says, "*Cast him into the Nile, and he will come up with a fish in his mouth.*" Without laying claim to the uniformly lucky character which this proverb describes, I may say that having been providentially delayed in this country a few months longer than I anticipated, the present volume is the result. Unable to sustain the wear and tear and excitement of a tour through the churches, to inform those interested in our mission work, of what the Lord has done in opening the door of faith to the descendants of Ham, I trust I have not been presumptuous in the hope that in this way I could best serve His cause in that land.

This volume does not pretend to give a complete view of the work in Egypt; it describes only one of its departments. This department I am conscious furnishes a field for stirring narrative, and the description of exciting personal adventure, which might not be found in our more settled work in Alexandria and Cairo. It

(7)

is not, however, on this account that I have selected it, but because, from reasons stated in the
introduction, I alone have had of it the notes
which form the basis of the narrative.

I may here be permitted to state, that I think
there is, in our churches, far too prevalent a taste
for the stirring and romantic in mission reports.
The missionary who explores an unknown continent, who wades rivers, traverses burning deserts, and impenetrable thickets, and fights with
wild beasts, and even with more savage men, is,
on his return home lionized, and it *may be* right
that he should be; but should not then his more
retiring brother, who spends long years in the
hard back-bone toils of the study, or the tread-
mill of school and pulpit duties, come in for his
share of the glory? I would rather traverse
Africa from Alexandria to the Cape of Good
Hope, than undertake a second time to master
the Arabic language. The dashing adventurous
raid, and the crash and shock of contending
armies on the battle-field, furnish material for the
graphic and entertaining narrative; the more
laborious and tedious processes of the siege—
the hard toil with mattock and spade—are
despised. In Alexandria and Cairo we have
had committed to our care large numbers of
young, impressible souls; and in training them
in our schools as well as in the regular services
of the sanctuary we have spent years of toil.

We have been digging deep, and laying broad and firm the foundations, while our enemies have said, " What do these feeble ones ? If a fox go up he shall even break down their stone-wall." Under the mask of patience and hope we have labored on, and at length, God in his providence has removed the mask, and our enemies see with confusion that a deep trench has been dug and a solid breastwork built in front of their very citadels; and late reports from Cairo show that a strange, mysterious light from heaven is playing about our ramparts which attracts to it all eyes. This, the work of years in these great cities, I have not undertaken to describe; I have only attempted to give a view of the beginnings of a great work in the whole land of Egypt.

"Princes shall come out of Egypt; Ethiopia shall soon stretch out her hands to God." And they *are* coming out of Egypt. This narrative shows, that crushed and down-trodden though they be in that the "basest of kingdoms," poverty-stricken and despised by their proud rulers, and by all who behold them, there are yet many who in noble friendship and generous hospitality, and earnest adherence to truth, are indeed princes, and we trust that this may soon be true, not of individuals alone, but of *the people;* that the voice from heaven shall soon proclaim, " Blessed be Egypt, *my people;*" yes, and Ethiopia shall soon stretch out her hands to God. The first subject of that work of grace which is now in progress in Cairo, is the daughter of an Abyssinian (Ethiopian) woman.

I may state that the first five chapters of this volume were published some time since in the columns of the "Christian Instructor." Had time permitted they should have been remodeled and presented in a somewhat different form.

It is usual in the preface of a book to say something about the critics. All I have to say is, that missionaries who are faithful to their work must be content to forego the distinction of becoming *literati* in their mother language. This should be kept in mind by those who are disposed to complain that missionaries are dull and uninteresting in their narratives. I have endeavored to give a truthful account, as far as it goes, of the people of Egypt, and of the work of the Lord among them, and if the critics wish to break a shaft with me, it must be on Arab steeds and in the field of Arabic literature.

G. LANSING.

LISHA'S KILL, N. Y., *Feb.* 12*th*, 1864.

EGYPT'S PRINCES.

CHAPTER I.

In September, 1860, the Egyptian Mission of the United Presbyterian Church of the United States put into execution a project, which for some time previous had been entertained, of purchasing a Nile-boat, for facilitating the work of the mission in Upper Egypt. The reasons of this movement are briefly stated in the following extract of a letter, written from Alexandria to the Board of Missions in Philadelphia, under date of September 29th in that year :

"1st. We were convinced, from the experimental trips which we and other missionaries had made, and the representations of reliable men from Upper Egypt, that it offered us a missionary field of great promise. The people among whom we are especially called to labor at present are the Copts, and the Copts are mostly in the Upper country. There are but few of them in Lower Egypt, and scarcely any in Alexandria, except in summer, when a large

number of government scribes are here with the
court; and even in Cairo a large proportion of
the Coptic sect is in government employment:
a very unfavorable circumstance for our work,
as they must sacrifice their Sabbath days; and
the man whose interests, nay, in this case his
very livelihood (for these men are fit for nothing
else but this work, to which they have been
trained from youth), force him, systematically,
to violate his conscience in any one point of
known duty, is encased in an armor of brass,
invulnerable to the shafts of truth.   But the
Copts of the Upper country are, for the most
part, poor and simple-minded peasants, and it is
usually among the poor and unsophisticated that
the gospel has the freest course.   They are, as
to intelligence and wealth, in social character
also, the lowest of the eastern Christian sects;
but yet there are, in their condition, several
grounds of special hope.   They are a thoroughly
humbled race.   The iron heel of despotism is,
and long has been, upon their necks.   From
your stand-point you may not be prepared to
regard this as a ground of encouragement; but
if you had known, as I have, the self-sufficient
pride and upstart vanity of *young Syria* (caused
by the spring and re-action of a too sudden deliverance from despotism), you would understand what I mean.   'It is not the whole, but
the sick, that need a physician.'   Christ now, as

in the days of his flesh, calls not the righteous, but sinners, to repentance.

"2d. They have never enjoyed (or rather been cursed with and ruined by) a European protectorate; and hence they do not regard, as do the Greek and Catholic sects, Russia and France as their Gods. Israel trusted in Egypt, rather than in God, and the broken staff pierced their hands. Thus has it been with the Christian sects of Syria; and even now, in this respect, they revolt more and more, and we believe that they will therefore be stricken yet more.

"3d. They have, at the same time received substantial benefits from England; and they regard Englishmen and Protestants as their friends, and in a special manner us missionaries, from the good service which we have rendered them, both by our books and personal efforts, in resisting the proselyting encroachments of the Jesuits and other Catholics. Meshakah's* Controversial Works are eagerly sought and read by them. They use them as an armory against Popery, and in the end they find that they have undermined their own superstitions.

"4th. Their priests have never taken a stand

---

* Dr. Meshakah is a native of Syria, resides in Damascus, and is a member of the United Presbyterian Mission Church in that city. He is a man of rare abilities and worth, and is the author of several valuable works well adapted to meet the peculiarities of the native mind.

against the Bible as the priests of the other sects have; and the extent to which it has been purchased and read by them is, as compared with the other sects, remarkable. This is the people to whom Providence is, for the present, calling us to direct our efforts.

"5th. We cannot undertake this work by personal, permanent residence among them. Their land is the valley of the Nile, from Alexandria to Assouan, a distance of seven hundred and fifty miles, and each mile has its village or villages, and many of these contain Copts. To occupy this field would require an army of missionaries, and you have given us but little hope to expect so many for some time to come. While in most of the villages that contain Copts there are only a few families, or a few hundreds of souls, there are only a few large towns like Osiout, Girgeh, Esneh Negadeh, and Ekhmim, in each of which there is a population of a few thousands; but even these we cannot attempt personally to occupy, for we have not the men; and, if we had them, it is very doubtful whether families could live in the hot climate of Upper Egypt during the summer season, and at any rate they could not be sent there without physicians. In this state of the case, we have concluded that all we can do for the present is, to settle at the chief points as fast as we can secure the services of reliable and trained men, schoolmasters and evangelists, whom we must visit as often as practicable, in a boat, during the winter season, staying at each place as long as may be possible, and at the same time visiting the unoccupied villages, or distributing books, and directing itinerating work. Thus we will be able to exercise a strict supervision over the men whom we may employ, and they will gather a nucleus for us in the towns in which they may be placed, and in other places the way will be prepared for more permanent settlement.

"6th. To attempt this work we needed a boat of our own. Egypt is becoming more and more every year the sanitarium of the north. We could only make our trips in winter, and in winter there are crowds of invalids and other travelers here, who have raised the price of boats to from two to three hundred dollars a month, an expense which we could not think of incurring. Nothing remained for us, if we would undertake the work which I have described, except to purchase a boat for ourselves.

"7th. We were induced to undertake this enterprise now, because as you have determined to send two more families here, we feel that we will then have a sufficient force, and be in other respects in a position to undertake this work.

"There is another very important consideration. We have no mountains here to which we can resort for a change of climate in summer.

We have found the summers, both at Alexandria and Cairo, very trying, especially for the children, and the experience of the English residents also is, that they need to spend every third or fourth summer in England, which we think is oftener than you will want to see us. A change to a Nile boat for two or three months is, in a *sanitary* point of view, a very profitable one, and our plan is to employ in this Nile service the invalid family whichsoever one it may be.

"Such, briefly, are the grounds on which we have taken this new and important step, and Providence favored us with the offer of a boat admirably suited to our purposes, and at a very reasonable price. We purchased it of our friends, Messrs. Corlett & Fleming, of whose kindness, in times past, in giving us the use of their boats for short trips, when it was not the season of travel, we have already informed you. It is an iron boat, called the "Ibis," eighty-three feet long by twelve feet in the beam, with three masts, a large cabin, and four staterooms, pantry, etc., in the centre, and a short deck at each end. We have paid for it $1,500. This is a large investment, and we should, perhaps, have first asked your advice, and made an appeal for the money. As to the former, we were all so fully convinced of the wisdom of the measure, that we were sure you

Egypt's Princes.

THE NILE BOAT.

P. 16.

would approve of our action; and as to the latter, our experience of the delays and comparative failure of appeals has been such, that we felt it was our duty to take upon ourselves personally the pecuniary responsibility of the enterprise. We have, therefore, put together our little private purses, and this not being sufficient, we have taken the liberty of making a draft upon the "Building Fund" for the balance, which, as it has not yet reached proportions sufficient to warrant our commencing that enterprise, we are not likely to need for some time. Nor have we done this without a reasonable prospect of replacing the money. The season of travel is about eight months, viz., from September to March, inclusive. From two to three months are needed for the trip, (most of the travelers perform it in two,) so that three trips can be made in a season. Our plan is to make one trip in early autumn, so as to be back by the last of November, which is the height of the season for travelers, and then let it for a couple of months, which we can readily do at the above-mentioned rates. In this way we propose paying our debt to the Building Fund, and after that supporting the enterprise; and, as I before said, we have taken the entire responsibility. The expense to the Board will be the wages of the boatmen, about $50 per month, *while the boat is engaged in missionary work,* unless the exigencies of the

2*

work should be such as to demand that we forego the opportunity of letting her for a trip during the season of travel, when the expense will
be heavier.

"I have been engaged the last week in fitting
her up for her special service. The bathing
room has been transformed into a book depot,
and in it and in the hold thirteen large cases of
books have been securely stowed away. I have
also made forms and tables for two schools,
which we hope to be able to open at Osiout and
Thebes, and next week Brother McCague* proposes starting. I could say much of the bright
prospects which this enterprise opens up to us,
but I prefer waiting until we can write history.
In the meantime we ask your special prayers for
this work."

Brother McCague, who undertook this first
trip in the "Ibis," was forced on reaching Luxor
hastily to return to Cairo, on account of the illness of Mrs. McCague, when it was agreed by
the Mission that I should undertake a second
trip, and the following are the notes of that
trip:

I have long entertained a strong prejudice
against "missionary reporting." While ready
to admit that those who support missionaries in
foreign lands have a right to know in general

* Rev. Thos. McCague, of Ripley, Ohio. He sailed from this
country for the missionary work in Egypt, Sept. 30, 1854.

how they employ themselves, and what measure
of success they meet with—while I know too
that the continued interest of many in the good
work, and the amount of support which they
contribute, depend in far too great a measure
upon the success they meet with—and while I
also know that the continued interest of many in
the good work, and the amount of support which
they contribute, depend in far too great a measure on the motives and incentives which may be
brought to bear upon them from abroad and not
upon the more solid foundation of Christian principle, and the motives which are furnished by
the love of the Saviour shed abroad in the heart,
and his revealed will as our King and Head, and
that taking human nature as it is, it is our duty
in a measure to fall in with this desire; I still
feel that missionary reporting has been in many
cases overdone, and that many evil consequences,
both at home and abroad, have resulted.

I have, therefore, seldom kept a diary, and
still seldomer thought it prudent to send it
home for publication. To keep one, however,
during our winter's sojourn in Upper Egypt
was a necessity. The work was, in many respects, different from the one which we are called upon to undertake in our regular stations in
the large cities. I was continually meeting with
new faces, mingling in new scenes, and acquiring new and often novel experiences, and, much

of the time, so rapid was the change of scene, that even had I anticipated a speedy return over the same ground, the brief record which I have made of facts and memories would have been very profitable for future direction. But since I will probably be followed in the work by other brethren of the mission, to leave such a record of acquaintances formed, and experiences acquired, of names and facts, and statistics, as shall enable them to begin where I have left off—to sow where I have passed over, and water what I have sown—to beware where I have erred, and to labor harmoniously in carrying on that which has been well begun, and thus to build upon the foundation which (not I, but) the Lord has, I trust, laid for a great and permanent revival among the Copts of Upper Egypt,—becomes not a matter of either vain glory or of mere expediency—but a necessity.

My notes were for the most part hastily sketched in pencil after the day's work was over, and they are now presented to the public with the hope that they may be instrumental in exciting an increased interest in the truly interesting field which the Lord has opened for us in Upper Egypt, and in securing that earnest prayer for our success, and that increased supply of men and means which we so much need.

Of the purchase of the " Ibis," and of the general plan of work which we thus proposed to ourselves, an account has already been given. Brother McCague's hasty trip as far as Luxor was a proof of the wisdom of the step we had taken, and an earnest of still greater results yet to be hoped for. He was absent only a month and a few days, and was then forced to return so hastily, that he only had time to call at eight principal places, and yet he sold books to the amount of $120, and opened schools at Osiout and Luxor.

On the day of his return, (November 8th,) the remains of our little one were buried from our sight in the cemetery of Cairo. Having given up our house in Alexandria to Mr. Hogg, we had been unable to secure another suitable one. By long continued attacks of ophthalmia, together with watching with our child, both Mrs. L. and I were much reduced in health, and thus Providence indicated, and the brethren decided that we should follow Brother McCague in the work which he had so well begun—and with heavy hearts we set about the necessary preparations.

We took with us Faris, a converted Maronite priest, who had come to us well recommended by the brethren at Beirut, and who, during a few months' residence in Cairo, had proved himself zealous and able in the work of the Gospel.

We left Old Cairo on Wednesday, the 21st of November, at 8 o'clock A. M. The wind was light at first, but it soon became strong, and

continued thus all day, of which we were not
sorry, as there are but few Copts residing between Cairo and Beni-Souef.   At the latter
place we would gladly have stopped, as Brother
McCague had left an interesting record of acquaintances formed there—but the wind was
fair, and in going up the Nile the true policy is
to stop only when the wind fails.   In coming
down, one has the stream always in his favor,
which, with the oars of his trusty crew, give
him, as it were, both ends of the rope in his
hand, and he can command his movements; except when a strong North wind baffles both current and oar; but in going up he is dependent
upon the wind; and if it fails, or is contrary, he
must lie by, unless the men "track," or drag the
boat by a long rope from the shore, which is so
slow and laborious a process, that I could seldom allow them to do it.   We passed Beni-
Souef at midnight.

22d. Awakening early, I found we were an-
chored just above Bibbeh.   We filled a bag with
books, and started up for the town, inquiring
our way to the Coptic quarter, which we found
to be quite on the north side of the town, and a
long-before-breakfast walk.   Faris, and Abdallah
our servant, were praying for a "propitious
opening" to our work, to which, in every great
undertaking, the Arabs attach much importance.
As for myself, I must confess that I went with

a heavy and misgiving heart. Indeed, my heart had been buried in that little grave in Cairo, and I felt much more like musing than working. How prone is the mind, under such circumstances, to lose interest in transitory things, and even in that good work in which our hands should do with their might whatever they find .to do, and to prey upon itself. At first, my forebodings seemed about to be verified. We were led to the church, and in it we found the Kummus.* He said they were all supplied with books, and he was evidently disposed to turn a cold shoulder upon me and my books. All I could say, I could not interest him. Stunned and staggered as I had been by the blow of God, and weak and faint with our long walk, I was about giving up in despair when a couple of boys coming in, I told them to run away and tell their parents and friends to come for books, and I sat down in the court of the church to see if any would come. In a short time I was rejoiced to find that twelve or fourteen had made their appearance, and one of the first who entered was a man who almost snatched the book, saying, "I'll take it and spend my evenings reading it!" and he kissed it and pressed it to his bosom with evident delight. Soon after another came in, and taking a copy, said with an

* The Kummus is the third in order of the Coptic priesthood, being beneath the bishop and above the priest.

emphasis which was not feigned, "It is honey-comb! it is honey-comb!" Another excited a no less deep, though a painful interest. He was an aged and venerable-looking man, and the principal speaker. He said that their religion was to fast when the priest fasted, and feast when he feasted. When I opened the Testament and read, he said that the Kingdom of God as likened to hid treasure was the Virgin Mary, and he showed the low state of morality in the place by making, in the midst of the conversation, and in the courts of the Lord's house, and before old and young, an unblushing mention of a sin, with the name of which I dare not blacken this page.

We conversed with them about an hour, and I was much pleased with the interest which some of them manifested, and with the skillful manner in which Faris managed his part of the conversation. When we left, we found that we had sold but three Bibles, but the interest with which they listened, and the sad degradation and ignorance which they manifested at once encouraged us, and drew forth our sympathies. I felt the torn and entangled tendrils of my rift heart interlocking again with this good work, and entwining anew around the poor people of this dark valley, and raising me up from prostration.

We reached the boat at 9 o'clock, and imme-

diately set sail. The Coptic population of Bibbeh is only about forty taxable males, but we
were told that there were many more in the surrounding villages who here attend church.
The church was a large and fine one, recently
built; indeed, not yet finished. They said that
it had been built by the purse of St. George;
and a rude likeness of the fabulous cavalier,
with his dragon, was carved above the door.

We sailed all day, and at midnight passed
Minyeh, the second "bender," or large town.
The night was dark and stormy, and the "Ibis"
inclined and tossed so much as quite to give us
the feeling of being at sea. We found in the
high wind the advantage of her peculiar rig.
She has three sails, the large one being in the
centre, while the native boats have but two, the
large one being quite in front. To a light breeze
they can spread as much canvas as we can; but,
under a heavy wind, they must lie by entirely,
lest their big sail should capsize them; while we
can scud under our foresail. We passed a number of Dahabiyehs containing travelers, who had
left Cairo several days before us, to their no little mortification.

23d. We sailed again all day. During these
two days I became much interested in reading
Syriac with Faris, in which I found him an ac-
complished scholar. He could correct the vow-
eling of the Bible Society's edition of the Pesh-

3

ito, and give the grammatical reasons for his suggestions.

Thus to fly along under full sail is most delightful and exhilarating. The only drawback was that Mrs. L. had been suffering since we left Cairo under a severe attack of neuralgia, which made us fear that we, too, might be forced, like Brother McCague, to turn back.

We reached Osiout at eleven o'clock at night, having been just sixty-three hours from Cairo, including seven hours of stoppage at Bibbeh. The distance is 254 miles!

As Osiout is the largest and most important town in Upper Egypt, I will leave the narrative of what took place in it for another chapter.

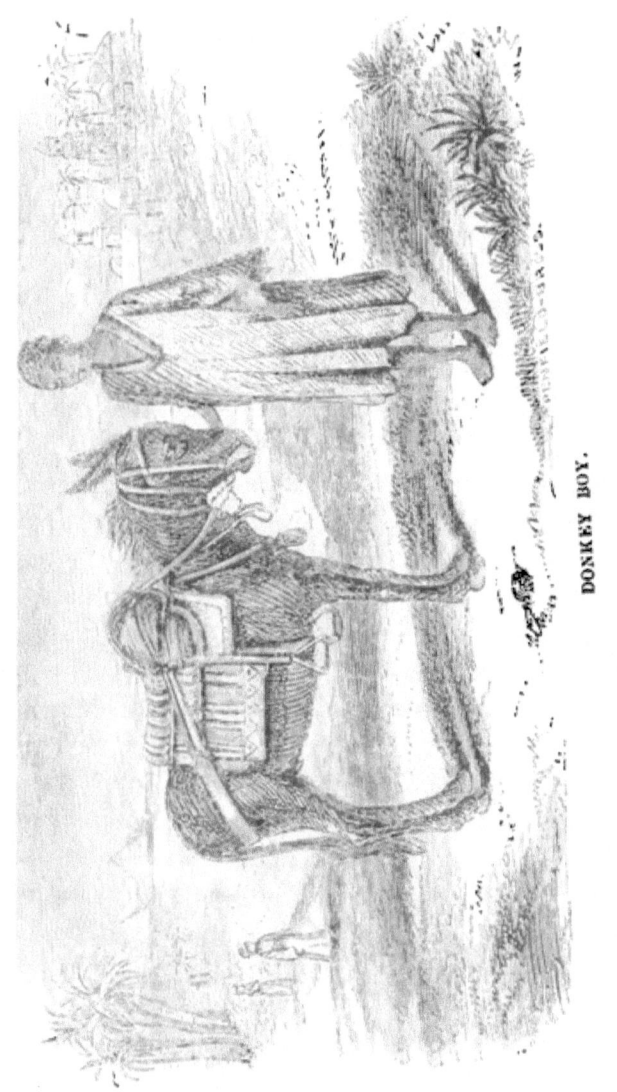

DONKEY BOY.

CHAPTER II.

Osiout, 27th November. Taking a hasty break-fast, Faris and I secured donkeys, and started up to the town, which, unlike most other large towns, is not on the river's bank, but about a mile and a half inland. The road to it is over a raised cause-way or dyke, called in Arabic a *jisr,* (bridge,) which keeps the communication with the river open, even in the time of the inundation. These "*jisrs*" are very common all through the valley of the Nile; they are from six to ten feet high, and serve for roads between the villages, as well as to detain for irrigation the waters which by the inundation and the canals are distributed over the land. The building and keeping of these in repair, as well as the digging of the canals, is a great slavery for the poor fellaheen.* The ride up to the town is delightful, amidst green fields, and luxuriant fruit gardens. The gate of the town presents one of the best specimens I have seen of the oriental institution of "the gate." Within it is a fine open space, shaded by a few large lebbekh trees, and on either side are the Government offices and

* The common people.

court rooms, occupied by gaudily dressed, portly Turks, and lean, Coptic scribes in black. These are the "Elders sitting in the gate." Oh, when in all the cities of this land, shall the walls be salvation, and the *gates* praise? Then, when that Church shall be established against which the *gates* of hell shall not prevail?

We found our way up to the house of Wasef, who is the American Consular Agent and a Copt, and, after making our call of ceremony, went to the school, where we found Ibrahim, the teacher who had been left by Mr. McCague. There were but five boys in the school, but we were pleased to find him at his post, and busy, especially as it was Saturday, when neither his contract nor the example of our school in Cairo, which he had attended, obliged him to teach, and he had no previous notice of our coming.

I must here go back a little, and bring up the history of this movement. When Brother Mc-Cague came with a teacher, a number of the leading Copts, and also the Bishop, manifested a good deal of joy in the prospect of having a school; and the Bishop furnished a school room. But he had scarcely left when the "*Areefs*," (the blind schoolmasters,) whose influence with the people is in many places even greater than that of the priesthood, took the alarm lest their trade of teaching, (not the young ideas how to shoot, but the young throats how to shout—viz., the psalms and dead Coptic prayers,) together with their small, resultant gains, should be cut off, and, accordingly, they set themselves to crush the school in the bud. The Bishop is an old man, more noted for his monkish austerities than his powers of government, and the Areefs easily persuaded him to take their view of the subject, and call a meeting of the sect, at which the Areefs, with all the vociferous clamor for which they are noted, insisted on expelling Ibrahim, with his new-fangled school books and apparatus from the town. This would have been done, except that the Consul and a few of the "pillars" of the people, the parents of the five children, interposed their veto, and so it was decided to write to the patriarch on the subject, asking his opinion, and requesting of him a teacher of a class superior to the Areefs. This request they had made some time before, and he had declined acceding to it, and they now agreed that if he did not send one, they would support our school. His answer had not yet come, though ample time had elapsed; but it was easy to foretell what it would be, as to the general question of supporting our school, whatever he might do in sending another teacher. The Patriarch, elevated to his seat by the influence of the English Consul at Cairo, and in spite of the strong opposition of Abbas Pasha, who was then on the throne, had forgotten the Protestantism which he pro-

fessed while yet a monk, and violating the
pledges of reforming the Church which he had
then taken, had recently been guilty of various
acts of opposition to our cause, and petty persecutions of Protestants; and it was, therefore,
easy to divine what his decision would be. I
saw that a heavy cloud was gathering; nay,
had already descended upon our infant movement there, and as Ibrahim was young and inexperienced, I determined to leave Faris to take
the helm and endeavor to outride the storm.   I
had hoped to be able to take him with me to assist
in the work of book distribution, and to pursue
with him my Syriac, but I saw that it was more
necessary that he should remain.

In the mean time, I did all I could to prepare
the minds of those whom I met for the Patriarch's answer, and I found the occasion a very
opportune one, for the Patriarch had just sent
his agents to levy on the sect a heavy tax to
assist in building the new church, which he had
recently commenced in Cairo. This "*scheme*"
was already a very unpopular one with the people, and it did not help it any when I told them
that I had been credibly informed before leaving
Cairo, that he had sent to Europe an order for
25,000 piasters* worth of images for the new
church, (the Coptic, like the Greek Church, does
not use images, but only pictures.) The Copts,

_____

* A coin about 3¼ cents in value in Egypt, and 4½ in Syria.

besides, have never been accustomed to the expense of building, nor the luxury of worshipping in marble cathedrals. Their churches are all very plain, and they are strongly possessed of the primitive (not present,) Wesleyan notion, that this best befits the simplicity of the gospel, and I found they had most extravagant reports of the thickness of the walls, and the costliness of the materials of the Patriarch's new Cathedral in Cairo. Human nature, too, is everywhere the same, and I found them very ready to listen to me in a matter in which their pockets were concerned. They were greatly scandalized by another fact, of which I informed them. The Patriarch had recently set up with the money of the sect, a printing-press, when, sending for one of the beautiful reference testaments of the Beirut press, he asked at what price the Americans sold it, and when told at 13 piasters, he said we will leave the printing of Bibles to them; we cannot print them at that price—and the first book he undertook to print was, "the Story of Antar," —a vile Mahommedan novel, which is read in the Cafés. Word had also reached us at Cairo a few days before, that at Bosh, (near Benisouef,) where he was at that time, he had prohibited the people from buying Bibles from Lord Haddo, (a step for which the Coptic Church is not yet at all prepared;) I told them that the answer which they would probably receive from his Holiness would be, that they must neither receive our books nor our teachers, but must wait until his edition of Antar should be published, and that then he would send a quantity of them, together with a teacher to teach their children to read them.

They fully felt and admitted the force of these things, and much more that I said; but, alas! the Copts generally are fully persuaded that the priests, however ignorant, or perverse, or degraded they may be, are yet the vicegerents of God, and hold the keys of the kingdom of heaven, and, until convinced of the contrary, they may despise, but they will still obey the priesthood.

25th, *Sabbath.* Having been invited by the Consul, Faris and I went up to his house and spent the day. He had provided an abundant dinner for us, which we would have enjoyed more had it been on another day. We spent most of the day in religious discussion and instruction, and trust good was done, although most of the time only three persons were present. We went to call on the Bishop, but he was not in, for which we were not sorry. On a pillar in the court of his house a notice was posted, indicative of the state of morality among the Copts. With many apologies for the apparent breach of the established usages of society, it informed guests that arrack could not be furnished them when they called.

On our way back to the boat we met Bakhtor,

and here, again, I must return to bring up the
thread of the history. Bakhtor is a priest, who
five years ago when I first came to Alexandria,
used to come to us on Fridays, with some other
Copts, for instruction. He has lately spent most
of his time in Cairo, and been under instruction
with the brethren there. He had been truly
enlightened in the knowledge of the truth, and
was convinced, while at the same time it was
evident that he was not very brave or decided
in its profession. He is one of those timid
spirits, who are made for peaceful times. He,
however, offered to labor for us in Osiout. His
native village, Benoub, is near this place, and as
he there has some little property, we agreed to sup-
plement his livelihood by a salary of four dollars per
month, and so he came up with Brother McCague.
When the Areefs raised their little storm, he
feared and fled—at least he made an excuse
to go to Benoub, his native village, and Mr.
McCague, on his return from Luxor, on finding
him absent without sufficient reasons, left word
with the Consul, that we should no longer consider him in our employment. He was just
now returning, and our meeting him was very
providential. He immediately saddled his ass,
and followed us down to the boat, and I heard his
explanation of his leaving. It appeared that he
had better reason for going than we had thought,
and, besides, he had labored under certain little

misunderstandings, into which I need not now
enter. Suffice it **to** say, that I was satisfied
with his explanations, and told him that if he
would **resume** work, (colporteuring and talking
with the people in Osiout and the surrounding
villages,) I would pay him his wages on my
return, **to** which **he** agreed. I spent the evening in conversation and prayer, **with him and**
Faris, and Ibrahim, endeavoring to prepare them
for the work and the trouble which I foresaw
here in store for them.

26th. We hoped here to have overtaken Lord
Haddo, (since Lord Aberdeen,) who had left
Cairo thirteen days before us; but those thirteen
days had **been** days of prevailing south wind,
and we were sorry to learn, on inquiring from
other boats coming down, that **we** must have
passed him in the night at Minyeh. As his Lordship's **name** will hereafter be much connected
with this journal, **and as we** are much indebted to
him **for** his zealous co-operation and assistance
through the winter, **I** may as well at once gratify
the desires of an innocent curiosity, by saying, that
being a great invalid, he had come out from Great
Britain to spend the winter in Egypt for the bene-
fit of his health, and that unlike many Christian
travelers, he had brought his Christianity with
him, and was anxious to do all he could for the
promotion of the Master's cause, and especially
in the **work** of Bible distribution.

He had taken from us at Alexandria, a quantity of Scriptures and publications, of the Beirut press, and I had a further supply for him on board the "Ibis," which he had ordered before leaving. We had also given him Father Makhiel, a converted Coptic priest, to act as colporteur. He had invited me before leaving Alexandria, to come up in mid-winter, and spend a month with him in the work, but there was then but little prospect that I would be able to do so; and, of course, he was not aware of our present undertaking. I was anxious to see him, in order to deliver the books which I had brought, and to arrange our plans for future work; but he had not yet come, and might not for several days, and as we did not wish to lose so much time, we could only leave a note and proceed on our journey. His lordship having been received as the guest of the government, a fine large Dahabiyeh* had been placed at his disposal by the Viceroy, who in such matters is most liberal. He had also given him a firman to all the sub-governors in the Upper country to treat him as became the royal guest. This, it will be seen in the sequel, greatly facilitated our work in many places, and gave to it a prestige which it could not otherwise have had; but, on the other hand, it was not without its disadvantages. We have always found it best to do our

* Nile-boat.

work as humbly and quietly as possible; and
thus, as far as possible, avoid attracting the
public attention. " He hath chosen the weak
things of the world to confound the mighty."
" The kingdom of God cometh not with observation."

We bade adieu to our friends and left Osiout,
at 9 A. M. The wind was light, and at 2 P. M.,
just as we were at dinner, it failed us altogether
opposite Abutij. We took this as a providential indication that we must stop, and I sent
Abdallah and one of the sailors up with a basket
of books. After dinner I attempted to follow
them, but a canal between the river and the
town made a long detour necessary, and, after
walking about half an hour, a severe headache
warned me to beware of sun-stroke, and I returned. Several of the people, however, came
down, and I sold them a number of books. Abdallah soon came back, when, on making our
accounts, we found that we had sold books to
the amount of about $15. They told us there
were 4,000 Christians in Abutij, and some of
those who came to the boat to purchase said
they were from Ez-arabeh; a place some distance inland not put down on the map, in which
they said there were also 4,000 Christians, but
that they had no church: the Moslems would not
allow them to build. One of those who called,
I am sorry to say, asked for arrack before leav-

ing, and Abdallah found, on counting his books, on his return, that two or three of the smaller ones were missing, having been stolen in the crowd and confusion with which he was surrounded while selling in the town. We left again at half-past 6 P. M.

27th and 28th. Winds light and varying most of the time, but still fair, and we made no stop.

29th. At 8 A. M., opposite Ekhmim, where we would gladly have spent a little time, as it is one of the largest Christian towns in the country; but the wind was fair, and we pressed on.

Reached Ghinneh at sunset, and just after a heavy rain-cloud appeared over the eastern hills. The wind suddenly went down, and it became very warm and sultry for a time, which was followed by a smart shower of rain. The north wind was piercing and cold all night.

30th. Went up to Ghinneh at 8 A. M. Though thickly clad, I think I have never before, in Egypt, suffered more severely from cold than in the ride up to the town, which is about a mile from the river.

As I had by mistake written Negadeh on the list of books left here by Brother McCague, for sale, I was not aware that he had left any; and as one of our sailors said he had gone to the Dewan and sold books, I concluded to try the church, and gave orders to the donkey-boys accordingly. They took us through many winding

4

streets to the farther side of the village, when
we were brought to a stand at the door of what
they said was the church, beside which, under a
shed, we found an Areef, with nine urchins.
He started to bring the keys of the church, but
we stopped him, and, after some preliminaries,
told him that we wished to sell books, and asked
him where the priest was, or the men of the sect,
who would buy.　He said the priest was at Farshoot, and the people scattered about through
the town at their work; but that if we would
leave the books with him till over Sabbath, he
and they would see them, when they came to
the church, and might buy.　At the same time
he looked over the title-pages of the books, and
remarked, "All from one press, all from London."　This smacked of Rome, and aroused my
suspicions, and a few leading questions brought
out the following facts, viz.: that this was the
church and school of the Coptic *papal* church;
that the sect consisted of one hundred souls (I
was afterwards informed that this was a large
story), and that the absent priest was an *Italian*,
to see whom I made no promise of remaining
over Sabbath.　As the Areef had his eyes on
the books, he was turning on a little foot-lathe,
preparing beads for the sect, which gave employment to his hands, eyes and feet, while his mind
(no, that was sold to Rome), his ear was engaged
in hearing the sing-song repetitions of the pupils

of Coptic prayers, to him, and to them, unintel-
ligible; yes, dead Coptic prayers! Oh, Rome!
true is thy boasted " *semper et ubique eadem*," for
dead Coptic in Ghinneh is the *same* as dead Latin
in the rest of the world. Only thy motto might
better have been, " Always and everywhere,
anything ;" *anything* that will take with the people; anything that will deaden the intellect and
crush the soul, and further thy selfish ends.

We gathered up our books and left. On our
way back, Es-seyed, one of our sailors who had
accompanied Brother McCague, said that he had
left books to be sold, with a man in the city, and
so we threaded our way through the intricate
streets to his shop, which we found in the main
bazar. This man's name was Ibrahim, a deacon,
and evidently a nice, intelligent, young man. As
he had only Bibles and catechisms, and I had
other kinds of the Beirut publications, I took
my seat beside him in his little shop, and hailing
every man with a black turban* who passed, we
sold during the forenoon to the amount of 220
piasters, which, added to the 430 piasters which
he had sold of the books left by Brother Mc-
Cague, made 650 piasters in all. Good business,
this.

After securing a stock of vegetables and other

---

* The different classes of the people are indicated by the
color of the turban. The Copt wears black, the Moslem white,
and a descendant of the Prophet green.

necessaries from the well-stocked market, we went down to the boat. The brother of the French Consular agent and a number of others accompanied us, and we had with them an interesting conversation. Having heard of our schools in Osiont and Luxor, they urged us very strongly to establish one here also, which I think we should do as soon as possible, as this is a large and important place.

I saw very few signs of that licentiousness which travelers take so much pains to describe. Only in one street I saw a few of the *Ghawaze** sitting at their doors.

As Ibrahim was about to shut his shop and remove to Erment, to accept a situation as secretary in the sugar factory there, I took the books which he had remaining, and closed accounts with him, of the necessity for which I was very sorry, as he had evidently done his work well and faithfully.

The Coptic sect in Ghinneh numbers between 4,000 and 5,000. They have no church, but are forced to go to Denderah to worship, which is full five miles distant, and on the other side of the river. During the time of the inundation, they can often scarcely get there at all. This is a great hardship, but it is the law of the land that no church shall be built without a special permit from the Government, and it usually re

* Dancing girls.

quires a great deal of bribery and influence to
obtain one, and the Muslems in the place in
which the church is proposed to be built, usually
interpose as many obstacles as they can. They
told me a long and sad·story of the efforts which
they had made for a long series of years to obtain a permit. As far back as the days of Mohammed Ali, they had by some means procured
one, and commenced building, when the Muslem
Sheikhs arose and said that Ghinneh was one of
the stations of the holy Haj (many of the pilgrims come up the Nile as far as this, and then
cross over to Cossier on the Red sea, and so to
Mecca,) and that it could not be polluted by a
Christian church.   Both parties represented
their cause to Mohammed Ali, and he at length
decided that the walls which had been raised
should be torn down, but that the Christians
should be refunded the expenses which they had
incurred in building from the public treasury!
Here, you will say, was "even-handed justice,"
in the midst of the grossest injustice; for why
should the Christians not be permitted to build
wherever they have the land, and the means, and
the power to do so?   But alas! you know little
of the spirit of Islam.   The Catholics, however,
have a church, the permission to build having
been secured by the French Consul, and in this
they possess a great vantage ground for proselyting from the Copts, and yet they have succeeded

4*

very poorly. The more I see of the Copts, and learn of their history, the more I admire the constancy with which they have withstood for ages, the persecutions and annoyances of the Muslem power, and of late years the machinations of Rome also. I often wonder that the very name and every trace of Christianity have not long since been swept from the land. It would have been so, but that the Copts are a most constant, earnest people. Truly they deserve our deepest sympathies and earnest prayers, and in reference to this matter of church building, the Consuls of the Christian powers should unite to insist on the removal of the present restrictions; and were they to do so, I am confident they would succeed. But alas! too many of them have their own private ends to compass with the Government.

We set sail at 2 P. M.

December 1st. Found on awakening that we were becalmed on the western bank. Took a cup of coffee, and started out for a morning's walk. On reaching the top of the bank, I saw the ruins of the temple of Karnak, (the most Northern of the Theban temples,) and yet, the wind being south, and the course of the river very tortuous, our poor men toiled against the heavy current until 4 P. M., ere reaching Luxor. The day was bright and calm, and the temperature delightful—the first day we had which at all

met my ideas of the Egyptian climate. All the
way from Cairo we had had it most uncom-
fortably cold, and especially at night; the difference between the temperature by day and by
night surprising me—the night being very cold,
and even by day the winds were raw and pinch
ing, having a strong smell of Alexandria and
the sea in them. But to-day, all was mild,
and genial, and bright—and as we sat on the
deck, winding amidst the historic scenes and
classic ruins of ancient Thebes, it was a time for
sentiment and poetic musing—but I will spare
my readers. My business is with modern—not
ancient—Egypt; with its moral ruins, and not
its pictured tombs and stately temples. These
latter have been a thousand times described by
others who have leisure and talent for the task—
and who can see in them all, and much more,
than I can to admire. One sound touched my
heart more than all the voices coming down
from antiquity. It was the song of the turtle-
doves in the acacia groves on the banks. This
has always been to me a most affecting song.
It speaks of the condescension of our God.
Under the Jewish economy, the poor believer
who could not bring his bullock or goat was
directed to bring two turtle-doves, or two
young pigeons, to be offered on the altar of his
God as a sacrifice for his sins. It was the poor
man's offering. In almost every grove, and often

in the courts of the houses, these doves may be found in abundance, so that they were always accessible, and no man could plead excuse for wanting an offering. They are usually seen in pairs, and the mates are seldom far apart, and the plaintive ditty with which the day long they respond to each other, always brings to my mind a sentence which it not a little resembles in length and division of sound—"*Unto the poor the gospel is preached.*"   Before we had left Cairo, a friend had given Mrs. Lansing a pair of Meccan doves, which not a little resemble the turtle-dove, only that it is often pure white, with a black ring around the neck. Their song is also shorter, and the Muslems fancy that it resembles the words—"*Ya Kareem,*" (Oh, most merciful One,)—and hence they call them Kareemies, and esteem them much. But our poor male bird had been killed by some evil cat which had found her way to the deck of the boat the night we were in Ghinneh, and the mate was now sitting disconsolate and with ruffled feathers, mourning her loss. There are voices in nature which speak most touchingly to the soul. But oh, how often we are forced to feel that there is in our hearts a sad want of harmony and unison with them !

As we neared Luxor, the men and boys, recognizing our boat, flocked down to the shore to meet us. I went up with them to Monsur's room, but did not find him in.* He had taken advantage of his Saturday's vacation in the school to go over to see the ruins on the other side. The Bishop, however, soon came down, and invited me up to his house. It consists of three rooms on the roof of the church, and a fine view is obtained from it of the ruins of Karnak, and the magnificent plain of Thebes. The valley of the Nile is here very wide, and clothed as it is in the richest green, and thickly dotted with clumps of acacias and palms, marking the positions of hamlets and water-wheels, with here and there the columns and gateways of the ancient city towering above all, and enclosed in the distance by the yellow Arabian and Lybian hills, which, at sunset, would glow like a framework of burnished gold; it was a most charming picture—one which I could never weary with admiring.

Monsur soon came, and our coffee having been finished, the Bishop took us down to the church. He himself has built it, mostly by the aid of donations received from the travelers to whom, during the winter season, Thebes is the great centre of attraction. It is a large and solid building, with two rows of pillars in the midst supporting a raised roof, through the win-

---

* He is a teacher whom Brother McCague had left here. He is a Syrian, a graduate of Abeih Seminary, and a very promising young man.

•

dows of which light is admitted. A raised place
in the back part—about one-third of the whole
area — constitutes the women's department,
though it has not yet been partitioned off by the
usual lattice-work screen. Here I was happy to
find the school forms which I had had made
before Brother McCague left Cairo; but was
sorry to find that the native carpenter had made
a very bungling hand of setting them up.
Brother McCague had established the school in
the house of the Prussian Consular agent, who
is a Copt, and who at Cairo had offered us a
room for the purpose. But as the season for
the travelers drew near, he seems to have hoped
that some invalids wishing to spend a few months
at Thebes might need it, and prove more profitable tenants; and so he had sent Monsur notice
to move the school to some other quarter. In
this emergency he went to the Bishop, who received it into the church—with what ulterior
ends, the sequel will show. The first interview
with him led me to suspect the purity of his
motives; for as we came out of the church he
pointed to a vacant lot just beside it, to which he
had brought a large quantity of bricks and building material, and on which he said he wished
to build a school-house, as it was not fitting, he
said, that the school should permanently remain
in the church; but that he was in need of the
wherewith to go on with the building. I told

him we would help him all we could, but determined not to commit myself too far. The Bishop failed us in the end, but he never deceived me. In looking over my letters written to Cairo at the time, I find, under date of the succeeding Monday, the following :" The Bishop professes great devotion to our cause, but of course has his ends. Still, it is a favorable breeze, to which, for the time being, we must open our sails, making the most of it."

2d, Sabbath. The Bishop having invited us to attend services in the church, and Monsur informing me that he thought they would allow me to preach, I sent up on Saturday evening to inquire what would be the Scripture lessons for the morrow. That in the Gospel was Mark x. 17–31. I could not have asked a better text, and spent till one o'clock in the morning in preparing to preach from it. The exciting anticipation of having the privilege of preaching in a Coptic church, awoke me by starlight, but withal I was not early enough, for I was but just fairly seated at my coffee and eggs, and the sun, not yet up, was beginning to gild the western hills, when two messengers came from the Bishop to tell me to come, as the services had already commenced. I hastened up to the church with my Testament under my arm, and was pointed to a chair beside his reverence. They were reading and chanting their prayers, partly in Arabic, but mostly in

Coptic. When the time came for reading the
"Lesson" from the Gospels, the Bishop first read
it in Coptic, with a deacon standing on each side
of him with a lighted candle. He then asked
me to read the translation in Arabic, and I took
my place behind the stand on which the books
were placed, (there being no pulpit.) One of the
deacons came to me with a lighted candle, but
looking up to the windows in the roof, I remarked that there was light enough, and I could
see to read, which provoked a smile from those
around, and he took his seat. I read the passage above mentioned, when the Bishop asked
me to expound, and I commenced my sermon.
The men and boys, large and small, were sitting
around on mats, and the women in the raised
place in the back ground, where the school is
kept. There were, I should think, from 150 to
200 present, and they were all very attentive. I
spoke about three-quarters of an hour, when I
could see that the Bishop was getting uneasy,
and I stopped. He had good reason for uneasi-
ness, for he had not yet had his breakfast, and I
found that they had yet the long services of the
mass before them. When all was over I found
that it was nearly nine o'clock, which, considering that the service commenced before sunrise,
made a long—not *sederunt*, for as the church, like
most churches of the East, was unfurnished with
seats, the people *stood* most of the time. The

Copts are as noted in the East as the Covenanters in the West for the length of their services, and when we consider that they are almost altogether in incomprehensible Coptic, we must at least admire their patience. As I went out of the church I could not help exclaiming, Poor, poor people who have no food but this for their souls.

But to return to the mass, or Kuddas as they call it. The Bishop asked me to go into the Holy of Holies, which, as I had never witnessed the ceremony in Coptic, I did. The inner room, which I have called the Holy of Holies, as it corresponds to that department in the Jewish temple, is a small room about ten feet square, arched over-head, with a narrow door on each side, leading into small dark vestry rooms. It is separated from the body of the church by a chintz veil, into which an opening is cut, large enough for the entrance of a man: (this veil occupied the place of the panelled and carved partition or image-stand in finished churches,) and back of the veil is the altar, (a stone one, and not a wooden table which the high-church-men would doubtless rejoice to learn,) covered with a cloth much greased by the droppings of the candles. The officiating priest, a fine-looking young man, whose acquaintance I had made the day before, was dressed in a dirty white linen robe, with a shawl of the same material over his head,

5

and around his face, on which were embroidered
fancy designs and crosses. He stood in front of
the opening, just within the veil and before the
altar, and of course with his back to the people.
Besides him and myself there were in the inner
room a deacon, (who swung the censer which
was occasionally replenished by the priest from
a little box of frankincense beside him, from
which he each time took a pinch, at first with
his naked fingers, but after he had washed his
hands for the manipulations of the mass, with
an intervening cloth,) and four boys, one of whom
was also robed. The service was altogether
Coptic, and was chanted; the deacon and boys,
and also at times the people outside joining in
the responses. The bread was a round cake,
about three inches in diameter and one in thickness with a square figure like a Jerusalem cross
in the center, which they say represents the Saviour, and around it twelve other similar smaller
crosses, for the twelve apostles, and five small
holes pierced into it to represent the five wounds
of the Saviour, and around this figure the passage, "Glory to God in the highest, on earth
peace, good will to men," in the Coptic. The
silver platter containing the bread, as well as
the cup which was placed on a raised stand in
the center, were each covered with several small
silk embroidered cloths of different colors which
were slowly removed, two by two, by the priest,

and then held up in succession beside him on a level with his shoulders, while he was repeating the service. After removing all the cloths, he performed various manipulations over the bread, such as crosses, passing his finger around the edge of the cake, placing it over the cup, and holding it in one hand and placing the other over it while he was constantly repeating the service. He then broke the bread into, I think, five pieces, one of which he dipped into the cup, and then pressed it upon the other pieces successively. He then ate a part himself, and the rest he administered to the boy in robes, the latter walking around the altar after each mouthful, holding a cloth closely to his mouth, to prevent the possibility of a crumb being lost. The wine was then taken with a spoon also by the officiating priest and the boy. Throughout the whole ceremony, the greatest care was taken to prevent the waste of a crumb of the bread, or a drop of the wine. Every time the priest lifted or touched the bread, he very carefully rubbed his fingers over the platter, and after the bread was eaten he first carefully picked up the crumbs, and then rubbed the platter over and over again, with his forefinger, which he each time licked off with an appetizing smack, which must have made the teeth of the poor people who were fasting outside water. The bread was elevated several times to a level with his head, when the people

bowed most of them half way, but many of them
with their faces to the ground. At particular
parts of the service, too, the people repeated
prayers, apparently very devoutly and earnestly,
with their hands and eyes lifted to heaven.
When all was over, the Bishop came within,
and standing before the opening in the veil,
blessed the people by putting his hand upon the
face of each as he passed, and repeating the
words of the benediction. He then broke and
handed to the people without one of the cakes,
over which they had a good-natured scramble,
each trying to get at least a crumb. This of
course was not considered as part of the sacrament, as the bread had not been blessed. It is,
I think, the love-feast of which we read in early
church history. In the Greek church I have
seen a large dish of bread thus distributed. He
then gave Monsur and me each a loaf, and one
for Mrs. L. when we left. A Coptic priest can
seldom be met on Sabbath after mass but he will
take from his bosom and offer one of these
cakes; and it is done with an air which shows
that it is regarded as an act of Christian recog-
nition and brotherly good feeling.

Afternoon. Saw a man whom I knew, from
his black turban, to be a Christian, fishing with
a net ; called him to the boat, and remonstrated
with him for breaking the Sabbath. He said,
"You are a priest, are you not?" I said,

"Yes." "So am I," he answered. "Then," said I, "you are a successor of those who were fishers of fish, and the Master made them fishers of men, and you should this day be engaged in this latter work." I talked with him a long time, but evidently without making much impression. He admitted the truth of what I said, but appeared to be a man whose mind had been embittered against religion. Speaking of him to another priest, in the evening, the latter told me that he had not been at church for years; that he was so hardened a man, that on one occasion he saw him beaten by order of the bishop, until he seemed almost dead, and the boils broke out all over his body, and yet he was obstinate; he would not yield. In thinking of this afterwards, it seemed to be a very pertinent illustration of Deut. xxiv. 3 : "Forty stripes he may give him, and not exceed; lest if he should exceed, and beat him above these with many stripes, then thy brother should seem vile unto thee." This man, by being over-beaten, had "become vile" in the eyes of his fellow Christians, and lost his own self-respect. It requires some insight into oriental character to understand this. We certainly would judge the contrary, viz.: that his power of endurance and strength of will, in not yielding, would be a matter of pride and boasting to him. We certainly, under like circumstances, would be apt to say, "The bishop

5*

whipped me until he was tired, and I did not give up," and claim from others praise for manliness and strength of character.

The fact of his being thus beaten, thus inadvertently mentioned, shows what episcopal authority and church discipline are among the Copts. Jacob, the Bishop of Minyeh, who died a few months ago, was noted for the free use which he made of the naboot.* He is said to have had several of different sizes, which he had named after the names of some of the apostles and fathers. These he had standing in the corner of his room, and his custom was summarily to deal with each case coming before him, by ordering the offender on his face, and then ordering one of his deacons to bring St. Paul or Peter, or Cyril or Athanasius, according to the gravity of the offence. He is said to have killed two men under the naboot. Thus he, as well as we of the Westminster Assembly, had degrees of church censures. It seems hard—but what can be done with a people who have no keen sensibilities except in the soles of their feet, and with whom admonition, reproof, rebuke, etc., and even excommunication would be little more than empty sound or idle wind. With a people such as the Egyptians, I believe in the bastinado. They are grown children, and for children Solomon pre-

* The naboot is a heavy club of about six feet long, and an inch in diameter.

scribed the rod, and Solomon was wiser than our modern suasionists. I would, however, far prefer seeing the rod in the secular hand.

This Episcopal power seems to be a remnant of the old Egyptian regimen, when the priests of towns were their governors, and the temples were at the same time the palaces. Joseph married the daughter of the "prince" or priest of On. Our marginal Bible gives the second meaning as a various reading, but his father-in-law probably united in his person the two offices, which we know from the sculptures was the custom with the ancient Egyptians. The name was preserved after the two offices were separated. In 2d Sam. viii. 18, David's sons are called " chief rulers;" literally "Kohenim" (priests). But they were not priests, for that would have been against the Jewish law; and, besides, we are informed in the preceding verse that Zadok and Ahimelech were the priests. The word is the same, but the offices had now become distinct.

While on the subject, I may mention two other analogies between the modern and ancient priesthood. In Gen. xlvii. 22, it is said: " Only the land of the priests bought he not; for the priests had a portion assigned them of Pharaoh, and the priests did eat their portion, which Pharaoh gave them ; wherefore they sold not their lands." From this we learn that the priests were proprietors of land. And when the land

of Canaan was divided under Joshua, the priests
also had their cities, with their suburbs, assigned
to them.   So the modern Coptic priesthood do
not consider it derogatory to their sacred character to be possessors of houses and lands.   I
was reliably informed that Jacob, above mentioned, possessed at his death 2,000 acres of the
rich land of the Nile valley, and that cash to the
almost incredible amount of $80,000 was found
in his coffers, which all fell to the Patriarch of
Cairo, as being the heir of the Church, or rather
of her heirless bishops.   So our friend, Father
Makhiel, pointed out to us on Saturday, from
the roof of his house, his lands and possessions,
both in the town and beyond on the plain.   This
system has, we think, *here and in the present state
of religion and society*, great advantages.   It
renders the priesthood independent: an advantage which our English friends boast of as the
result of their establishment, with its " regium
donum;" but to my mind, on many accounts, a
much less dubious advantage here than there.
It enables men like Bukhtor, who has some
property of his own, to come out on the side of
truth, without any fear of being starved by the
people on whom he is dependent, or a cruel
mother church; and where the weekly functions
of the priesthood do not require a week's laborious study and preparation, but consist for the
most part of an hour's senseless vociferation and

manipulation, it is much better that the priest
should spend his week days among his cattle
and crops, than in the houses of his parishioners,
and that he should earn his bread by the sweat
of his brow, by plying the plow and the mattock, than that he should be left to depend for
his livelihood upon the low arts of a selfish
priestcraft, and the cunningly devised rites of a
superstitious and secularized church, that he
may thus reach through the enslaved consciences
of a debased and abject people their tightly
drawn purse-strings. Whether I am right in
ascribing the fact in a great measure to this or
not, it is nevertheless the fact that the Coptic
priests do not assume nor possess that absolute
power over the consciences of their people which
the priests of the other eastern sects do, notwithstanding their occasional use of the naboot.
And in this fact is one of our strongest grounds
of hope for the Copts.

Another point of analogy was the special favor
shown to the priesthood by the government.
The land of the priests bought he not, and
yet their necessary portion of daily food was
assigned them of Pharaoh. And thus to the
present day the priests have many immunities
and privileges. To us, the wisest of these appear to be that we missionaries are allowed to
bring into the country Bibles, books, and whatever else we need, free of custom, and that we

have the privilege of traveling free on the government railway between Alexandria and Cairo.

Monday, 3*d*. Two other priests called. They asked for instruction, saying that they were ignorant. I handed one of them the Testament, and he opened it and read the parable of the ten virgins. I called their attention to the great lessons therein taught—that a large portion of those that are in the church or kingdom of Christ, will be found foolish virgins, who, in the last day, will find the door of the kingdom of heaven shut against them; that the foolish and wise virgins appeared as to externals the same; that the difference consisted in the oil of divine grace being found in the hearts of the wise and not in those of the foolish ; and that it was their duty first as individuals, to ascertain their own state, and then, as priests, to do all they could to save their people from the awful dangers of self-deception. This latter duty I further urged upon them from another passage which he next turned up—viz. " Whosoever offendeth one of the least of these little ones that believeth in me, offendeth me," etc. They appeared attentive and teachable, and I gave them some directions how they should pursue the study of the Scriptures, and promised to instruct them further on my return.

We went up to the school, and a good sight it was. Forty boys were present, fine looking fellows, with the old Egyptian contour of face, and bright eyes, only one pair of which seem to have suffered from ophthalmia. Heard about fourteen of them read, who read very well in the Testament.

Next called on the Bishop : he again spoke of building a school-room, and said that the materials were ready, only that he had no money to pay the workmen. I promised to endeavor to obtain some assistance from the travelers on my return from the South. Noticed the inscription above the church door. It stated that the church was built by Father Makhiel, (the present Bishop) that it was dedicated to St. George, and its date was 1574, from the martyrs, a memento of the bloody reign of Diocletian.

We started at 4 P. M., but the wind being unfavorable we did not make much progress. Noticed that most of the peasants were naked, with the exception of the white cotton cap, which many of the children were without, and the apron or bandage about the loins just as they are delineated in the sculptures.

4th. Reached the sugar factories of Mustapha Pasha, at Erment, at 2 P. M. The appearance of the settlement from the river is the most beautiful I had seen since leaving Cairo. The dull brown bank of the river, which, with the yellow hills in the back-ground, is almost all that can be seen, day after day, from the deck of the boat, was here covered with a coat of luxuriant halfeh grass—from the water's edge a winding stone stairway led up to the top of the bank, on each side of which was a fine antique statue, with a couchant lion on a block of granite. Along the bank was a fine avenue of acacias, with an underbrush of tall reeds on each side— in the back-ground were the extensive factories and works, with the houses of the operatives, all built in a modern and chaste style, and neatly plastered—and over the corners and sides of some of the snow-white houses were creepers of deep green. On the one side were the picturesque pigeon towers, with their myriad flocks of circling tenants, giving life and cheerfulness to the scene, and on the other side was the tasteful mansion of the Pasha, surrounded by what was evidently a well arranged and well stocked garden, and over all towered three tall chimneys, one of the sugar factory and the other two of the steam pumps which poured their life-giving tide into the vast plain of luxuriant sugar-cane in the back-ground. Nor was it as it is usually the case in oriental scenery, distance alone which lent enchantment to the view. On closer inspection, the details were found to sustain and strengthen the general impression. All was neat, and clean, and tasteful, and the Pasha's garden, with its vine-trellised walks and bowers, and every variety of flowers and vegetables,

and shrubbery and fruit-trees, (the latter including even the apple and pear of more northern
climes) was a delightful combination of the useful with the beautiful, and took us back to lands
where taste has been long and studiously cultivated, and where horticulture has become a
science; and when, with Mr. Scott, the chief
engineer, I visited the pump and factories, and
examined their immense machinery, it was difficult to realize that we were in Africa, and 500
miles from the sea-board.

This settlement shows how easily Egypt might
be made the garden, as it has for ages been the
granary of the world. These tasteful and comfortable houses were altogether constructed of
sun-dried bricks, with rafters of the split trunks
of the every where abounding date palm, covered
with the branches and leaves of the same, and a
layer of earth; and there are no heavy rains to
melt the frail materials. Where stone is necessary, as for supporting the heavy machinery, it
is everywhere at hand in the neighboring lime-
stone ranges, which enclose the valley, or in the
adjoining temples, the most of which (antiquarian
research and æsthetic enthusiasm to the contrary, notwithstanding,) could be put to no
better use—and labor is cheap. There is a
teeming population, and the necessaries of life
are few and easily obtained—so that the wages
of a master mason are 25 cents a day, and of a

common laborer 7 cents. The bright sun and
genial climate, the matchlessly fertile soil, and
the great Nile, which pours its tide of liquid life
through the length of the land, and with its
canals and lesser water courses, which carry its
fertilizing and vivifying stream, even to the feet
of the Lybian and Arabian ranges, and its annual
overflow, with its rich deposit, make its soil
perennially a virgin soil. These are conditions
of agricultural prosperity which I believe are
found in no other known land, and under their
influence the more tardy and slowly maturing
wonders of the vegetable kingdom, as well as
the more speedy and useful annual crops, spring
up under the hand of culture, and come to ma-
turity as if by magic. Of the latter, wheat, Indian corn, rice, cotton, and sugar-cane are the
chief, and they are staples in the world's market.

Modern enterprise and the modern code of
political economy would say that there is one
thing wanting, viz. : coal, that powerful agent
which generates steam, and has in modern times
made the wilderness and the solitary place to
blossom like the rose. But coal can here be dispensed with, for if Egypt becomes the producer
of the world's necessities she may well afford to
continue dependent on others for the few luxu-
ries which she needs. The vessels which bear
cotton for the hands, and wheat for the mouths
of the overworked denizens of Manchester, may

continue to bring back a few bales of cotton
stuffs, for the thin blue shirt and the heavy white
turban, which are alone needed by the unsophisticated dwellers of this genial clime. What! you
will say, depend on the fickle winds and sullen
stream of the Nile to bear the wealth of Egypt's
productions five hundred or one thousand miles
to the sea-board! Yes, for the navigation of
the Nile has facilities which no other river in the
world possesses.

For nine months of the year the famous Ete-
sian winds blow steadily from the north by day,
wafting along the lateen-sailed craft with a rapidity which almost equals steam; and by night
the swollen and rapid stream quietly bears down
the heavily-laden craft with almost an unequaled
rapidity, so that I believe were the Lybian hills
coal, and the Arabian iron, it would be a long
time before steam and steamboats could compete
with the clumsily made native djerms. It could
not until that passion for rushing ahead which
has possessed, and is ruining the Western nations, shall have taken possession of Egypt also;
and I trust that day is far distant. No! the
cheery songs of the Nile-boatmen are better than
the crash and roar of the steam-engine—and
what though you be sometimes becalmed?
An occasional day of quiet meditation on the
deck of a sailing boat, and under an Egyptian
sky, is far better, even if material and temporal

interests alone are to be consulted, than the little extra headway that might be obtained amidst the fumes and steam and heat, and the consequent wear and tear both to body and mind, of a steamer. Nor do I believe that the shallow and ever-varying bed of the river would admit of steam navigation, except as an amusement for the Pashas, with their pretty playthings of steam yachts. All that seems wanting in this department are the iron plates from Glasgow, for a class of capacious flatboats to take the place of the present clumsy native djerms; some cotton presses from the United States, by the introduction of a few of which some enterprising merchants are this year realizing their 100 per cent.; and a few sugar factories, the machinery and coal for which the proprietors can well afford to import from England; these, and instead of the powerful steam pumping machines, for the setting up and working of which a Pasha's estate and purse and forced labor are called for, some contrivance for raising the water for irrigation, which, I believe, is yet to be done by the screw which Archimedes formerly introduced here, or as the marshes were drained in Holland.

Also, the wheat is still ground in many places here *by the north wind,* and the man who introduces the contrivance will deserve from the land of Egypt, and especially from the poor blind-folded cattle who labor in the tread-mill of the creak-

THE SAKIA.

Egypt's Princes.

ing sakias,* and from the naked "drawers of water" who toil in the hard service of the Sha- doof, a monument of brass as tall as Cheops. Nay, Egypt can prosper without coal, for it has in it the elements of a great agricultural coun- try. But it has a need, nay two, which must be supplied before it can become the great and prosperous country for which it is intended.

1. It needs the Gospel to deliver its people from their degrading superstitions and abject ignorance, and that Gospel alone can procure for them and prepare them for a free, liberal, and fostering government. Egypt is now truly the basest of kingdoms. It is such because the Lord has fulfilled his threatening, " I will make the rivers dry, and sell the land into the hand of the wicked; and I will make the land waste, and all that is therein by the hand of strangers. I the Lord have spoken it." The Lord *has* smitten Egypt. He has smitten and he has promised to *heal* her, "And they shall return even unto the Lord, and he shall be entreated of them and shall heal them."

The second thing needed, and which will follow as the result of the former, is a wise and liberal government. The present government is a cruel despotism, and the people, alas, are prepared for no better. The attempt to force upon them a

* Water-wheels for raising water from the river to irrigate the land.

6*

better before they are prepared for it, would be to introduce confusion and anarchy and every evil work. The ruling house, since the days of Mohammed Ali, has made the attempt to introduce not a liberal and fostering government, under which the land might prosper, but despotically to force upon the people the arts and sciences of European civilization, and the result has been a failure. It has crushed the great mass of the people into deeper misery and degradation, and such must ever be the result of such a scheme.

Western civilization is in this soil an exotic. It is like the apple tree brought from Northern climes under this ardent sun. It has degenerated from a tree to a stunted shrub, and its fruit is rotten before it is ripe.

But I have wandered far from the sugar factory of Mustapha Pasha. I was anxious to know who was the presiding and forming genius in this scene of beauty, and I soon saw him, under circumstances which caused a sad revulsion in the feelings of admiration which his handy work had caused. On landing, I went directly to the dewan of the Coptic scribes of the establishment, in order to inform them that I had Bibles for sale, and also to find John Markus, a Copt, who had bought a large number of books from Monsur. Entering the room where some dozen or fourteen of these were sitting "a la Turk," on their cushions, behind their little desks, and with

their great account books in their laps, and all
in the usual Coptic confusion and disorder, I
looked around, and choosing the most intelligent-
looking one on the other side of the room, I stepped up to him and asked him if he knew John
Markus. "I am he!" he answered with an exclamation of surprise at my knowing him, as he
asked me to be seated. I sat down on the floor
beside him, but I had hardly finished the compliments and coffee, when I saw a strange sight
from the window, the description of which I will
have to leave for another chapter.

CHAPTER III.

I was sitting beside John Markus as I heard
a strange clatter and a beseeching cry of distress, and, stepping to the window, I beheld, for
the first time during my residence in the East,
the judicial administration of the *bastinado*. A
spy from the overseer of the works, Ameen
Effendi, had been out the night before, and had
found the guard, who should have been on duty
watching the sugar-cane, asleep at their posts;
and twenty-five of them had been brought up
for punishment. The place for the administration of the punishment was the most public one
in the village—in front of the café. The Effendi, who had been the judge in the case, sat by
with a few of his men—thus the punishment
took place in the presence of the Judge, according to Deut. xxv. Each man stepped forward
in turn, and apparently without any reluctance,
and, lying down on his face, raised the soles of
his feet. Two men sitting on the ground, one
on each side of the culprit, firmly grasped his
extended hands, and then placed their feet
against his sides. Two others, sitting likewise
on the opposite sides of his knees, held his feet

(68)

in their place by means of a stick about four feet long, with a noose in the middle, which was wound around the ankles, they also placing their feet against his knees, so that he was held as if in a vice. The *torturers* were two strong men, who had their flowing sleeves tied up about their shoulders, so as to give the right arm free play; and the instrument of torture a *karbash*, which is a heavy whip much like our cowhide, about five feet long, and made of hippopotamus skin. Each man struck his foot. The whip, which is a very heavy and severe one, was raised high in the air, and came heavily down, with a crash which reminded me very much of our old-fashioned threshing with flails. The number of strokes was twenty-five. Some, whose hardened feet did not seem to suffer so much, received a few more; others who squirmed very much and besought the Effendi very piteously for mercy, were let off with less. Most of them did not move, and when they rose, after limping a few steps, they put on their shoes and walked off as if nothing had happened. It was to me a most sickening sight, and yet it has not changed my opinion before expressed of the expediency of such punishment with a people such as we have here. The law of Moses was made for such a people. It prescribes the rod for various offences, and he who enacted that law was wiser than all our Solons.

I may be permitted to say a few words in defence of this opinion, which, I anticipate, will sound very barbarous in delicate and civilized ears:

1. The *Naboot*, or *Karbaj*, simply inflicts corporeal pain. It does not, as it would with us, entail degradation and infamy, such as would make a man vile in the eyes of his neighbors, and take away self-respect.

2. It is prompt and severe, and appeals to the corporeal instead of the moral feelings, and this punishment should do good among a people whose moral feelings are so imperfectly developed. To children and a child-like people it is the rod that giveth wisdom. I feel confident that our code, with its tardy but strict (even strictness is sometimes well dispensed with in dealing with children) justice—its delays in administration—and its lingering imprisonments and heavy fines, with the sufferings which in this poverty-stricken land they would necessarily inflict, not only on the culprits, but on their families—more misery would be entailed and less crime prevented than by the present system. To the Church in its nonage the ceremonial law contained in Leviticus was an admirable pictorial gospel addressed to the corporeal senses of those whose mental and reflective powers were not yet sufficiently developed to appreciate a more abstract exhibition of truth, and so

it was with its moral code with its appended
system of corporeal punishment; and it is now
equally applicable to a people of like mental
habitudes. When the gospel comes with its
higher cultivation, it brings with it freedom
from these beggarly elements and this intoler-
able yoke.

3. I do not believe that the *Naboot* is in as
frequent requisition here as many passing travelers represent. That which I have described is
the first time I have witnessed its application
during a residence of ten years in the East. I
do not think that the Turks deserve the reputation for wilful and despotic cruelty which they
have received. Cases of gratuitous and unreasoning tyranny doubtless exist, but I believe
they are rarer—and popular opinion has a more
powerful influence than is usually imagined.
There is a freedom of intercourse and a community of feeling between the rulers and the
ruled, which we seldom see in more enlightened
lands, and it has its effect in smoothing down
the rough edges of arbitrary power—so that,
notwithstanding all that has been said of Turkish cruelty, I have no hesitation in avowing my
belief that the Naboot is far better in the hands
of Turks and Arabs than it would be in the
hands of imperious Englishmen and nervous and
excitable Americans.

4. There are here checks and balances which,

though very different from those which keep the
machinery of Western governments steady, are
yet very effectual. True, we have no free press
here to expose the irregularities of mismanage-
ment and mal-government; but we have the
everlasting clatter of a thousand tongues, which
are swifter than the pens of ready writers, or
the types of steam-presses, and they are in the
heads of a people who know everything and tell
every body all they know. We have no regular
constitution nor written code of law and jurisprudence, except the crude apology for them
contained in the Koran and traditions, but we
have an all-powerful popular opinion, regulated
and enlightened by many wise maxims which
have come down from a remote antiquity, and
by the influence of contact and intercourse with
surrounding nations of various political systems
—a popular opinion which is all the more jeal-
ously guarded and insisted on from the absence
of other safeguards of public weal. True, we
have not here legislative, judicial, and executive
departments, each acting in its peculiar and well-
defined province, and each acting as a balance-
wheel to the other. These are, for the most
part, united in the persons of the rulers, each
one of whom is made all but absolute in his department; but there is a subordination of per-
sonalities and an amenability of lower to higher
tribunals, and of all to the decision of popular

opinion, which, in a measure, secures the ends of
our limited monarchies and constitutional governments. The Sheikh-El-Beled is subject to
the Nazir, the Nazir to the Mudir, the Mudir to
the Viceroy, the Viceroy to the Sultan, and the
Sultan to the conscience of enlightened Europe
and the balance of European powers, so that
absolutism, in the strict sense of the word, cannot be said to exist. The higher tribunal is in
all cases accessible to the complaints and statements of grievances from the subjects of the
lower; so that every man who is entrusted with
authority, is also literally a man under authority,
and it is thus made his highest interest to secure
the respect and good-will of those over whom
he rules. Thus, while each man may be absolute in his own department, he is very far from
being independent or irresponsible. The different departments are connected by the bands of
a chain which cannot be broken, and each man
is enclosed and limited by the bands of an unwritten law, which he cannot burst asunder, and
above, beneath, and around him is an atmosphere of public opinion from which he cannot
escape.

I could produce numerous examples of the
harmonious and beneficial working of this system, but to do so would carry me far beyond
my prescribed bounds, and I prefer referring to
a couple of Scriptural parables which beautifully

7

exhibit the working of that system which I have attempted briefly to explain, Matt. xviii. 23–38 ; Luke xvi. 1–12. I find that the author of "Village Life in Egypt," (an acute writer, but one whose opportunities of observation were limited,) represents the above facts and principles as producing a contrary effect to the one which I have observed, and which is described in the above parables. He says, " From these anecdotes it will be seen that the office of *Nazir* is no sinecure, and it is perhaps natural that men who are themselves subject to such arbitrary treatment should go and do likewise to their inferiors. In the less princely way, but with equal severity, do the *Nazirs* treat the subordinates, and especially the Sheikhs of villages. These again, it is true, in order to ease the smart, make free with the shoulders below them. So that a cuff from the Pasha of Pashas eddies away sometimes to the very depths of the population, and is felt in its consequences from the Bahairah to the Said. It is impossible to calculate how many square feet of human back used to require poulticing within a few days after one of Mohammed Ali's interviews with his naughty children."

The "anecdotes" which he had related, viewed from my stand-point and interpreted by those maxims of human, and especially of Arab, nature which I have been led to adopt, bring me to conclusions very different from those expressed in the above extract.

[NOTE.—While copying these notes, I am able to add, that about a month after the date of the above, Ameen Effendi himself was degraded from his office, bastinadoed, put in irons and thrown into prison, and all that most justly, if popular report concerning his crimes be true; and while I was calling on a friend a few days after, an agent of his called to ask most humbly for a loan of a few thousand piasters. Now I think that when he gave judgment against those poor men, and sat over them during its execution, he must have felt: "I myself deserve the like of that, and ten-fold more, and my reckoning may also come to-morrow;" and that this feeling would mitigate his severity, and, though conscience might be dead, selfishness and pride would lead him to conclude, "I, too, may soon need the pity and good offices of this sympathizing crowd of spectators, and it illy becomes me now to compromise their good will by injustice or undue severity." It is at least certain as to this particular case, that twenty-five men who would desert their post, and leave the cane of a large district exposed to the depredations of the villagers around, deserved twenty-five stripes each; and, in general, I must repeat, and sorry I am that I have to do it, that more cases of unreasoning barbarity and gross injustice have fallen under my notice committed by Franks than Arabs. The difference may be explained on various accounts. The ignorance of the former as to many of the customs of the natives, and their consequent mistakes and misunderstandings, their nervousness, caused by a debilitating climate, and many little vexations to which a residence here subjects them, and the different and higher code of right and wrong, according to which they judge—these may be mentioned as causes of the difference.]

But this long digression has caused me to leave far behind John Markus and his fellow-scribes. The open ears of the latter, and the watchful eye of the overseer of the corps, who was sitting before an open window in an adjoining room, did not allow us to enter into religious discourse, and so I invited him to call on me at the boat, in the evening, and bade him good afternoon.

In the evening he came with two of his sons, and we had a long conversation, during which he asked me particularly concerning our views of justification by faith, and transubstantiation, and we spent most of the evening in the discussion of them. He was from Negadeh, and had evidently been tampered with by the Catholic priests there. In the morning he came again, bringing with him a friend, who bought a number of books. The rest of the scribes did not buy, as they said they had already been supplied by Monsur, and that their pay being in arrears, they had no ready money.

5th. Left Erment at 10 o'clock, and, with a pleasant breeze, were carried to Esneh, which we reached in the evening.

December 6th. Spent at Esneh, to allow our men to bake bread. They had purchased about eight bushels of wheat at Erment, which they here had ground and baked. This is their usual system. They generally need to stop at Osiout and Esneh a day for that purpose, but as we had had an unusually quick passage to Osiout, the supply which they brought from Cairo lasted them to Esneh. The bread, after it is baked, is cut up into slices and dried on the cabin deck. The men take two meals of this a day, one at eleven o'clock and the other at sunset, and they prepare it for mastication by soaking and stirring a sufficient quantity for each meal, in a large wooden basin, until it becomes of the consistency of a thick pudding, and then sitting around the basin as closely as possible (spoon fashion, as we would say), they help themselves, each with his right hand, which has been previously washed for the purpose, and which is supposed never to be used except for pure purposes. It is marvellous how soon they

7*

will despatch a dish of this paste; and this, with a raw onion and a cup of coffee following, and with a change of a dish of lentiles, and an occasional sheep, for which they depend on the liberality of their Khowajeh,* these form their "table de hôte;" and it is remarkable how much hard work they will perform on so slender a fare. They are a most docile and faithful race, and those travelers who have trouble with them are usually themselves to blame.

Arming myself with a letter of introduction which the Bishop of Luxor had given me to the Kummus Ibrahim, I started up to find him and to see the temple. At the latter I met our friends, Messrs. ———, whose *dahabiyeh* had kept us company most of the way from Cairo. The temple, or rather portico (for it alone is visible, having been cleared out by order of Mahommed Ali, in 1842), is very magnificent. The guidebook says it was built by the Cæsars; but I was greatly amused by the answer of our friend's dragoman, who, when they asked him who built it, answered, "Rameses II.;" and then taking them to one of the side walls, where a large birdnet flourished prominently among the hieroglyphics, informed them, with an air of true antiquarian impudence and presumption, "and this is his cartouch." Our travelers gazed very sagely at the confused jumble of marsh-weeds

* The Frank or foreign employer.

and aquatic fowls, some entangled in the meshes of the net, and some flying away as if frightened by the artist's flagrant disregard of all rules of perspective the birds being doomed to soar most awkwardly, with one wing on their backs, and the other on their breasts. This was about enough for my poor risibilities; but they were doomed to a farther trial, for, standing a few moments after before a pictured column all covered with hieroglyphics, one of my friends at my side asked me, "Are these characters Arabic?" I answered, "No, they are some other language," and turned away, musing on the mania of sight-seeing and lion-hunting.

I went to the church, but did not find the Kummus Ibrahim in, to whom my letter of introduction was addressed. I then started through the streets inquiring for one Keddes Makarius, to whom I had been warmly recommended by Monsur as having assisted him very much in selling books, in a visit which he had made to Esneh some weeks previous. After a long search, I found that he was not in town, when I again started through the Christian quarter of the town, informing those whom I met that we had books for sale in the Dahabiyeh, and also for the same purpose visiting the Christian schools, which I found wretchedly kept, the one by a youth who was a relation of the bishop, and the other by two blind Areefs. They all said that

they had been supplied by Monsur, and I returned rather discouraged ; nor did any one call
during the afternoon, which was far from being
a pleasant one, as we were fastened to a dirty,
dusty bank, and were constantly annoyed by
beggars and Ghawaze. Esneh has the reputation of being the most religious town on the
Nile, but it had disappointed my anticipations.
Pleasanter experiences, however, were in store
for the future. Left towards evening, and sailed
all next day.

7th. The winds were light and the climate
and temperature pleasant, which we enjoyed
very much, after the high winds and piercing
cold which we had experienced most of the way
from Cairo. Saw a crocodile on the sunny bank,
the first we had seen. In one place we saw the
peasants plowing. The plow had two handles
and a share and coulter, rude in construction,
but more western in shape than any we had
seen in the East, which have generally only one
handle. It was, however, exactly the form of
those in use centuries ago, as depicted on the
sculptures. Nearer the water's edge a man was
sowing barley on the strip of mud which had
been left by the retreating Nile. He sank up
to the thighs in mud at every step. This was
sowing in a good and deep soil, one in which an
abundant harvest might be anticipated almost
as a certainty. There were neither thorns nor

stony places; still there was danger of the fowls of the air devouring it, for they were flying about in myriads, and the sun and wind had covered the surface with a thin, dry crust, into which the seed would not sink; so that boys were following in the track of the sower, floundering in the mud, and, as they went, harrowing in the seed with their fingers. Such has hitherto been *our* seeding time in the valley of the Nile. We have found a deep, rich soil in the Egyptian mind. In the little patches into which we have been able to cast the seed of the Word there is promise of a golden harvest, and already a few handfuls have been given us as an earnest of that harvest; but it has hitherto been the lot of the sower to go forth with weeping—waist-deep, in a mire of difficulties. "But he shall doubtless come again with rejoicing, bearing his sheaves with him."

This is that sowing to which Solomon exhorts, in Ecc. xi. 1 : "Cast thy bread upon the waters, for thou shalt find it after many days." Some commentators understanding too literally the particle "*upon*," which in the margin is given "upon the face," have gone to the Indian rice marshes for an example of the actual casting of the seed upon the surface of the water. But the phrase may mean, "*in the presence of—beside*" the waters; and this agrees with the fact, as we daily witness, of the peasants going forth and sowing the seed *beside* the retreating and drying up waters of the river, the pools and canals, and in the broad fields through which it can be distributed by the water-courses; and the prophet Isaiah xxxii. 20, says, "Blessed are ye that sow beside, literally '*upon*,' all waters." This use of the phrase "*upon* the waters" is yet common in Arabic. When the people would go out for a pleasure excursion, they gather up their pipes and coffee-cups, and say, "Come, let us go and sit *upon* the waters;" meaning beside the waters, on the banks of some neighboring stream; and the converse phrase is frequently used in the Koran, in the constantly recurring promise to the believer of "Gardens, *beneath* which flow rivers of waters."

Saturday morning, the 8th—reached Edfou, and immediately went up to the town, which is about half an hour from the river, armed with a bag of books, and an introductory letter to the priest. Of this document the following is a translation:

[THE SEAL.]

"*Makhiel, Bishop of Esneh:*

"The promulgation of this perfect blessing and comprehensive grace is unto our beloved son, the Priest Makhiel. May God bless thee with heavenly blessings.

"We inform you that the most honorable and

pure priest, Mr. Lansing, together with his wife, who are our most particular friends, are about to leave for your parts. He wishes to visit and see the southern country, and we desire you to receive him with a perfect reception, that he may return praising you. And that you treat him with the honor that is due to him, since he is a man of learning and high position; and also give peace to all the brethren who inquire concerning us; and may the most high God preserve you.

"1577, 25th Hatur."

In the other letter which he gave me to the priest of Esneh, he had, "In the name of the Lord Jesus," in the introduction, and Monsur told me that in the one which he gave him he had added, "And in the name of Mary and the saints and martyrs"—a discriminating mind. I found said priest Makhiel, who received me very cordially, and urged the people to buy books. They were evidently a poverty-stricken people, but they took books to the amount of 70 piasters, which they said was the number of Christians in the town. They had no church, but worshipped in a convent in the mountains. One of them, an intelligent-looking man, having heard of our school in Luxor, expressed a very strong desire that they might also have a school in Edfou, and said that he himself would attend

with the children. I told him that if he would
read the Bible with diligence, and seek the enlightenment of the Spirit, he would learn the
truth, which the priest seconded most earnestly,
saying, "The Bible is the life of the soul. It is
the life of the soul." Another hesitated at taking the four gospels, in Coptic and Arabic, at
20 piasters, saying that it was dear; when his wife
(an Abyssinian) interposed, saying, "Do you
say it is dear at 20 piasters?—one word of it is
worth 10,000." The priest invited me in to
coffee, but, poor man, he had only a dark, low-
doored house to which to invite me, and I preferred remaining outside in the sun and filth,
to walking, nay, creeping in. I gave them an
exhortation, to which they listened very attentively, and I left them with a much more favorable impression of their knowledge and piety
than Mr. Jewett obtained on his visit. He attempted to speak to them through his interpreter,
but found them "almost destitute of ideas."
(Perhaps his interpreter did not convey or awake
many.) He found that none of them could read!
and says, "It was impossible to suppose that
they were Christians, on any better ground than
because their parents were such." He should
have known them better, before passing so harsh
a judgment. For my part, I see much in their
Christian character to admire, and I think no
one can be intimately acquainted with the crafty

art and unblushing tyranny which have for centuries been employed by the Muslems to seduce or force them to apostatize, without feeling a deep sympathy with their sufferings, and admiration of their constancy.

I next went to the temple, which is the most perfect one in Egypt, and must excite admiration in all beholders. I would be tempted to undertake a description of it, but that I have positively determined to leave the ancient Egyptians and their works to the warm imaginations and glowing pens of those who can neither understand the language nor appreciate the character of their modern descendants. My work is with the latter, and I can only stop to express the hope that the building of the temple was not such a work of tyranny as the clearing out of it has been. Three years ago the government issued an order to have the rubbish, which by the accumulation of centuries had almost filled it, cleared away, and for three years the poor peasants of Edfou and the surrounding villages have been engaged in the herculean task, and of course all is done by forced labor. The inside has been all emptied, and about fifty men and children were at present engaged in removing the heavy bank of rubbish which had accumulated around the outer wall. The men filled the baskets of the children (boys and girls), and the latter carried them away on their heads, and

emptied them on a high mound adjoining. The
task-maker, kurbaj in hand, took us through the
temple, when he sued for a present. We gave
him a small coin, and a much larger one to the
children, who in his presence did not dare raise
the usual shout for bak-sheesh. Perhaps travelers would not manifest so much impatience at
the "eternal cry of bak-sheesh" (as they love to
call it), were they more intimately acquainted
with the circumstances of their innocent tor-
mentors. Were I called upon to act as umpire
in this controversy—a controversy which, I am
ashamed to say, is too often settled by the stick
or kurbaj—with which, on coming to Egypt,
too many travelers arm themselves (and which
to keep up the fierce prestige of their new-grown
beards and moustaches, they are very free in
using), I would decide that each decipherer of
hieroglyphics and admirer of ancient temples
should pay to the poor people who disinterred
them a bak-sheesh proportionate to their admiration and appreciation of them when uncovered.
Instead of this, some officious (or as they doubtless esteemed themselves) public-spirited travelers have complained to the government of the
annoyance of the boys, and the result was that
a government official accompanied us all through
the town with a long naboot, with which he cruelly belabored the poor children. So inconsist-
ent is human nature. These public-spirited ones

will whip and complain of the boys, and at the
same time praise the liberality and public spirit
of the Pasha, who, to gratify his foreign guest,
to enrich his museum with the antiques which
may be disinterred, and to employ the faithful
hands and crush the faithful hearts of which he
has so many thousands at his disposal, orders
the work. But our travelers are "*on principle*,"
opposed to the system of giving presents. "It
encourages mendicancy and indolence, and every
evil work." It might do so in those whom want
and the lash do not force to be industrious. We
think, however, that a little sympathy, or at
least consideration, might be exercised by those
who bear the Christian name.

Learning that but few Christians were to be
found between Edfou and Assonan, with not a
very large community at the latter place, we
took down our big sail and turned our faces
northward. It required a little self-denial to
turn away from the interesting ruins which were
yet to be seen on the way to the first cataract,
and especially at the far-famed Philæ, but sight-
seeing must be made a recreation, not a pursuit,
until the seed of the Word shall have been sown
in all the land of Egypt.

We left Edfou at 1 p. m., and floating down
the river, with the help of oars and a light south
wind, reached Esneh at midnight. Rising early
next morning, I found we were moored below the

town, in a much quieter and pleasanter place than
the one we had occupied before.   On the bank
above was a beautiful acacia grove, and just below a palace which was built by Mohammed Ali,
with a fragrant garden, and an old dilapidated
factory in the back-ground.

As it was Sabbath (the 9th), I took a hasty
cup of coffee and light breakfast, and hurried up
to the church, which I reached just after sunrise.
The services, which had begun at daybreak,
were already far advanced. The children at
least had been there long enough for their child-
ish impatience, for they were very restless, and
the Kummus Ibrahim was keeping them in order
with a long staff, which, as I entered, he was
freely using over their heads and shoulders,
while the service was proceeding. He provided
me with a seat in the most conspicuous place in
the church, beside the reading-desk, in the midst
of the congregation, who were seated around on
the floor, about one hundred and fifty in number.
At different points in the service, however, they
rose and stood, or bowed to the earth, and repeated the prescribed prayers and responses.
As the whole was in Coptic, which I did not
understand (nor did they), I did not think it my
duty to join in the dumb show, and kept my
seat. This seemed to act as a silent reproof, and
I could plainly see in the countenance of some
around me an expression of shame at their mean-

EGYPTIAN CHILDREN.

ingless performance. In the meantime the blind
Areefs, three in number, were taking the lead
most lustily in the chanting, which, together
with the sound of the loud cymbals which they
beat, and the screams of the boys, who chanted
in unison, only an octave higher than the rest,
made an almost deafening noise. Soon, however, a homily of Chrysostom, on the emigration
of Abraham from Ur of the Chaldees to the
land of promise, was read, which, though not
marked for depth of thought, was at least more
satisfactory than the Coptic. A passage was
then read from the gospel of Luke, first in Coptic
by the Kummus, with all the circumstance of
candles, incense, etc., and with the face turned
towards the east; and then, in Arabic, by a boy
about twelve years of age, and with his face
towards the west. He read very badly, and the
people were constantly correcting him from all
parts of the house. A servant of the bishop
being present from Luxor, I noticed he had
some conversation with the Kummus apart, in
which I suppose he informed him that I had
preached in Luxor on the Sabbath before, and
the Kummus coming forward, invited me to
speak. I took out my small Testament, and as
the character of Abraham had previously been
held up to them in the homily, I read the first
four verses of the 4th of Romans, and preached
a sermon on the free justification of Abraham by

8*

faith. I prefaced with expressions of brotherly love and union, telling them how happy I was to unite with them in the service of God, and that though of a different race, and land, and tongue, we were yet all one in Christ; that we had one God and Father, and one baptism, and one hope, and that we all trusted to reach the one home in heaven, prepared for all the people of God. I said, however, that there was one drawback in our Christian communion, viz., that I could not understand and unite in a large portion of their services, as they were in Coptic, which to me was incomprehensible, and that one word with the understanding was better than ten thousand words in an unknown tongue; at which some of them smiled, as if to say, " and to us also they are incomprehensible." All, even the before restless boys, arrested, perhaps, by the novelty of the thing, gave very marked attention; and I was particularly struck with the intelligent countenance, and hearty, audible expressions of assent of an elderly man, who was on the other side of the partition which separated the men's from the women's department of the church, and whose face only appeared in a small window. His name I afterward found to be Khaleel. We were to have a more intimate acquaintance, as the sequel will show. The commentary was next in order, but one suggested that my sermon would answer the purpose, which was agreed to by acclamation, and it was dispensed with, and they proceeded at once to the mass. This was performed by a young priest, and I was sorry to see that in the midst of the service he turned round, and elevating the host before the people, said, "Bow to God," which they did. He then made a circuit in the church, bearing it, and some of the people said, "Blessed be he that cometh in the name of the Lord."

The services closed at 10 o'clock, when I gladly staggered out, giddy and faint, and almost suffocated from the dust and the incense smoke, and my head reeling from the confusion of the worshipers, and the clash and clangor of the cymbals, and the Coptic prayers. In the passage-way was a seat, and I was very happy to accept the invitation of the Kummus to be seated and rest awhile, which we did over a cup of coffee, a number of people seating themselves around on the ground. A question arising concerning Paul's travels, I took the ebony staff of the Kummus, and, tracing a rough map on the ground, pointed out to them the track of his principal missionary tours, but my geographical enthusiasm carrying me beyond the bounds of Paul's journeys, to England, and France, and Russia, I was at length brought back by the remark of one present, "This is not spiritual converse!" It was Keddes, whom I before mentioned as not being in town when I went up, but who had since returned. We returned to "spiritual converse," in which we continued about an hour, when I returned to the boat, followed by Keddes and two others. These, after about an hour, were followed by the Kummus, Khaleel, and two others; and these again by other companies, and thus the day was spent in "spiritual converse." I was delighted with the acquaintance with the Scriptures, and earnestness which they exhibited; and though weak, and pained very much in the chest, I was able to continue the conversation until near sunset, when they at length gave me a "breathing spell." A day long to be remembered: one such a day is better than a thousand.

After they had left, I went up for a quiet stroll and meditation in the acacia grove above, when, passing the open gate of the factory above mentioned, my curiosity got the better of me, and I stepped in, for which I came near paying dearly. I noticed about the premises some black men, whom I afterwards found to be Darfurians, but the thought of danger from them did not enter my mind. So thoroughly tame by nature and the strong hand of despotism are the Egyptians, that one feels everywhere and always safe amongst them. But I had entered only a few paces, when I found myself surrounded by some twenty or thirty of them, gesticulating and vo-

ciferating in their gibberish in a most violent
manner, and apparently bent on mischief. One
of them especially, a tall, strapping, half naked
fellow, laid hold upon me, and with eyes flash-
ing like those of a wild beast, and with inflated
nostrils and raised fist, seemed on the point of
striking, and I only kept him at bay by looking
him fixedly in the eye and demanding, with all
the sternness I could command, that he should
let me alone. He, however, did not understand
me; but just then one of them came forward
and asked me, in Arabic, what I wanted. I
told him, "Nothing, only that I had walked in
to look about me," when he took me by the
other arm, and attempting to drag me in, said,
"Come, and I will show you." His friendship
was evidently little better than the hostility of
the others, and my apprehensions were brought
to the highest pitch, when I turned and saw
three or four of them tugging away at the heavy
gate to shut it. I saw that no time must be lost,
and so by one violent effort disengaging myself
from the grasp of my officious guide, I walked
out faster than I came in, but still with as much
deliberation as my excited nerves would allow.
Walking off, I met a man whom I asked who
they were. He told me they were Darfurians,
who had been brought from their native land by
the government, to be tamed for soldiers, and
that they were detained here for a time, because

the winter climate at Alexandria was too severe
for them; and he added, without knowing anything of my adventure with them, "They kill
folks when they get them inside." I scarcely
need add that I felt most grateful for my narrow
escape. Just before leaving Cairo, I saw and
very much admired a regiment of these men,
with their tasteful uniform of scarlet tarboushes,
surmounting their jet black faces, white eyes
and teeth, their scarlet jackets with silver but-
tons, and blue pants. I thought it a great improvement on the dusty brown faces and dirty
white uniform of the Egyptian soldiers. But I
shall take good care hereafter to keep at a good
distance from them, at least until tamed.

December 10*th*. When I arose, I found Keddes
and Sedhum, a tailor, who accompanied him yesterday. The former asked what hour we took
breakfast, and being informed, he went ashore and
spoke to a boy, who then started up to the town,
of the meaning of which movement I was not long
left in the dark, for the boy came down at break-
fast-time with two large dishes of fateer, the one
cooked in butter, and the other in milk. The
fateer is composed of very thin unleavened cakes
thus cooked in butter or milk, and then plentifully
sprinkled over with fine sugar. And it is delicious. He had brought enough for a breakfast
for twelve men, and besides a large bag of dried
dates for our journey. It was a rich present;

but principally pleasing to us because it was evidently given in the name of a disciple—a disciple of Him who has said that "a cup of cold water thus given, shall not lose its reward." Poor Keddes and his friend would not sit down with us to breakfast; when I found that the former was fasting—literally fasting, and not merely exchanging an animal for a vegetable diet, as is done by most of the Eastern Christians. The Coptic fasts are terribly severe. Taken together, they amount to about seven months out of the twelve; and it is the custom of the large proportion of the people to taste nothing till after the daily morning prayers; and then they eat no animal food, not even milk nor eggs. The most of them, during Lent, which is accounted the holiest of the fasts, and lasts fifty-five days, do not eat till noon—many until 3 P. M., and the more religious until sunset. Of this last number is Keddes; though this is not Lent, but the Fast of the Virgin. I talked with him and his friends a long time, endeavoring to teach them that the Master had not placed upon them this heavy yoke, but failed to convince them. He utterly disdained dependence on his fasting or other works in the matter of justification and acceptance with God, but contended that in these warm climates they needed these long fasts, in order to mortify the flesh and the lusts thereof. Poor man, I could only commend him to that

great Agent in our sanctification, who is held
forth in the Word—the Spirit, through the
truth. I found he was making use of the latter
most industriously. On a recent visit which he
had made to Cairo, he had purchased a copy of
a Reference Testament, recently published at
Beirut. He was spending his evenings until
late at night in reading this in course, and had
got as far as the 9th of Matthew, *looking out all
the references.* What a cold, ease-loving piety is
ours! Here is a man fasting and laboring all
day long for the support of his family, and at
night taking his light repast of bread and vegetables, and then sitting down over his little lamp
until midnight, and after it, in the study of the
Scriptures, until, although yet a young man, he
has already almost ruined his eyes by it. He is
not particularly bright in intellect, but he is a
most earnest character. May he speedily be
brought into the perfect liberty of Christ. And
he will be; for He whose word is truth has said:
"If any man will do his will, he shall know of
the doctrine;" and also, "If ye continue in my
word, then are ye my disciples indeed, and ye
shall know the truth, and the truth shall make
you free."

His friend was not so earnest a character, and
seemed to be somewhat influenced by the pride
of intellect; but he had proceeded farther than
the other in the doctrinal knowledge of Protes-

tantism. His narrative of the process by which he was led to this was interesting. He said that a book, called the "Thirteen Letters," had fallen into his hands (it is one of the Beirut publications, written by Mr. Bird against the papal errors.) He commenced reading it, when he soon found that it did away with confessions, the mass, the priesthood, image-worship, etc., until he began seriously to believe that it would leave nothing of the Christian religion, and was strongly tempted to burn the book; to which also the friends whom he consulted strongly urged him. But he said, "I at length determined to read it through, when, instead, I found that it only did away with what was superstitious, and had been superadded to our religion, and not with religion itself; and so," he said, "I continued reading the book, and am now very much pleased with it." I afterwards heard that our friend, the Kummus Ibrahim, had been reading this book, in company with some of his people, when he at length told them, "We must quit reading this book, for it is knocking all the pegs (cogs) out of our wheel" (referring to the well-known water-wheel.) Next to the Bible, Thomas A'Kempis' Imitation of Christ was most in demand with them. One person seeing Mrs. Lansing's pocket Testament, wished to buy it, though in English, evidently to use it as a charm.

9

A curious incident happened yesterday. The priest who had performed mass in the morning, came down with the others. The servant offered him a pipe, when he took from his pocket, and put upon the mouth-piece, a perforated nipple of wax, through which he smoked. In answer to my inquiry why he did so, he said that as he had partaken of the consecrated sacrament in the morning, he was holy for the day, and could not smoke from a pipe which had been in contact with other (profane) lips. The idea seemed to be that he was charged, as it were, with a holy fluid, and must keep himself insolated for the day. While on this subject, I may mention that I have met with Copts who were greatly scandalized by the report that in the English Church in Cairo what remained of the bread, after communion, had been eaten by the servants—Muslems and others. The Levitical origin of this prejudice is manifest. It is an offshoot from a more pernicious error—viz.: there is still in the Church a priesthood besides that of Christ, that the ministers of the Church are priests, who Sabbath by Sabbath offer up in behalf of the people, in the mass, a sacrifice for their sins, and thus their minds are turned away from that one Sacrifice which perfects forever them that are sanctified, to one which needs daily to be repeated, and which can only bring into remembrance, but cannot put away sin. This may be called the capital error of the Coptic Church. Oh, that she might be brought to see that the holy communion is a commemorative and not a sacrificial ordinance— that in it Christ is offered to them, and not to God; and that He possesses an everlasting priesthood, and can have no successor in the office! If the Coptic Church could be convinced of this, and could be persuaded to substitute in her worship the vernacular for dead Coptic, she might be considered a reformed church; but when shall these two corner-stones be laid?

Left Esneh at 10 A. M., and reached Erment at 4 P. M. Stopped for half an hour, during which time I had a short interview with John Markus. Reached Luxor in the evening, but found neither Lord Haddo nor letters from Cairo, both which we expected. The want of them left us in doubts as to what our future plans should be. Determined to wait a few days, and leave all to the disposition of Providence.

11*th*. Spent the evening with Mr. M. and company, who were moored in their dahabiyeh beside us. Mr. M. was evidently far gone with consumption. (He afterwards died at Cairo.) He inquired particularly about our work, and next morning sent us a note containing his best wishes for our success and a contribution of £5— an encouragement to us in our work. Oh, that grace and wisdom may be given us to use well the means which are placed at our disposal by God's people for the promotion of His work!

12*th.* The tenth anniversary of our first departure from Boston for the Damascus Mission. How little idea did we then have of either the work or the providences then awaiting us, or of the sad destiny which then impended over that dear Damascus Mission to which we then bent our steps! It is well that an impenetrable veil hangs over the future; and now, when all is past, how like a dream it seems! The last farewell and last receding sight of that honored parent, whom we then felt we were not to meet again in the flesh—the long wintry voyage—the first strange, vivid impressions of oriental life—the five years of earnest preparation and buckling on the armor for the Eastern work—and just as that work was opening in bright vista, a sick bed and another departure from a dearer home—dearer because consecrated by purer, by heavenly, affections. A short sojourn among the exciting scenes of the fatherland, and another parting scene, with three bright young faces in the foreground, one of them, oh, how soon to join the angelic band which hovers over this checkered pathway! Alexandria, with its Babel of strange tongues, and the heavy responsibilities of a new mission—another fount of joy springing up in the new and now desolate home, so soon to become a river of affliction to wade through—and now, in this still night, with the ripples of the classic Nile whispering beside me, and the wonderful remnants of old Thebes around, just entering upon a new and most interesting enterprise for the resuscitation of this ancient and apostolic, but now sunken Coptic Church. These are the outlines, and memory fills them up with light and shade upon much of which I would not dwell. And will I be permitted to spend another decade in this good work? The frail flesh and this pained chest answer—No! Yet, O God, grant it, if such be Thy holy will, and make me more faithful than ever yet I have been. And what will be the results of other ten years of sowing and reaping in this fertile valley? Egypt has her Nile, and it has made her what she is. Oh, that that river, the streams whereof shall make glad the city of our God, may soon overflow its banks, now so narrow and restricted, and carry spiritual life and verdure unto the uttermost bounds of this now barren valley, so that sower and reaper may at last rejoice together!

9*

CHAPTER IV.

December 13*th*. Heard that small-pox was raging in the town. Went up with priest Antonius to ascertain the fact. Seven children had died in the bishop's family (connection), and the one to whom I was now taken was the child of a slave connected with the family. It was a sad and most affecting sight. The passage-way into the house was close and confined, and reeking with unhealthy odors. Just at the door of the room into which I was led, several women and children were standing as if entirely unconscious of the deadly infection which surrounded them. The room, which was about six feet square, had no window, and the low door, opening upon a narrow passage-way, afforded but little ventilation; and there sat the poor black mother with the moaning child upon her knees, in the worst stages of confluent small-pox. Myriads of flies were swarming around its little face, attracted by the filth and the loathsome disease. I could only prescribe cleanliness and pure fresh air, the latter being most studiously avoided by the natives in this disease.

Being aware that the Government made it

incumbent on the barbers of the town to vaccinate the children, making them an allowance of
a piaster each, for all the children born; I immediately asked to be taken to this functionary
that I might learn the reason of his failure to do
his duty. I found him sitting in his shop, making out his report for the Government of the
deaths which had lately taken place. I asked
him why he did not attend to his duty and
vaccinate the children. He said he did it whenever the parents would bring their children to
him. I asked him to show me some specimens
of his work, when he took me to a house and
showed me a child in which the vaccine had evidently regularly taken effect. He told me that
the people were very unwilling to have their
children vaccinated, at which I could not be
surprised when I recollected the cry which in enlightened England was raised against poor Jen-
nings, for attempting to evade the decree of
Providence, and to bestialize his species by in-
troducing into their system diseased matter from
the udder of cows. I was afterwards informed
that the unwillingness of the people had a deeper
foundation—that it resulted from the fear of the
inoculation of the (so-called) Frank disease,
which is fearfully prevalent—the result of the
introduction of European civilization, or rather
licentiousness, into the East, and at Esneh, some
ten days previous, I had seen a child whose arm

was in a dreadful state of putrefaction at the
usual place of vaccination. (I doubt not from
this cause, though at the time I made no inquiries
into the matter, as I had no intimation of the
prevalence of the disease in the country.)   The
people also seemed to want confidence in the
protective power of vaccination, as they said
that a number of children had died who had
been vaccinated.   I think, however, that in
these cases the children may have taken the infection before they were vaccinated.   I was told
that many of the parents bribed the barber not
to vaccinate the children ; that he then sent in
his reports to the government, and received his
piaster for each child, and that when they died
of small-pox, he reported them as having died of
some other disease.   He himself told me that
many of the children who were dying daily were
dying of scarlet fever, but I saw no case of this
disease.

To finish this subject, while upon it, I may say
that I immediately sent to Cairo a statement of
the case, to be laid before the sanitary department, and also a request for fresh vaccine matter, as they said they would allow me to vaccinate their children.   The result of the former
was the sending of most stringent orders, and
the adoption of new measures to secure the desired end, by which the sheiks of the town were
made responsible in the matter, under threat of

very severe penalties. This caused no small stir among the latter, and I was then glad that in sending the complaint I had taken the precaution to request that my name should not appear in the matter, as I would otherwise have brought upon myself their high displeasure. I was present soon after, when, the Nazir having come from Ghinneh, they came to him in a body, bitterly complaining of the new arrangement, but he summarily drove them from his presence. The whole would probably result in their paying him a heavy bribe to be released from the onerous new arrangements, and then matters would go on in the old way; so hard it is, even when the government has good intentions, to have them carried out. During the whole of the three months of our stay, the disease prevailed. I cannot say how many children were carried off by it, but I think that from one hundred to one hundred and fifty is a low estimate. Funeral processions, with the blind sheiks in front chanting the Mohammedan confession, and the mourning women with their piercing shrieks, in the rear, the little corpse wrapped in a cloth, borne in an open bier on the head of a man, passed our door with hasty steps nearly daily, and the doleful wail of the bereaved mothers could almost constantly be heard by day and by night. Mr. Ridgeway, an English traveler, took the infection, as he thought, at Gournou, on the

opposite side of the river, where he came into
contact with a case of it, and was long detained
by it at Osiou, on his way down, when his wife
took it from him, and died at Cairo. I was subsequently informed that the disease was also
prevalent at Esneh, but my informants seemed
afraid to give me the facts particularly.

The prevalence of this loathsome disease added
another element of doubt to the question which
during this week was engaging our anxious
thoughts, viz., whether we should return immediately to Cairo in the "*Ibis*," or remain at
Luxor, and send her back. Into the pros and
cons of this question I need not now fully enter.
Suffice it to say, in brief, that on the one hand
the work seemed evidently to demand our remaining. It had thus far prospered beyond our
most sanguine expectations. There was already
a school of over forty children, and it in the
church; and to have the permission of preaching
in the same church every Sabbath with an audience of one hundred and fifty to two hundred
souls, besides the opportunities which were
daily offering of selling books, and conversation
on religion with a people who seemed so ready
to hear, were advantages for the pursuance of
our work which could not be lightly foregone.
At the same time, I saw that the bishop was a
man who would need so much of politic manage-
ment, that the future prosperity of the work

depended very much on the continuance of his
good will, at least until the truth should obtain
a footing in the hearts of the people, and that
Monsur, though he had done nobly, was quite
unequal to cope with his craft; and, moreover,
becoming disgusted with his duplicity, as well
as repelled and discouraged by the apparently
hopeless degradation of the people—a feeling
which, however natural, would, I saw, if not
checked, preclude his further usefulness, (for this
people, like any other, in order to be raised from
their abject state, must be heartily grasped in the
arms, and not merely touched with the finger-
ends,) so that I concluded, should I go, it would
be expedient to take him with me, which would
look far too much like putting our hands to the
plow and then looking back. Then, too, the
state of our health, which had been the first
occasion of our coming, demanded that we should
remain. Mrs L. was still weak, and the pain in
my chest, with which I left Cairo, had increased,
instead of diminishing, with the cold winds
which we had experienced most of the way up,
and we felt that it would be imprudent to go
back in mid-winter to the rains, and mud, and
dampness of Alexandria. On the other hand, I
was sure that poor Mr. Hogg and the work
there needed my presence and the help which I
could render. Besides, also, it was not pleasant
to think of going up to a native house and send-

ing back our boat, without knowing when she
might be able to return to us, and especially so
from the prevalence of small-pox, and in case of
sickness, we would be far out of the reach of
medical aid. These were the main reasons which
weighed on either side. We considered them,
and endeavored to commit our way to Him who
is the breaker up of their way before his people,
and can deliver from the "noisome pestilence,"
and protect from the "destruction that wasteth
at noon-day," and finally we concluded to remain.

December 14*th*. The bishop sent for me on
the matter of the new school-room. He wanted
two things: First, a master-mason from Esneh
to sketch a plan for him; and second, the money to commence with. As to the former, I
gave him a plan which met with his approval,
though in conversing with him on the subject,
I found that he had his mind fully as much bent
on securing a store-room for his crops, as a
school-room for the children, (the former occu-
pying for the present one of the three upper
rooms,) and so I shaped my plans for the accomplishment of the double purpose, with which he
was well contented. As for the money, I determined, as far as possible, to keep it in my
own possession, and a matter of hope with him,
depending for its gradual realization on the continuance of his favor, and, in fine, to trust him
with no more than would be a fair rent for our

present quarters, the church, and so I gave him a pound. He asked what a pound would do towards building a school, and I told him that it would at least begin the work, and that then we would see. I soon found that it would go a good way in his manner of working, which was to send his slave, Sarur, with his camel, for the stones, his servant Bakhum cutting them, and the boys, of whom, as is the custom, the congregation always leaves at his disposal a few, (as Levites, "to do the service of the sanctuary,") carrying the bricks and materials, and clearing away the rubbish for the foundation. Only two or three men receiving wages were employed, and his reverence sat by most of the time, in his morning dishabille and episcopal staff, overseeing the work. He was, after all, very well contented with what I gave him, and insisted on commencing the work on the morrow, (Saturday,) though I finally persuaded him to delay it till Monday.

December 15*th*. Spent in preparing for the services of the morrow, the "lesson" to be read being Luke i. 23–38.

December 16*th*. The pain in my chest and side was so severe that I could scarcely draw on my boots, and drag myself up to the church. I feared much that I should not be able to preach, but commenced, and soon found that the excitement made me forget all my pains. The text

10

generally have two great charges against Protestants concerning the Virgin Mary. The Copts
gave me an opportunity of explaining our sentiments, the origin of which I could never learn.
The one, that we pray upon the house-tops, and
the other that we say that the Virgin was a box,
or casket, containing a precious jewel—that the
jewel was taken, and the casket left empty, and
no better than any other; and that in general we
speak against her. I told them that this was a
slander, and false—that we never spake against
her, but in her praise—that as she herself had
prophesied that all generations should call her
blessed, so we did—that we always said that she
was the "Blessed among women," and the highly
favored of the Lord,—that he was "with her,"
and distinguished her while on earth above all
other women that had ever lived,—and that she
was now with Him, happy and perfect, and glo-
rified in heaven,—but that while saying all this
concerning her, we said *nothing* to her,—that as
she is in heaven, and we on earth, she could not
hear us, nor should we address her,—and that as
neither the angel Gabriel, nor Elizabeth, nor any
one else, is represented in Scripture as speaking
to her, except when present with her, so we could
not speak to her until we should enter heaven to
be with her,—that, therefore, we never prayed to
her nor sought her intercession, as we knew that
the Son was the only intercessor and mediator

between God and man,—and in short that we did
not allow her nor any one else to usurp his office,
nor depend on them to perform his work of
saving us. This talk I noticed pleased the people, but made his reverence quite nervous, until
seeing that he was on the point of stopping me,
I went on to the second head of my discourse,
viz.: The human and divine natures of the Son,
which as I took pains not to use the phrases
which are so obnoxious to their monophysite
dogma, viz.: "two natures in one person"
pleased them much. I told them, which is the
fact, that that whole controversy between them
and the other sects is a mere verbal one, they
using the word nature in the sense in which the
others use person, and that we all agree that our
Saviour was perfect God and perfect man united
in one, and that this alone was necessary, as
neither the term nature nor person was used
in the Scriptures. With this they seemed contented, and I closed with an application to the
women, telling them that Mary was a poor humble fellaha,* such as they were, and that they, too,
should strive to please God, and that they, too,
might be favored and distinguished by him to be
mothers of sons who should prove blessings to
the Church and to the world.

After sermon I strove to beg off from remaining to the mass, whispering to the bishop that I

---

* Peasant, or member of the lower class.

was not well; but he insisted on my remaining, as he said it would be a great shame to leave before the Kuddas, and the people would think strange of it; and, moreover, that they would soon be through with it. Thus I was forced again to sit by while they went through with the meaningless ceremony. It *was* gone through with in a hurry, which made it even a greater farce than usual. The bishop charged the officiating priest before entering the "heykel" to make haste, and the latter threw about him his priestly robes and addressing himself to the task in hand with all his might, his tongue running at even a more fearful rate than usual; the bishop meanwhile occasionally crying out from his seat outside, "Kowam, Kowam, quick, quick, skip that, skip that;" and this, with the poor Copts, is what has been substituted for the Lord's Supper! How different from that solemn, edifying ordinance with us!

17*th.* Moved up to the house of Mustapha Aga. As that worthy had not yet made his appearance from Cairo, though daily expected, we will leave a formal introduction of him for a future occasion, and at present introduce our readers to his house, a room of which was to be our quarters for three months to come. Parallel with the river, and on a rising ground, sloping down to it, extend, 800 feet in length, the "disjecta membra" of one of the ancient temples of Thebes. This vast skeleton is at present deeply imbedded in sand, and covered with the mud-huts of modern Luxor. Keeping up the figure, its ribs may not inaptly be called the double row of columns, twelve in number, which are twelve feet in diameter, and from thirty to forty in height, with wide-spreading capitals, representing the full-blown lotus, and superincumbent architrave of huge blocks of stone of corresponding dimensions. This double colonnade forms the pretentious portico to the house of Mustapha Aga, the most pretentious house of the most pretentious personage in the village. From its roof a man daily scrambled up, by the help of a palm trunk, to the top of the colonnade, and from a flag-staff on each end suspended the American and British flags—for Mustapha is the Consular agent for these two powers.

The house is built against and partly between the hindermost row of columns, between two of which is the front door, entering into the hall, on the left of which is the Consular office, and on the right our room, with a small store-room adjoining, and a small unglazed window opening upon a platform between the next two columns, and raised about four feet from the ground. To this platform I often retired with my Christian friends who did not feel free to converse among the Muslems in the more public

10*

hall; and, by way of being classic, I used to call
it my "Exhedra," while the hall in which I had
daily earnest discussions with the Muslems I
called "the Portico." The Exhedra commanded
a view of the open space between us and the
river, which was the place of general assemblage,
or "place de la concorde" (*discord*) of the village—the Dahabiyes of the traveler—of which
there were usually from six to a dozen bound to
the bank below, and in the background the vast
green plain on the other side of the river, with
its scattered temples and the vocal Memnon and
his mute companion immediately in front, receiving day by day, in silent and majestic dignity,
the first salutations of his "beloved Aurora;"
and in the background the bold circling amphi-
theatre of tomb-perforated hills. This was the
picture of Thebes *as it is*, which, day by day,
sunk deeper and deeper into my mind, and can
never be effaced.

Within, our dark little room looked gloomy
enough, and with its rugged brick floor and
mud-plastered walls, (which having ordered preparatory to our occupation to be whitewashed,
I found, on coming up to it, had been bespat-
tered with lime-water, no such a thing as a
brush being to be found in Luxor,) and its roof
of split palms, it was primitive enough. And
when, having sent up our little effects, and seen
the "Ibis" spread her sails for the northward

flight through "the land of the overshadowing wings," I went up to it and found Mrs. L. arranging our simple furniture, it looked truly desolate; and had she given me the least countenance in so doing, we would have sat down for a turn of the blues, and repentance for the step we had taken. But she did not. Slower than I had been in coming to the conclusion to remain, yet she was now prepared to meet with cheerfulness all that it involved, and before night I had evidence that female hands can make the most desolate place look home-like, and all was well again. Our style of living was very simple. A settee on each side of the room, which served for beds by night; a few small mats on the floor, a deal table from the school-room, and two chairs, three cups and saucers, ditto knives and forks, and a few plates. Robinson Crusoe, in his desert isle, possessed many more of the comforts of a civilized state. We learned how few are the necessaries of life, and with how little one can live and be happy. As to outward circumstances, Diogenes in his tub could scarcely have envied us. As to real happiness and solid contentment of mind, a king upon his throne might.

18*th*. Yakob the scribe, in the "Shoneh," or government depôt, who afterwards became our fast friend and most hopeful disciple, called with a friend from Pesht, a neighboring village, and we had a long and very interesting conversation

on the vitals of religion. On leaving, they re-
quested me to appoint a time when they might
come every day to receive instruction. I feared
that such a step might awaken the suspicions and
jealousy of the bishop and priests, and so told
them that I would see the latter, and have the
time appointed when I might meet not only
them, but others, at the church, or bishop's
house. To this they answered very significantly,
"That will not answer their purpose." And
when, on calling on the bishop in the afternoon,
I proposed the matter, I found they were right.
He said the people were stupid, and took no interest in religion, and would not come together.
I saw where the difficulty lay, and for the present did not urge the matter. He, however, went
on to say, in reference to my last Sabbath's sermon, that I would have to be very cautious what
I taught the people, that as yet they could not
bear sound doctrine, that I would have to advance step by step and very gradually; and
especially that I would have to be very careful
not to say anything against the "holy mistress,"
(Mary;) that they loved her very much, and
would not endure to hear anything against her.
I asked him whether what I had said was true.
He answered, "Yes." Then I said, "The truth
never yet harmed one, and as for the people,
I will take the responsibility of their being
offended." The truth was, that my doctrine

had pleased all who heard me except himself. I felt strongly tempted to break with him at once, and especially so when, in the evening, Monsur informed me that he had turned the most promising boy out of the school, on account of a private quarrel. The bishop has an aged sister living with him. This ancient dame, it seems, had been in the habit of patching up the episcopal revenues by writing and selling charms to the people; and the "head and front" of this boy's offending was, that he had shown disrespect to one of these charms: indeed he had torn it in pieces and thrown it into the Nile. This was an act of high daring which would greatly endanger the craft in the estimation of the people, and could not be suffered to go unpunished, and the decree went forth that the boy must leave the school. Monsur had protested and entreated, but to no avail; and I too, though strongly tempted to make it the breaking point, was fain to keep silent. The school was in the church, and by means of our friendship, hollow though it was, we were enjoying golden opportunities of reaching the people. Had the bishop been alone, it would have been a very easy matter to throw him overboard at once; but I knew the strength of the chain of priestcraft by which the poor ignorant people were bound to him, and for their sakes I determined to put off the evil day as long as possible.

19*th*. The bishop sent a turkey and twenty loaves of bread. The servants, who brought them, lingered about as if their commission did not end with the delivery of the present, and so I gave them a present in money to the full value of the articles brought, for doing which his reverence, on calling the next day, administered a gentle reproof, and I protested that it was nothing, only a little present to have the young men drink a cup of coffee, and keep them in good humor, and that his reverence was drowning us in the sea of his bounty, etc. Oriental compliments these, admirably adapted to promote reciprocal good feeling.

Hearing very near our house a more bitter death-wail than usual, I went up to the roof, when I beheld a company of women, in the court of our next neighbor's house, gesticulating and dancing in their usual frantic manner, the men at the same time violently walking to and fro in the street, giving vent to their exclamations of grief. As such scenes afterwards became very familiar to us, I will here give in order a few points of Scripture illustration which they suggested to my mind, some of which were new and very striking to me.

1st. *Covering the face and lips.* I noticed the men above mentioned had each a kind of shawl wound around the head and lower part of the face, their ordinary turbans being removed.

They were also barefooted, and I was particularly struck with the manner *in which they carried their faces upwards, never looking towards the ground, which (being so contrary to our ideas of the effects of grief as bowing the mourner to the earth,) together with their unusually quick step, and short vehement expressions, caused me for some time not to recognize them as mourners, and their conduct quite puzzled me until I understood their expressions. I was afterwards very much struck with the agreement of all this with the following expressions, Ezek. xii. 6: "Thou shalt cover thy face, that thou see not the ground, for I have set thee for a sign to the house of Israel," and verse 12. Ezek. xxiv. 17: "Forbear to cry, make no mourning for the dead, *bind the tire* (turban) *of thine head upon thee, and put on thy shoes upon thy feet, and cover not thy lips, and eat not the bread of men*," and verses 22 and 23. Also Micah iii. 7, Es. vi. 12, Jer. xiv. 3, and li. 51.*

2d. The "*eating the bread of men*," mentioned above in Ezek. xxiv. 17, refers to the following custom, still prevalent. The mourners, during

* The covering of the head and lips in this manner is used on other occasions to express sorrow and humiliation. The Christians in the upper country were forced always thus to appear among the Muslems, and I have seen them in church on the approach of the host hasten thus to cover their heads and lips. In these cases it seems simply a badge of humiliation and respect.

the days of mourning, do not bake bread, each of the neighbors sending in a few loaves, for the present supply of the family, and then when the "days of mourning are ended," they make a feast, to which the neighbors are invited. See also Deut. xxvi. 16, and Hosea ix. 4.

3d. *Going barefoot.* This is mentioned in the above passage, and also together with the covering of the head, in 2d Sam. xv. 36, and xix. 4.

4th. *Rending the clothes.* This is frequently mentioned in the Scripture as a sign of grief, and we frequently witnessed it. It is usually done by the women, and in the funeral procession they may frequently be seen, apparently in a very ostentatious manner, holding up before them, and tearing a portion of their veil or loose dress.

5th. Connected with this, the wearing of, and *girding with sackcloth*, is often mentioned, and one of the women above mentioned, had a strip of sackcloth around her waist under her loose dress, one end of which she held in each hand, these ends protruding outside her garment, while at the same time she was dancing in a most violent manner.

6th. *The employment of mourning women.* Their office is fully described, Jer. ix. 17: "Call for the mourning women that they may come, and send for cunning women that they may come, and let them make haste, and take up a wailing for us, that our eyes may run down with tears, and our eyelids gush out with waters." Also 2 Chron. xxxv. 25, and Matt. ix. 33. Many of these women are "skillful of lamentation." They usually describe in most hyperbolical terms the good qualities of the deceased, and lament the stroke of fate by which he has been taken away. Being exercised in the matter, they soon cause a great deal of sympathetic feeling among themselves, and as for the spectators, and especially the bereaved ones, their hearts must be hearts of stone if their eyes do "not" run down with tears, and their eyelids gush out with waters. Two or three points in their mourning deserve special mention, as being deeply founded in the laws of the human mind. 1st. They do not attempt to keep up a long continued sorrow. The period of mourning is more or less extended, according to the age, sex and social station of the deceased, but these cunning women do not attempt to keep up a long continued feeling. Human nature could not endure that. Every high excitement must have a speedy reaction, and consequently they only strive to produce a paroxysm of grief, violent, but short, and then they leave till the next day. 2d. Their gesticulations are most wild and frantic, and their expressions and shrieks of sorrow, short and piercing. They are entirely devoid of that idea of tender melancholy which we attach to grief, and often, espe-

11

cially as accompanied with instrumental music, and the not unpleasant song of the blind sheikhs, repeating the confession of faith, convey to the spectator the idea of a joyful rather than a mournful occasion. Their movements also correspond with this. The procession moves at a very quick pace, instead of slowly as with us, and the women dance, or rather jump up and down, in a manner so violent, that it is wonderful how they can long continue it. All this shows that tendency in human nature in all deep and violent emotions of the mind to pass from one extreme to the opposite. Shakspeare understood this principle well when he so often introduced in the midst of his most tragic scenes a clown or buffoon to relieve for a time the audience from their intense and painful excitement, and cause them to laugh at sayings and actions, which, on other occasions, would only have excited contempt ; and J. B. Gough doubtless owes much of his success as an orator to his skillful commingling of the pathetic and ludicrous in the arrangement of his anecdotes. It is wonderful to what an extent even the joyful is mingled with the violent and demonstrative grief of an oriental funeral. The procession is often preceded by a company of boys, who run about and frolic, singing as they go their school lessons from the Kuran in a most joyous strain. Then come the religious sheikhs (usually blind) chant-

ing in a not unpleasant manner, the Mohammedan confession of faith, "There is no deity,
but Allah, and Mohammed is the prophet of
Allah." Then follow the male mourners and
friends, who usually abstain in public from all
demonstration of grief. Then follows the bier,
not in sombre pall, but covered with a bright
colored cloth, usually a Persian shawl embroidered with scarlet. At its head, on an upright
staff, is placed the tarboush of the deceased,
often ornamented with jewels and tinsel. Bou-
quets of flowers and green and red flags, with
verses of the Kuran, are often carried in connection with it. Behind it, follow the mourning
women and the female members of the family
with their expressive and often violent demonstrations of grief.

7th. Connected with this I may mention the
voluntary and formal character of oriental mourning. They set about it as a *performance* which
the usages of society and the memory of the deceased demand of them, and they call upon the
wise, cunning women to come and assist them
in the work. Among the poorer classes who
cannot afford to call hired mourners, the neighboring women are expected to come and assist
in the work, and if they do not come, jealousy
and hard feelings are the result; and they may
expect to be left to mourn alone when their time
comes. So David called upon Israel to mourn

for Abner, 2 Sam. iii. 31, and this voluntary
character of the mourning makes it a fit subject
for legislation; and the government has recently
sent out an order that the women should not be
allowed to run into excesses in their mourning,
and passing one day through the streets with
Mustapha Aga, he scattered a company of
mourning women in a harsh and unceremonious
manner which would have seemed very grating
on the feelings had their lamentations been the
expression of true sorrow. How different is all
this from the subdued, chastened, and heartfelt
sorrow of the Christian heart!

The time prescribed by custom for the mourning varies. Children, and especially females, are
often hurried away to the tomb by the bearers
and sheikhs alone, not even the members of the
family following. Grown up males, and especially "an only son," require a longer time, and
the days of mourning are often extended to two
or three weeks. All the house of Israel mourned
for Aaron, and also for Moses, thirty days. Joseph and his Egyptian friends mourned for Jacob
three score and ten days, and afterwards at the
threshing floor of Atad, which is beyond Jor-
dan, they mourned with a great and very sore
lamentation, seven days, so that the inhabitants
of the land said, "This is a grievous mourning to the Egyptians," and the Egyptians
are still noted among all the orientals for

the length and grievousness of their lamentations.

8th. *Going about the streets.* Solomon says, Ecc. xii. 6, "And the mourners *go about the streets.*" It was always the custom in Luxor for the mourning procession to make the circuit of the town; and when the mourning extended over several days, they each day did so, going through the principal streets.

9th. *Casting dust upon the head,* and towards heaven. Job ii. 12. This is still the custom. On the occurrence of a death the women of the house often go to the coal house or ash heap, and sitting down cover themselves with coal dust or ashes, while screaming and tearing their hair and clothes in a terrible manner; and in the streets they often bedaub their faces and clothes with mud.

10th. *Exclamations apostrophizing the dead.* In the instance with which I commenced the men who were the sons of the deceased were crying out, "According to what God has judged, O my Father. In the religion of God, O my Father, O my Father! O my Father." This reminded me of David's expressions: "O Absalom, my son, my son Absalom," etc., and other Scriptural examples. 1 Kings xiii. 30; 2 Sam. iii. 33; Jer. xxii. 18.

11th. *Formal visits of condolence.* These are expected from the friends of the family of the deceased, and are often given when there is but little friendship or true sympathy with the bereaved, and sometimes a long journey is made for the purpose. Thus Job's three friends came to comfort him in his affliction, though their speeches did not exhibit much true sympathy. Two instances have come under my notice in which distant villages were visited for the purpose. In one of these, happening to be at the bishop's house, a messenger came from the family of the deceased, announcing the death of a mother, and asking for a friend to come and comfort them. The bishop ordered one of the priests to go, at the same time complaining of it as a hardship, saying that when she was living they wished her out of the way, but that now she had died, she had suddenly become very dear and precious to them. I asked them what consolations they offered on such occasions. He said, "Oh, we say that Adam died, and Abraham died, and that all the patriarchs and fathers died, and that we all must die—and the like empty talk." Three other priests besides the one about to go, and a number of the people being present, I made them sit down and gave them a specimen of the consolations of the gospel, and then having the priest bring his Testament, I turned down the leaves of the 15th of 1st Cor., and the 11th and 14th of John, and told them to read for them those chapters, and explain them as well as he could ; and the next day when he returned he said he had done so, and they thought it much better than the stereotyped phrases which they had been accustomed to use. Many of those phrases, however, are very expressive and pretty. I was struck with the following : in consoling for the death of a child, if there be other children, it is said, " The blessing is in those that remain"—and if an only child—"God will replace it by a better." But I will not give more, for such expressions lose their force in translating. They are mostly the maxims of a stoic philosophy. They do not offer to the smitten heart the strong consolation of Him who is the resurrection and the life, and truly they are " empty talk."

I might mention other points of Scripture illustration, but these are the most important.

It is important to remark that many of those customs exist only, and all of them in greater perfection, among the Muslems, and especially those of Bedouin origin, than among the Christians and Jews. The latter might have been suspected of copying them from the Bible, but the former cannot. Thus testimony is borne to the fidelity of the description of oriental manners and customs contained in the Scriptures, and thus strength is added to the strong chain of argument by which they are proved authentic.

Before leaving the subject I may be permitted

to mention a classical illustration. Most of the women carried in their hands in the funeral processions long staves of a kind of reed abundant in Egypt. These they flourished in the air over their heads, and taken in connection with their leapings and convulsions, they reminded me of the orgies of the Bacchantes with their thyrsus, staves. They seemed only to want the deerskin nebris, and the ancient Egyptian priests, as depicted in the funeral processions in the Theban tombs, wore a leopard skin. I have never seen elsewhere this carrying of staves, and it was interesting to witness it in Thebes, from which we know so much of the Greek and Roman mythology, as well as the Christian superstitions, have their origin.

The following description given by Herodotus, "the father of history," of what he saw in Egypt over 2,300 years ago, is also interesting, as illustrating a number of these customs. He says, "The following is the way in which they conduct their mournings or funerals. On the death in any house of a man of consequence, forthwith the women of the family beplaster their heads, and sometimes even their faces, with mud, and then leaving the body indoors, sally forth and wander through the city, with their dress fastened by a band and their bosoms bare, beating themselves as they walk. All the female relations join them and do the same. The men, too, similarly begrit, beat their breasts separately. When these ceremonies are over, the body is carried away to be embalmed. The sculptures on the ancient tombs represent the mourners as performing the same acts.

CHAPTER V.

Afternoon 19*th*. Walked out and met the man who came the other day with Yakob. Was sorry to learn that he was to return in a few days to his native village, Pesht. As this was a place not put down on the maps, and I had never heard of it, I asked him about it, when he told me that in ancient times it was a large town, but that a certain bishop in passing through the streets one day, some boys who were playing chanced to throw a missile, which put out his reverence's eye, when he cursed the town, and thus cursed it had ever since remained; and that most of its inhabitants, having learned by experience that they could not prosper in so ill-starred a place, had removed to other parts of the country; and that he had avoided the effects of the bishop's curse by building his house a short distance off from the town. Thus Egypt also has her Jericho. Josh. vi. 26.

20*th*. Went out as usual to seek some one to whom I might speak the Word of Life. Met Yakob, and for more than an hour we sat conversing in the sun, and on a disagreeable dusty bank. Found that he had spent most of his life in Khartum, far into the interior. I was delighted with the deep interest with which he received the truth, and his submission to the Word of God in all points of controversy.

Called on the bishop, and found him not at all well. He had been ailing ever since I came, and I had been giving him medicine which he thought did him great good; but he insisted on taking more blue pill than I wished to venture on administering, especially as he had a great antipathy to taking oil after it, thinking arrack would do quite as well. The latter, together with his fasting diet, was evidently causing his illness. He showed me the measure of the amount he daily took, and I persuaded him to come down to half his usual allowance, and also pressed him to break his fast. He said that he would willingly do so, but that the people would say that he had turned infidel. He expressed strong faith in my medicines. At the same time he talked strangely and mysteriously of visions which he had had during a former illness—of Mary and others of the heavenly host passing before him and speaking to him, and seemed to speak despondingly that he was not now thus favored. I told him that he should not regard this—that the wise man said that dreams come " through the multitude of business," and that therefore we should not regard them as either good or bad omens— when I was quite surprised to hear him say in answer that these were not dreams of which he spake, but actual visions, which he saw when wide awake. He said this hesitatingly and dubiously, as if he hardly thought I would believe him, as other and more superstitious ones had done—as if he himself hardly believed what he was asserting. To this I could answer nothing, as it took me entirely beyond my sphere of thought and experience. It was, however, to me an interesting incident, as helping to solve a problem which I was then deeply pondering, viz: how it came to pass that the ancient church, and especially the Coptic church, had been so imposed upon by "lying wonders." I was then reading a volume which I had before borrowed from him, viz.: The Life of St. Bakhum, (Pachomius of Church History,) and found it quite full of visions, dreams, apparitions, and miracles, and all narrated in a simple, artless style, and attended with circumstances which showed that the renowned saint himself, his cotemporaries, and the narrator, were all alike sincere and in earnest. I could not, (and yet for the time I did not see why I should not,) receive their united testimony, especially when we recollect the number of those who were deceived. More than 6,000 were following Bakhum to the convents which he established in this neighborhood. I see it now, and the bishop's visions helped to put me on the track. This tempts me, as usual, to go into a long digression on the subject, but I must for the present forego the pleasure, hoping if ever I get through with these notes, (and have any time left for writing,) to be able to return to the subject. I may here, however, be permitted to make a couple of general remarks, which, to those who think and have the imagination to transfer themselves to a different state of society from that in which they live, will suffice to lay bare the whole subject. These "lying wonders" seem to require in the age in which they are produced and received two conditions:

1. The existence of a superstitious, wonder-loving people, whose minds have been deeply stirred and excited on religion, but who, at the same time, are not living under the full blaze of Gospel light—who have some knowledge of unseen realities, but who, at the same time, have not had them revealed to the eye of faith, with that clearness with which it is the province of the Gospel to reveal them.

2. Certain men, (and in such a state of society these will not be wanting,) who will supply the demand which is thus created for lying legends. These legend mongers, judging from their works and the books which describe their lives, may clearly be divided into two classes: First, Barefaced impostors — men who deliberately and craftily set themselves for their own private ends to furnish food for the popular craving

which we have described. They boldly and
unblushingly put forth their cunningly devised
fables, and lay claims to lying wonders, and they
are readily received by a people not disposed to
be skeptical, nor competent, (were they so,) to
sift evidence and detect imposture.

The second class are a simple race—a "feeble
folk"—like the conies, and like them they "make
their houses in the rocks." They are the true
monks; not the men who are led by either craft
or indolence to assume the monkish robe. They
are themselves deceived, and self-deceived before
deceiving others. They are men of ardent but
not well-balanced minds. Their imaginations
are warm, and they are inflamed by meditation,
and fasting, and prayer, and solitude, until, in
their disordered conceptions, the inner and the
outer worlds become all confused. They lose
the power of always discriminating between the
ideal and the real, the subjective and objective,
fancy and fact. They mistake their internal
impressions for external perceptions. They hear
voices which come not from without, but only
from the depths of their own spirits. They see
visions which are only painted on the internal
surface of the retina—they receive visits from
angels and demons, which are the creations of
their own disordered imaginations—they believe
what they wish to be true, and these crude creations of their own fancies they throw out upon

a credulous public, too ready to receive, and once afloat, they do not suffer diminution as they pass from mouth to mouth.

This second class is by far the more danger- ous of the two; for sincerity carries with it a power which with the masses can (even in more enlightened communities) disarm skepticism, and dispense with proofs. Of the former class was the author of the Memoir of Sit Damiane, (the famous saintess of the Coptic Church,) with her forty virgins. He was a bold fabricator who cut his story, as we would say, "from whole cloth." Of the latter class was Pachomius. He was a sincere and earnest man, and his dis- ciple, Tadrus, (Theodorus,) was a singularly simple and transparent character. It is pleasing to find in his memoir, mixed with much that is superstitious, such strong evidences of true and sincere piety, and also that he was so free from many of the corruptions which have since been superadded to the Coptic faith. He possessed, too, with all his simplicity, good administrative powers, and a keen discernment of character. His power, as well as the favorable attitude of the public mind towards such a delusion, and the depth of the moral disease, and especi- ally the licentiousness which it was sought thus either to cure or flee, were shown by the suc- cess which attended the movement of which he was the leader. There had before been ascetics, who had fled to the living death of the desert; but though not the founder of the monastic life, he was the founder of regularly organized monastic institutions. His first convent was founded on the island of Tabenna, near Ghinneh, and he preached monasticism with such success, and built up his convent for the reception of his followers so industriously, that he soon found himself surrounded by a company of fifteen hundred monks. These he left under the charge of Tadrus, and went to Edfou, and built a similar convent, and thus he and a few of his faithful followers successively swarmed from hive to hive, until, at his death, he found himself at the head of a large number of convents containing about 7,000 monks. His brother, John, succeeded Tadrus as his right-hand man, and his sister also founded a convent for women, which flourished.

On a future occasion, I may write something about the rule of life which he prescribed to his followers; for the present I must proceed with the narrative. We cannot help admiring the self-sacrificing spirit which led these men thus to renounce the world, and devote themselves to the austerities of a monkish life. Had that self-sacrifice and devotion been employed in the evangelization of Africa, it would have carried the Gospel to the Cape of Good Hope.

In speaking of the two great needs of Egypt,

it will be seen, from my making the second item the *result* of the first, and from the manner in which I speak of a *forced* civilization, that I do not sympathize with those theorists who would make steam and modern improvements in the arts and sciences the great agencies which are to regenerate the world, and make it enlightened and happy. The opinions which I then had in my mind to oppose, are well set forth in the following extracts, which have since fallen under my notice:

"Steam is the acknowledged new element of advancement by which this age is distinguished from all which have preceded it. By its magical power distance is set at naught, and the productions of the antipodes are brought rapidly together. Coal must therefore henceforth be the motor and meter of all commercial nations. Without it no modern people can become great, either in manufacture or in naval art. As an illustration of this, if the disgression may be allowed, the mighty transformations which are this day taking place in the countries about the Mediterranean, especially among the Turks, where lives the presiding genius of Muslemism, might be adduced. The paddle-wheels of European intelligence and enterprise are there daily breaking up the stagnant waters of oriental superstition, ignorance, and despotim. Not a steamer plows the waters, from the pillar of Hercules to

12*

the Sea of Japan, that goes not as a herald of
civilization and Christianity to those benighted
nations.   Already has steam navigation wrought
a mighty change.   It has changed the whole
moral, political and social world.   It has brought
nations into neighborhood, made them acquainted
with one-another's advantages, disadvantages,
virtues and vices, and thus struck a death-blow
to a thousand prejudices and superstitions, and
made many tribes of rude barbarians ashamed
of their ignorance and barbarism, and resolved
to imitate their improved neighbors.   It has
wrought a mighty change on the habits of the
sluggish nations of the East. The paddle-wheels
of improvement, and the terrific puffs of the
fire and smoke of reform, have broken up the
stagnant waters of every nation, from Constantinople to Japan."—*Quarterly Review.*

"But the innovation of the mightiest magni-
tude, the one which has done most to break up
the stagnation of Turkish Orientalism, is the
introduction of steam navigation.   This has
opened a new chapter to the sluggish mind of
the East, and portends a revolution, moral, political, social and intellectual, of vast interest to
the Christian philanthropist."—*Read's Hand of
God in History.*

These extracts contain a modicum of truth,
but their expressions are far too strong and enthusiastic; and, if I mistake not, their authors

have fallen into the common error of putting
the effect for the cause. They would doubtless
point to Egypt as the brightest example of the
truth of what they assert—and I will briefly
state the case as it presents itself to my mind
here in Egypt.

1. Mere contact and familiarization of the
mind with the steam-engine, or any other work of
art, is not enough to raise and enlighten a people.
If this were the case, the Egyptians must always
have been enlightened, for since the days of
Thothmes and Rameses they have always had
before their minds monuments of science and
art, in comparison with which the steam-engine
is a child's plaything. The sight of an engine
may lead a few inquiring minds into investiga-
tions into the nature of a piston and a valve, of
the properties of steam, and the power of a
vacuum, which may, to a certain extent, enlarge
their capacities and spheres of thought; but
then the question is, whether this enlargement
will be used to subserve any good, social, moral
or political end. The mere contemplation of a
work of art will no more make men enlightened
and happy, than natural theology will make
them Christians.

But the fact is, that very few will inquire or
investigate. It is too far above them. It is an
intruder into their "stagnant waters," which
they content themselves with gazing upon in

stupefied amazement, as people would look upon a ghost, intruding into the common walks of life. This is not a figure of speech. A friend told me that one day, when, from some accident, the train stopped in its course and would not proceed, he overheard a fellah saying to his neighbor: "The affreet (demon) of the Franks is bewitched to-day."

But 2. It would not accomplish the ends proposed were it otherwise—were the engine not a foreign intrusion, but a result of self-developed enterprise and intelligence. For such in reference to the *ancient* Egyptians were the monuments of science and artistic skill to which I have alluded, and which have been to this day the wonders and the models of the world, and yet the people who conceived and executed them were a nation of miserable slaves. The gods which they worshipped were cats, and serpents, and beetles and hawks, and crocodiles — indeed, almost every creeping and living thing, so that it was said that it was easier to find a god than a man in Egypt; and if it be true that men become assimilated to that which they worship, we need bring no further proofs (which we might abundantly do, were it necessary) as to what they were, morally, politically, socially and intellectually; and like causes produce like effects. Were it otherwise—were the theory of the authors whom I have quoted correct, France should be, as to her "moral, political, social, and intellectual" character, one of the first and happiest of nations, one to which the Christian philanthropist might point with pleasure; and yet, what is the fact in France—poor, corrupt, hollowhearted, enslaved, unhappy France? Something more effective than art and science, more mighty than coal and steam, or the civilization of which they may be the "motor or meter," is needed to regenerate her and make her happy.

But 3. Our authors evidently attribute the "mighty transformations" which they imagine have here taken place, or are about to take place, as the result of steam navigation, to the contact which is thus brought about between "European intelligence and enterprise, and Oriental superstition, ignorance, and despotism." We suppose their idea is that each steamer must be "a herald of civilization and Christianity to those benighted nations," because each steamer bears to them civilized and Christian men, and not from any inherent virtue which the steamer itself possesses. This might be the case, were all who are brought civilized and Christian men, and were they, after coming here, true to their principles. But the contrary is, alas! the fact. It is a low estimate to say that nine out of ten of those who come have not been prepared by their previous training to exert an influence for good upon those to whom they come, but rather for evil. Thus the influence

of the few who have had a different training is
more than counteracted; and, even as to themselves, they soon find it much easier to glide along
with, than to oppose, the overpowering current
which on every hand they must breast. Unless
their good principles have been cast in a very
stern mould, they soon wilt and wither like plants
transplanted into an arid soil and under a burning
sun; and it is lamentable to see how even Englishmen, instead of raising to their own high level
those around them, are dragged down to the very
earth by the inert mass which on every side at-
taches to them. There is in morals, as well as in
physics, a law of gravitation. There are some
bright exceptions to these general remarks. Their
influence is good, and they deserve all praise.
Such being the case, the influence upon the natives is such as might have been expected. They
learn the vices but not the virtues of the new-
comers. They fail of the "advantages," but secure for themselves and entail upon their children
the "disadvantages" of civilization. Steam navigation *has* opened a new chapter to the sluggish
mind of the East. But it is a chapter whose head-
ing is, "A spurious and hollow civilization," and
whose subdivisions are, "A grasping avarice, an
unbounded licentiousness, and a flippant skepticism." It *has* "made them ashamed of their ignorance and babarism," but unsophisticated ignorance and barbarism are better than a painted

and polished corruption. It has destroyed superstition, but superstition is easier dealt with—is
nearer the truth, than hard-hearted infidelity. I
am now in a position to make the comparison. I
have found in this journey among the poor peasants of Upper Egypt, a sense of want and a
desire of improvement, a readiness to part with
their scanty earnings for books on religion and
science, and an earnestness in their study such
as I have never met with in Alexandria and other
seaport towns where intercourse with the Franks
has been enjoyed. Difference of race may in part
account for the marked difference, (for these
descendants of the ancient Copts are an earnest,
inquiring people;) still the fact exists, and it is
significant.

The following is a type of the new class of philosophy which is springing up under the tuition
of their European teachers. On my last trip
between Alexandria and Cairo, I had sitting just
in front of me a sprig of what may be called
Young Egypt, a youth just entering his teens.
He was decked out in the usual style, with cloth
coat and pants, silk vest, and massive gold chain.
He was reading (as attentively as his constant
smoking of cigarettes would allow) an English
book, which I found to be "Female Life among
the Mormons." (In a trip which I had taken a
few days before, I had as "companion du voyage" one of these chaps reading "Barnum's

Autobiography" in French.) It would take me a long time to describe the *airs* which he put on at the different stations at which we stopped, with his compeers of the telegraph service. One expression will serve as a significant index of the whole. The train was moving rather slowly, when he impatiently looked out of the window, and, puffing out a volume of smoke, he said, "This driver, d—n his eyes, is going very slow!" This boy had spent five years in a Protestant mission school, and as he was engaged in the telegraph service, his subsequent associations had been with Englishmen. What might I tell of those, and they are the large majority, who have had their training in Jesuit and Lazarist schools, and whose subsequent intercourse has been with the low Italians and French, of whom we have thousands in Alexandria, the off-scouring of Europe?

4. Steam navigation, and the other modern improvements of which it may be considered the type, must (in order to accomplish the great results expected from it) be the result of native development, (assisted, it may be, from without, but still native and indigenous,) or those expectations will be disappointed. It must not be an exotic—a foreign "intrusion into the stagnant waters" forced upon the people before they are prepared for it, and against their wills. The contrary has been the case here, and it has been and

is ruining the country and crushing the spirit of the people. Mohammed Ali initiated that policy, and his family has since followed it. It has given Egypt an appearance of prosperity which has made many people loud in its praise, but I cannot agree with them; for it is for the most part only an appearance—a glittering mask seen at Alexandria and, in a measure, at Cairo; behind it is poor, deformed, down-trodden Egypt. I will give a few examples to illustrate my meaning. And, first, we will mention one of the first acts of Mohammed Ali's reign, which has obtained a world-wide notoriety—the digging of the Mahmudiyeh Canal, between Alexandria and the Nile. For this work it is said that 250,000 or 300,000 of the poor peasants were driven together, and under great privations and the lash of the task-master, they performed the task in a month. 23,000 men are said to have fallen victims to the hardships endured, but even this oblation on the altar of Alexandria's prosperity must have been a small matter compared with the crushing effect of such an act of despotism on the other 275,000, their families and villages. The dam over the Nile, just below Cairo, was hardly a less work; and it was performed in the same manner. It never has answered any purpose, except to serve as a toll-gate for the annoyance of passing boats and the increase of the already swollen revenues of the Government; and there it stands, a monu-

13

ment of the folly of an ignorant despot, undertaken at the suggestion of an ignorant French
engineer. Factories, foundries, bridges, colleges,
etc., were built all over the land, and, empty and
unused, they have since been falling to ruins;
young men were torn from the bosom of their
families and sent to England and France, some
of them to school, and others to learn trades—
apparently a wise though a despotic measure;
but it has not met the expectations which it in-
spired. Most of the young men came back with
that little learning which the poet declares to be
a dangerous thing. As most of them were sent
to France, they came back infidels, and nearly
all of them on their return met with obstacles to
the carrying out of the purposes for which they
were sent, which rendered the whole measure
next to an entire failure. Take one example. A
young man was sent to Glasgow to learn the
trade of carpet-weaving. He spent some years
there, during which time he made a profession
of Christianity, and was baptized. He came
back with all the necessary machinery for a large
carpet-factory. This he set up, and one carpet
was made, when it was found that carpets could
be imported from Europe much more cheaply
than made here, and the enterprise was abandoned. This young favorite of the Government
has since been retained in its employment, but
at work for which his former training gave him

no special fitness, and, of course, at a rate of wages much higher than he has deserved. Soon after he returned from England he essayed to take a stand as a Christian, when Mohammed Ali called him up and asked him whether he had sent him to England to learn Christianity or carpet-weaving. This question from such a man as Mohammed Ali, was sufficient, and he has never since dared to manifest any Christian tendencies.

And this is the policy which has since been pursued by the reigning house. Gangs of laborers—men, boys and girls—may everywhere be seen driven like cattle to their work by the bayonet of the soldier and the lash of the taskmaster, and humanity hardly knows whether to rejoice in the fact that that lash is seldom needed, except for a threatening crack. Yet so it is. So degraded have the people become, so accustomed to regard themselves as the slaves and mere tools of Effendina, the Pasha, that they have come to regard this trampling upon their rights as men, as a matter of course, and the cheerful songs of the long lines of children which file along with their baskets of earth or hods of mortar upon their heads, usually supply the incitement to their heavy toil, which would otherwise be administered by the lash.

The following dialogue will illustrate the *esprit du corps* of these gangs of Egyptian peasants.

In one of my donkey rides one evening, outside of the gates of Alexandria, I overtook a boy, about twelve years of age, going out to the palace which the Pasha was building for his sister on the Mahmudiyeh, in which work he, with hundreds of others, was engaged. I saluted him with

"Good evening, my boy; where are you going?"

He returned my salutation, and answered, "To the works."

"From which village are you?"

"From such an one," he said, mentioning a town near Cairo.

"How many people are there here from your village?"

"A hundred."

"And how long are you to remain here in the works?"

"A month."

"And then who will come to take your places?"

"Another hundred from our village, and each village sends its share."

"What wages does Effendina give you?"

"Nothing; would Effendina give us wages— he is our master!"

"And what do you eat during all this month?"

"Bread; here it is," pulling out of his bosom and handing me a hard black loaf.

Handing it back to him—"And did you bring bread enough with you for the whole month from your village?"

"No; we brought all we could carry, and when it is finished, we will have to bake. But keep the loaf—keep it, you are welcome to it."

"You said you carried it; but did you not come here on the railroad?"

"No, we came afoot."

"How many days did it take you to come?"

"Four days."

"And will you go back also afoot?"

"Certainly."

"And why not by the railroad?"

"The railroad is Effendina's. He built it for the Franks."

By this time we had reached his stopping-place beside the road under an acacia tree.

"And is this your house?"

"Yes, I sleep here." There was his store of black bread in a large net-work bag made of palm leaf rope. It was a cold, raw night, and as he, barefooted and ragged, nestled down beside his bag of bread which lay rolled in the dust, I turned away with a full heart, saying, "Good evening, my boy, and may God give you patience till the day of deliverance."

And thus it is that railroads, factories, fortifi-

13*

cations and palaces, almost without number, are being raised throughout the land. Their towering walls are laid upon the very heart of poor, crushed Egypt. Their stones are cemented with her people's blood. The poet Thomson wrote well concerning the pyramids and other works of ancient art which remain unto this day:

> " Instead of useful works like nature, great,
> Enormous, cruel wonders crushed the land.
> And round a tyrant's tomb, who none deserved,
> For one vile carcass perished countless lives."

But it may be objected,—The poet's sentiment is not altogether applicable to the present works; for many of them, such as railroads, factories, etc., *are* "useful works," and, therefore, the good which will in the end result from them, will at length more than counterbalance the temporary evil incident on their first construction. I deny it. They *are not* useful works. A railroad which is built as I, a little more than a year ago, saw the one between Cairo and Suez being built, by 10,000 forced laborers, who, from overwork, insufficient food, and the bitter cold of the desert nights, were dying by hundreds—the privileges of which, when built, can be available to but few of the natives of the land on account of the high rates of fare—which, in short, is built simply to accommodate the overland passengers from a distant nation, and to swell the overgrown revenues of one man—revenues which are expended, not for the good of the people, or to promote the permanent prosperity of the land, but foolishly lavished on the whims of a despot, and to enrich a crowd of sycophants and parasites, mostly foreigners—such a railroad *is* NOT a "useful work." Its iron rails are laid upon the necks of the people, who are crushed to the very earth while a few ride triumphantly over them. It is an engine for the accomplishment of that which has always and everywhere been the chief function of despotism—the exaltation of the few at the expense of the million, and to render still more wide and impassable the gulf between the rich and the poor, the nabobs and the serfs. Such a railroad *is not* a useful work. And so of other similar works. A sugar factory—the expense of furnishing the machinery for which can be undertaken only by a Pasha, which, to pay, must be built and worked by forced labor, which must depopulate a dozen villages that their lands may serve for its wide cane fields, and the profits of which are absorbed by one man, or a favored few, and not divided among a large company of that middle class of society which, wherever it exists, is its pillar, its stay and hope—such a factory *is not* a "useful work." And even taking that which we have admitted to be the most hopeful measure of a

forced civilization, viz., the sending of young
men to the schools and workshops of England
and France, how signally and how naturally, too,
has it failed.   Take, for instance, our friend, the
carpet-weaver,—what must be the results to
himself and to his countrymen of his sojourn in
Glasgow?   As to himself, the first feelings
which would result from his being thus violently
torn from the bosom of his country and his
native land, and sent away to a land of infidels
and among a people of strange customs and
tongue, would be anything but pleasant.   But
this feeling would naturally soon wear off, and
then (and the attention which he would receive
abroad would assist in the matter,) he would
come to look upon himself as the protege of a
king, and a favorite of government, soon to return to his people a traveled hero and a prodigy
of modern science.   He naturally comes to regard himself as a made man, one whose livelihood, nay, fortune, is sure; and the incentives
to that strenuous effort and stern self-discipline
which make *men*, are wanting, (nor do his early
training and associations supply them,) and he
comes back the possessor of that "little knowledge" which the poet says "is a dangerous
thing,"—an empty pretender, who is fit for little
but to be an on-hanger of the court—a weak-
minded, emasculated sycophant, who, when ques-
tioned as to his faith, dare not say that his soul

is his own. *Men* are not made of such stuff, nor under such a regimen. Sammie Arkwright, the barber, was not thus made Sir Samuel Arkwright, the inventor of the spinning jinney and the founder of England's manufacturing wealth. Such sturdy oaks are not grown in the "hot-bed of royal patronage," but in the native soil where they must contend with the tempest and the blast.

Thus much as to the results to the man himself. Then, as to his countrymen, the income of one village, at least, is required for such an experiment. To send this young man to Scotland; to support him while there; to purchase and bring out the machinery necessary for the senseless project of a carpet factory in Egypt, and then, when it has failed, to support this young favorite in some government sinecure— these things require, at least, the income of a whole town; that is to say, a whole town must be kept for years in a state of serfdom, in order to support this experiment.

A nation is not thus made great, prosperous and happy. The process by which this is effected, is one which commences with the lower classes of society, and by raising them, raises all. It is the distinguishing trait of Christianity to do this. It commences with individuals, and the lowest and the poorest of them. It, first of all, enfranchises them from the bondage of sin and

Satan. It makes them "free *indeed*," with that
liberty with which Chirst makes his people free,
and thus it lays the only true foundation for
their regeneration and amelioration "intellectually, morally, socially and politically." Other
influences may conspire to assist in the work.
Foreign civilization may lend a helping hand.
Government may foster and encourage native
talent and industry. Modern inventions and
improvements in the arts of life may furnish a
high and advanced starting point, but still Christianity must ever be the "motor and meter" of
true civilization—the regenerator of a people.
It is a true sentiment, that "the nation is only
the aggregate of individual conditions, and civilization itself is only a question of personal improvement." Christianity alone is the system
which brings forth the *individual* and the *personal.* The system which I have spoken against,
exalts the few into the high places of temporal
wealth and position, and divides the mass into
two great classes—a crowd of spiritless, fawn-
ing sycophants and aspirants for office and royal
favors around the throne, and behind, the undis-
tinguished and degraded mass, without ambition,
hope, or motive to manly exertion and self-
improvement.

I am conscious that, in this chapter, I have
given one side of the subject, and that some
things could be said somewhat to enliven the

dark features of this picture, but with the restrictions which I have given, I can trust to the bright and glowing minds of my readers to cast sufficient light upon these dark pages.

CHAPTER VI.

20th. This evening Lord Haddo came. Seeing us descending to the beach to call upon him,
he sent off his small boat, when one of the boatmen insulted Mrs. L. This I resented, which
called forth an insolent rejoinder from one of
them, that "they were accustomed to deal with
big folks, and that it was a pity if they could
not properly hand my lady into the boat." At
this I refused to go off with them and turned to
find another boat, when, as their master was
observing them from the deck of the dahabiyeh,
they came to terms. This was my first encoun-
ter with these men, and I cannot explain what
tribulations I was destined to suffer with them
the next three months. His Lordship had received his dahabiyeh for the winter as a cour-
tesy from the Viceroy, and its crew of sixteen
men, puffed up with pride by their gay liveries
and connection with royalty, and pampered by
luxury and indolence, were the most unmanage-
able crew of lazy, hasheesh-smoking Arabs I ever

met. I had many rich scenes with them, which with the pen of a Stephens might prove very graphic in the recital; but with this general notice I will leave them, referring my readers to the narratives of Nile travelers for abundant details of similar scenes. I have read many of these, and have besides been called upon to mediate in many quarrels between travelers and their men, and I must confess that the men are generally in the right, and, with the exception of this crew, I have never met a more trustworthy, tractable, and industrious race of men than the Nile boatmen.

I found his Lordship not much improved in health. He had sold books for 4,000 piastres, though he had met with several drawbacks. First, he had not in sufficient quantity the books needed, viz., the Bible and parts of the Bible, which is the book most in demand in Egypt. Second, Father Makhiel, whom we had given him to act as colporteur, had been unwell the first twenty days of the voyage, and Lord Haddo had been under the necessity of making his boatmen colporteurs. This the latter liked very much after they had once overcome their Muslem repugnance to having anything to do with the Christian book, for as his Lordship sold beneath our regular prices, it gave them a margin to fill up in the way of securing pipe money for themselves, and consequently, when Makhiel recovered, and was able

again to resume the work, they were unwilling
to resign their commissions into his hands.
Thus a very unhappy rivalry arose, the effects
of which were bad on those who purchased; for,
first, the varying prices shook their confidence in
us Bible sellers as men of one word and one
price, (a character which we had labored hard
to establish,) and thus sent them back to their
old Arab custom of cheapening and higgling, and
second, they were often forced to receive the
book from the Muslems with remarks not very
complimentary to either the book or those who
professed its faith, and thus their sensibilities
were often sadly outraged, so much so that
Makhiel told me they often bought the book,
not because they needed it, but simply to get
it out of the hands of those vile Muslems. But
Lord Haddo knew nothing of all this, as Makhiel, not knowing English, could not inform
him, and Ali, his dragoman, was afraid to do it,
and so they did what was far worse, they themselves attempted to fight the men, a battle in
which I need hardly say they came off second
best, and when they reached Luxor they were
in the habit every night of retiring to bed with
the fear of being thrown overboard before
morning. Of course, all this cut the sinews of
Makhiel's energy in the work, and the men having a selfish reason for diligence, Lord Haddo
had come to the conclusion that his Muslems

were more diligent than the Christian in the good work. I had unconsciously given these men the key-note of my course of policy with them in the affair of handing Mrs. L. into the boat, and was able ever after to manage them, though often with great difficulty, and especially after their Ramadan* commenced, when by night they would only give themselves to gluttony and hemp-smoking, and by day their empty stomachs and hasheesh-burnt brains made them willing subjects of the demon of irritability.

21st. Spent the forenoon in company with Father Makhiel in a visit to the Bishop. The two having been old friends, had many past reminiscences to recall, and I found them in cordial sympathy in their dislike to the Patriarch. His edition of Antar and his order for Russian images for his new cathedral in Cairo were severely criticized.

Saw Lord Haddo in the afternoon. He proposed that we should go up with him to Assouan, and then he hire for us a smaller boat, and we spend a month in exploring and distributing books in Nubia. But though this would have been very pleasant, I clung to the proverb that "a bird in the hand is worth two in the bush;" and I could not in Nubia nor anywhere else expect to enjoy better opportunities of preaching the truth, both in the church and in private,

* A Muslem feast of forty days' duration.

than I then had in Luxor, and so I declined.   An
acre of ground well cultivated is better than a
plantation run to weeds.   There is no need of
tracing, like Alexander the Great, our outlines
of flour over a larger surface than we at present
are prepared to build upon.   Jowett explored
and marked out all Egypt, and, indeed, all the
East, and what did it result in?   When we are
ready to occupy Nubia, it will be time enough
to explore it; and besides, on the Nile, it is a
principle to push up the stream when the wind
blows, and we were now enjoying a wonderful
breeze of priestly favor, which, by the time we
could return from such a trip, might have subsi-
ded into a dead calm, or be succeeded by a
counter-gale. Already I found I had to trim my
sails very skillfully in order to keep them full,
and a short time after a side flaw struck us
which, like a gust from one of the steep cliffs on
the eastern shore of the river, set us all upon
our beam ends in a moment.

I may here as well go back a little and bring
up the history of our relations with his Reverence the Bishop.   I have already stated that
Brother McCague, on his visit here last autumn,
established the school in a private house, and
that when this was needed by the owner, the
bishop had kindly removed the school to the
church.   He evidently had a two-fold motive in
this: first, to secure our help in building a

school-room and some store-rooms for the Episcopal tythes, on the lot beside the church, for
which he had already collected the materials,
and second, to secure our influence with the
Frank travelers who might sojourn there, as it
had been principally by means received from
them that he had built the church, and he judged
that we would be able to secure a continuance
of their favors. Besides he knew that he was
in bad odor with Fadil Pasha in Ghinneh, and
he thought he might need some political protection for the work. For building the church,
he had obtained, from the Government, through
the English consul at Cairo, a firman, and it had
enabled him to build the church by forced labor.
He often used to boast that that church came as
easy as water. There was another strong bond
by which he was bound to the school. He had
convinced Brother McCague, when there, that
besides Monsur their regular areef (or schoolmaster) was necessary in the school, and also
Priest Antonius, his nephew, a lazy fellow, who
had spent a few weeks in Mr. Leider's school in
Cairo, where he had acquired a few words of
English, enough to enable him to palm himself
off upon the Luxorites as a prodigy of learning,
and upon the verdant among the travelers the
false scarabæi* which he spent his time in manufacturing. Each of these two was to receive a

* Images of beetles as worshiped by the ancient Egyptians.

14*

pittance of wages per month, and the areef richly earned his, for he was a good teacher, and the school was so large that he was needed. And Antonius had also in the beginning done good service by using his priestly influence in bringing in the children, but now he had nothing more to do, and I found on reaching there that he had no more conscience of either his school or priestly duties than to spend his time sitting in the street on the sunny side of a wall, carving with his knife false scarabiæ to palm off on the travelers. His want of conscience in the matter was so great that he even boldly asked me a few days after reaching there, for the loan of my Wilkinson, that he might copy from it the cartouches of the kings, from Menes down to the Ptolemies to serve as patterns for his art. I said to him, "Very well, go with me to the house and get it;" but when there, I took him aside and gave him such a lecture that he was glad to get off without it, and henceforth he abandoned the trade, at least in public. Still it was a great problem to know what to do with him. In securing to our cause such a priest, we were put in the position of the man who got the elephant. The next question was to know how to feed him and what to do with him. He could not be dismissed without giving mortal offense to the bishop, and this, in our circumstances, would not answer; and to pay him even the pittance of $4 per month of mission money, for the mere exercise of his influence in keeping the children in the school, this still less would answer. So I did the best thing I could think of for the time. I was reading the life of Pachomius, and other Arabic manuscripts, and found the hand-writing very crabbed, and trying to the eyes, and so I proposed to use him as eyes, to read to me several hours in the day. But this was looked upon by the bishop, who could not understand my scruples in the matter, as only a wedge to foist him altogether out of our service, and besides it was too much like work for poor Antonius, and he soon discontinued. This was the first bucket of cold water upon the new zeal of the bishop. Then, secondly, my sermons in the church were soon found to be quite too popular with the people. All his objections on this score he put on the ground of my disparaging the Virgin. But this I never did. I extolled her virtues and piety in the highest terms, but I said she was a mortal, and we should not pray to her. But, thirdly, he found he was not getting all the money out of us he had hoped for. The system of doling the money out to him for building the new school-house, only about as fast as we were getting the value of it in the rent of the church as school-room, did not meet his expectations. If Solomon had lived in the year 1577 of the martyrs (they don't date there A.D.

but from Diocletian) he would have added the Bishop of Luxor to his list of things which cry, give, give. I kept my hand hard clenched, but I assure you it was a hard task to do so. The building had now been going on a month, and I had only given $5, and was determined to give no more for some time to come; but it was very amusing to see all the artifices which he set on foot to cause the hard muscles to relax.

About this time the bishop undertook to take me in with a *coup d'état*, and I am sorry to say that for the time he succeeded. The whole story extended over several weeks, but I will now undertake to tell it all, so that the thread of the narrative may not be broken, and then go back for my scattering notes.

Fadil Pasha of Ghinneh, who was then the Governor of all this district as far as Assouan, was a terrible tyrant, but withal a man of a good deal of decision and rough justice for a Turk. He was then just levying forced laborers from all his district to dig in the canal on the opposite side of the river. This, as is usual in such cases, he did by demanding from each village their quota, to be apportioned among the inhabitants and sent on by the shaikhs of the villages. The bishop came to me with the story that George, the Christian shaikh of Luxor, was his inveterate enemy, and that he was making this conscription a pretext to annoy him by taking away the men who were at work on the school-house, and that, men who according to the rules of apportionment were not subject to the draft, and that he had been guilty of other outrages, such as interfering with the men who brought stones for the work, etc. This also touched me, although I had told the bishop from the first that we would undertake no responsibility in the building, except that of furnishing our mite towards the work, and that when done the house would be his, and that we only wished him to allow us to serve the community by keeping a school in it. But still it seemed too hard to have our work thus interfered with, and in an evil day I consented to make a representation to the Governor on the subject. On this the bishop immediately brought in a scribe, who —with an abundance of dark phraseology, and rhetorical flourishes, for which the Coptic scribes are noted, by which they so cover up the sting of a communication that it can only be detected by one initiated—wrote what purported to be a request that our men, to the number of twenty, might be allowed to go on undisturbed in the work, and complaining of the malversations of the shaikh. I noticed that the document did not say categorically that these men were not subject to the draft, and called their attention to it, but they insisted that it was all right, and I confess the truth I was simple and did not see

the plot, and so it was sent as it was. I also represented the case to Lord Haddo, and wrote
a note in French, asking the kind attention of
the Governor to the subject. The Governor
took it as a claim of exemption for these men
from their just duty in the canal, and wrote
us each a very polite note, reminding us that it
was the law of the land that no church nor school
should be built without a license from the Viceroy, and that if we had received one from headquarters, he would be very happy to furnish the
men to execute it. To this document I did not
see fit to return any answer, except through
Mustapha Aga, our consular agent in Luxor,
"that we were not fellahs, and under Turkish
but American law—that we were living in the
country with the knowledge and tacit consent
of the Government, and that our business was
to establish schools and labor for the enlightenment of the people, and that we only claimed
the same right of being allowed to pursue our
avocation unmolested which courtezans and grog-
shop keepers and other unlawful characters enjoyed, and that besides, even in their law, we
had never read that school-houses were included
in the prohibition of churches." This to him;
and to the bishop I said, "We will still go on
with the work with such men as we can get, and
if they take them all away, we will labor with
our own hands. We shall not admit his right

to prohibit our building." Had the bishop been either wise or honest, he would have fallen in with my whim and set the Government at defiance, and the result would propbably have been that the case would have been referred to Cairo, where we could have got the consuls to back us, and a precedent might have been established for building churches and schools throughout the land without a government permit. But the bishop was neither wise nor honest. I could not then bring him to take that view of the subject, nor did he, until in the case of Faris, six months later, he and all Egypt learned our power. After that I saw him in Cairo, and he freely admitted his error. So at the time he was immovable, and the work stopped. This led me to study his conduct, and finally to see through his plot, which was simply to secure exemption from the work in the canal for twenty men, when he could readily get so many to work for him, *gratis*, and then he would *eat*, as the Arab phrase has it, but perhaps I might say, with a nearer approach to truth, *drink*, in the form of arrack, the money which he should receive from me and the travellers for paying his workmen, and besides it would put into his hand a large patronage, and make him almost as important for the time being as a consular agent. And from the first this had been a great point which he had striven to carry with me, viz., that

I should use my influence to have him appointed
American Consular Agent in the place of Mustapha the Muslem, and, all I had been able to say,
I could not convince him that it would not be
fitting for a bishop and an ambassador of the
Great King of Heaven to stoop to an agency for
one of earth's little kings.

By the time I had come to the above sage
conclusion as to his motives in the movement,
(and I should have done so before, had I not
been of that race of Dutchmen who never see
the point of a joke till the next day,) Fadil
Pasha had received my answer, which was truly
Dutch in its sturdy obstinacy, and he sent down
an agent to inquire into the matter. I now had
nothing to say but that I still clung to the doctrine of the message as to our rights in the
matter, but that the bishop had deceived me, and
I had thrown him overboard, and would do
nothing more in helping him build the school.
This, of course, brought him down with his full
weight upon the bishop, and it was not long before all the males in his family connection, who
were to have been so neatly exempted, were,
right or wrong, in the canal under the lash of
the taskmaster, and when some of them showed
themselves refractory they were sent to Ghinneh
to engage in the honorable occupation of sweeping the streets, with a long iron appendage to
their feet. I need hardly say that from that

day our school in the church was doomed. The bishop finally saddled his pony and rode to Ghinneh and humbled himself before the Pasha, when, after a sharp reprimand, his offence was pardoned. I will now return to the thread of my narrative.

22d. The bishop being in high spirits about our proposed letter to Fadil Pasha, I thought I would strike the iron while hot, in the matter of securing his consent to a proposition which I had already mentioned to him, viz., to have also an afternoon service in the church. I went in the evening and found the priests and some of the people in the church saying prayers. On my return I stopped with them till midnight. It was the Feast of the Virgin, and they were repeating the twenty-four chapters of fulsome and blasphemous praise to her which the Coptic Church has borrowed from the Greeks. Oh! how sickening are these exhibitions of blind superstition! I found the bishop ready to admit the force of my plea for an afternoon service to explain the Epistle, as we did the Gospel lesson in the morning, and the matter was arranged. All his own opposition to the measure he endeavored to put on the shoulders of the people, saying that they were too indifferent to the subject to attend, but I agreed to be responsible for them.

23d. *Sabbath.* Preached in the morning in the
15

church. The lesson of the day was in continuation of the one of last Sabbath—Luke i. 39 to 55—so that I was obliged to give them a third sermon on the Virgin. The bishop was evidently very uneasy under it, but still bore it well, and I was happy to observe that when the deacons came to him to burn incense and bow to him, he motioned them away, and he had a custom which much amused some of the people, of occasionally interrupting me by saying, "Yes, it is just so; I knew it all once, but have forgotton it." These expressions at length became by-words among the people, who expressed sorrow that their bishop had forgotten so much.

In the afternoon a large audience—about 100 men—was present, and I was allowed to conduct the service in my own way; so we had no mummery of dead Coptic prayers. When, however, I proposed to pray in my own way before sermon, he interposed that it was not necessary; but I carried my point, telling him that prayer was good on all occasions, and especially when we meet in the church for God's worship. I gave them an exposition of the first part of the first chapter of Romans. It was a good sight to see so many sitting around so attentive to the word, and Monsur and Makhiel tell me that the people were much pleased with that style of worship.

25th. Received a letter from Faris at Osiout

that the Patriarch had sent there an excommunication against all the parents who should send
their children to our school. About the same
time word also came from the brethren at Cairo
that he was there moving heaven and earth
against us, and had even caused public prayers
to be made in the church against our work in
the upper country. Was strongly tempted to
send up a counter excommunication against him
for printing Antor and importing Russian idols,
and did anathematize most vigorously in my own
little circle, but soon afterwards he was taken
away by a sudden and mysterious death, and thus
the sun of this so-called Protestant Patriarch set
in darkness. Many of the people interpreted
his death as a judgment for his opposition to us.

26th. Called on the bishop and found him
with the Testament and also a volume of Church
history open before him. He was in a very
dejected frame of mind on account of the Pasha's
answer to us which had come to hand the day
before. He seemed almost ready to renounce
the world and retire a second time to the desert
and a monkish life. When I left him he was in
a more cheerful or at least resigned frame of
mind.

Went in the evening with a party of Americans to see the temple of Karnak by moonlight;
and Karnak by moonlight, the donkey-boys on
the way assured us, in phrases which they had

picked up from enraptured sight-seers, was "magnificent, charming, *exquisite*." (The latter they gave as an American adjective.) I shall leave the subject with this their description, for I have no other adjectives at command that will convey any adequate conception of these stupendous ruins. They must be seen, and I was so much impressed with that moonlight view of them, covering as it did all defects and obscenities of sculpture, and bringing all out in such magnified and yet mellowed proportions, that I was almost tempted to decide that they should be seen *only* by moonlight. I cannot, however resist the temptation of giving a bit of gossip. After wandering about for a long time through the ruined courts and sculptured colonnades, and when we had gathered together to leave, and the donkey-boys with their donkeys were around us, it was proposed to have a song, and after some discussion the hymn commencing "Before Jehovah's awful throne" was settled upon as the most fitting for relievieving the surcharged poetic sentiment of the company. I must confess I did not see the force of singing that hymn before those nasty old gods, and not being a singer, at any rate, I stepped back. The circle was formed in the midst of the great hall, and the first line was sung when the donkeys, not waiting for the proper pause, joined in with such an uproarious chorus that the young people of the party were at once forced to change their tune to a loud hah-hah! The graver members of the circle still hung to it, but at the end of the third line the paroxysm of the braying beasts being yet in full blast, they too broke down, and we all had a hearty laugh, and then mounted. I have never before seen so plump a fall from the sublime to the ridiculous.

27*th.* Went to see the Memnonium and the vocal Memnon and his sister on the other side of the river. For description see the guide books and travelers' journals, *passim.*

In the evening, with the little company which gathered nightly at Monsur's room. The Christians who were shy in coming to me in my Muslem quarters' were in the habit of meeting here, and Makhiel and Monsur strove to instruct them in the way of life, while I labored with the Muslems at Mustapha Aga's. I found many of them very willing to listen, and especially Yuseph the mufti of the town, who was an intelligent, and seemed a very upright and virtuous man. He was a graduate of the Azhar, the great Muslem university at Cairo, and it was a pleasure to talk with him. As he was a satellite of Mustapha, writing his letters and doing his other business for him, he came in almost every evening, and thus I had frequent opportunities of conversing with him, and established with him, I think sundry new canons of interpre-

tation applicable to the revelation of Mohammed. Mustapha, too, being consular agent for several European powers, and the recognised head
of the Muslem clique of the town, his house was
the great resort for the neighbors, and thus we
usually had a good audience of droppers-in to
hear our discussions.

Apropos of our rebuff from Fadil Pasha, he
was made the subject of our gossip this evening,
after more important matters were disposed of.
Each one present had some story to tell of his
tyranny, and by Muslems and Christians alike
he seemed to be feared and hated. Father
Makhiel on his way down had visited the prison
at Ghinneh. He found in it about 500 prisoners,
and on inquiring for what crimes they were
there, he concluded that most of them were
there wrongfully. One man was pointed out
to him who had been there a year and a half because he failed to produce his dead son when
the lot fell upon him for the army, although he
brought testimonials of his death from the shaikh
of his village, the doctor who attended him the,
grave digger, and other witnesses. Six others
came to him and said they were the remnant of a
family of eighteen, who had been imprisoned
three and a half years because a young man of
the family had deserted from the army. Most
of them were there for debt—that is, for failing
to pay the Government taxes. The tax on each

acre of land is here from $3 to $4.50, besides forced labor and many other improvised exactions; so the burdens of the poor fellaheen are heavy enough, and one cannot help exclaiming with the Psalmist, O Lord, how long?

Still it must be admitted that since the reign of this Governor the country has been in a state of quiet and security not known before. Then murder and robbery were rife, now peace and order reign. And after all it cannot be expected that a man who must so systematically harden his heart by the constant use of the rod, should be tender and considerate when humanity or even sound policy point them out as the better plan. The present conscription for the canal is an example of this. The whole young wheat crop of this section has just been cut off by the worm, and the people were just beginning to plow and re-sow the ground when this order came. The state of the case was represented to him, but he would not delay the work for a couple of weeks, though it might as well have been done; and the result will be an almost total failure of the heaviest crop of the country, and hundreds more of the poor fellaheen will next spring have to suffer the naboot and imprisonment for failure to pay the taxes.

29th. Went to the Tombs of the Kings and Deir El Bekre and Asaseef. I had now been here nearly a month, and had not seen these

great sights, and I found that the travelers who
had come from the ends of the earth to see
them, were beginning to put me down in their
books as a strange, if not a stupid man, for my
indifference to these ancient and wonderful
works of art, and so I started out, determined
to kill the last lion. Perhaps I should not speak
so lightly about them, for truly they were wonderful, and I found before I left that the longer
I walked in their shadows the deeper did the
impression of their vast proportions and exquisite workmanship sink into my mind. Still I
must confess that a living specimen of a modern
Egyptian is to me a greater curiosity, and an
object of deeper interest than a host of mummied kings; and I can find more to interest me
in digging among these ruins of society and religion, than in musing among the sculptured columns of ruined temples.

On our way we passed the canal, and saw the
men, about 5,000 in number, at work. They
were in gangs, those from each village working
together under their shaikh as task-master, and
the work was measured out to them by the
square dra (the dra is twenty-two inches.) The
men cut the ground loose with mattocks, and
filled with it the baskets which the children carried to the top of the bank on their heads. The
Egyptians know no other way of doing this
kind of work, and when Mohammed Ali im-

ported wheelbarrows for them, they carried them, filled with earth, upon their backs, and soon concluded that after all they were no great improvement. The digging of these canals for irrigating the whole land in this manner, and annually clearing out of them the thick layer of mud which the overflowing Nile brings down, is a Herculæan work. But even this was not enough, and the Suez Canal had to come to crush the poor fellah still further into the earth. Let France build the canal if she will, England to the contrary notwithstanding, but let *Frenchmen do the work*.

While there, we saw one man nabooted for attempted desertion. One would think—at least one who carried with him American ideas—that the people could be induced to do these works voluntarily, as they are for their own good, and they must starve without them; but here we have no such public spirit. The people are like children who must be driven to their tasks. Over-government and over-guidance have taken away from them the stimulus and necessity of self-government. They cheerfully fall in with this order of things which would be so galling to us, and think that everything must be done by legislation. They have never yet come up to the truth " that the function of government is negative and restrictive rather than positive and active."

We brought a supply of books with us of which the scribes who were over the works bought freely.

30*th*. Preached in the morning in the church on Luke i. 57 to the end, and in the afternoon on Romans i. Also at 11 A. M. to a company of fourteen travelers on Mr. Fellow's boat. The dahabiyehs of travelers were now coming in great numbers, and we who had before longed for some one occasionally to speak a word of English to us, had now a plenty of gay society. We were now in the midst of the holydays and almost every evening were invited out to dine, which after our long dieting on the dry market of Luxor was very grateful.

CHAPTER VII.

31st and January 1st. Terribly cold, windy days, so that we were not able to get out much, and inside too we were forced to sit in the dark, as to keep out the wind we had to close the shutter of our only unglazed window, and even then a storm of wind and sand came in through the crevices around it. This was a south wind, and all winter I noticed that our *cold* winds came from the *south*. This particularly struck me as it was so contrary to our experience in Cairo, where our south wind is always a hot wind, or sirocco. It is also very contrary to the theory framed by Herodotus 2,300 years ago. This is such a precious bit of philosophy that I cannot forbear quoting it. He says:

"It is the sun, also, in my opinion, which, by heating the space through which it passes, makes the air in Egypt so dry. There is thus perpetual summer in the upper parts of Lybia. Were the position of the heavenly regions reversed, so that the place where now the north wind and the winter have their dwelling became the station of the south wind and of the noonday, while on the other hand the station of the south wind became that of the north, the consequence would be that the sun, driven from the midheaven by the winter and the northern gales, would betake himself to the upper parts of Europe, as he now does to those of Libia, and then I believe his passage across Europe would affect the Ister exactly as the Nile is affected at the present day. And with respect to the fact that no breeze blows from the Nile, I am of opinion that no wind is likely to arise in very hot countries, for breezes love to blow from some cold quarter. Let us leave these things however to their natural course, to continue as they are and have been from the beginning."

So we too will return to the thread of our story, and let these things take their natural course until Professor Maury can come over and set them right, or at least explain why they are as they are.

We may, however, be permitted to remark that if the above extract be a fair specimen of the state of Grecian philosophy in the time of Herodotus, he should not be accused as he is by Plutarch of " malevolence towards the Greeks " for admitting, as he often freely does, that the Greeks were indebted to the Egyptians for most of their scientific as well as mythological ideas ;

and Cicero, who received at second hand from the Greeks the few ideas which he was accustomed to propound, so bombastically flattered his Greek masters at the expense of truth, when he said that Mercury (the Egyptian Thoth) went from Arcadia to Egypt and gave laws and learning to the Egyptians, and that Actius, the son of Sol, being an Astronomer, went from Greece to Egypt, where he founded the city of Heliopolis.

2*d*. Took Father Makhiel and a bag of books and started for Zeiniyeh and Negah El Hattab. At the former village, which is about an hour's ride to the north of Luxor, we found a few Copts who bought nearly all our books, and so we turned back. On our way back we met another Copt who was from Negadeh to whom we also sold a Bible and a Testament.

3*d*. Makhiel took a fresh supply of books and returned to the latter place, where he found about 500 Copts to whom he sold books to the amount of 166.20 piastres. The Christians of these two villages have no churches of their own, so they must worship at Luxor, and on feast days and great occasions they go to the Convent of Pachomius, about two hours' distant in the edge of the Eastern desert.

To-day I had a high scene with the bishop. The time had come around for paying the areef and Antonius their second month's wages. The

16

former, Monsur had paid last month through the
bishop—at least he had given the bishop the
money for him, but the poor areef complained
that but a small pittance of it had reached him,
and this month he wished the money to pass
directly from "our hand to his." So on reaching
the episcopal palace I said that the time had
come around for paying them, and asked that
the areef might first be called up.   This called
forth a good deal of heming and hawing, with
sundry nervous twitchings on his chair, and a
hint that he could hand him the money; but I
persisted, and finally the areef had to be sent for,
though the point was yielded with the apprecia-
tive remark, "I suppose you wish to pay him
his wages in his own hand."   When he came
up I said, "O Areef, your wages are seventy
piastres, are they not? commencing at such a
time; and you have received one month's wages,
and now another is due, is it not so?"   He hesitated and did not answer, when the bishop made
a terrible effort, and brought up from his poor,
fasting stomach a most emphatic "Yes," though
the effort made the perspiration start, which in
another moment came rolling down in great
dirty globules like peas.   The areef did not dare
contradict him, and so I paid him his month's
wages and sent him back.   But now came the
more difficult case of Antonius.   I had not been
able to bring this worthy down to anything like

work. He would neither come regularly to read with me, nor would he study the Testament as I urged him much to do, that he might be prepared for the discharge of his priestly functions, and my duty in his case was plain. It was that indicated by Paul in the aphorism "that if any would not work, neither should he eat;" so, after sending for him, I commenced with his reverence by stating certain broad principles on which we act in such matters, which are embodied in the phrase "*quid pro quo*," and also as to our responsibility in the sight of God for a right application of mission money; but he could not see the point of all this, and I was finally forced to meet the question point blank and refuse to give him anything until he should earn it, either in the school, or in reading with me, or in discharging his duty as priest. This, of course, called forth a tremendous outburst from the bishop, and in the midst of it he laid bare the whole subject in one sentence by saying that "Antonius was his nephew, and had been well brought up—that he had made him priest only to save him from the conscription; that his spirit was too big to beg his livelihood from the poor fellaheen, and that he *must* live." That was it; in shorter phrase—"Too proud to beg, and too lazy to work." Still I carried my point, and am proud of my diplomacy when I say that I did it without a final break with his reverence. This

I knew must come at no distant day, and *then*, as often before, I was strongly tempted to throw the old bishop overboard with his crew of ignorant priests and all belonging to him. But I knew that should I then do it, the poor people would have to go along with him, and so for the time I concluded to be patient, and strive slowly to unloose the knots and bands of superstition and priestcraft by which they were bound to him, and then farewell forever to this system of policy. So I bore with him, sometimes storming, sometimes flattering, meeting craft with counter craft, and I felt that I was fast acquiring the wisdom of the serpent, if not the meekness of the dove. And yet they say he is the choice of the thirteen bishops of the Coptic Church. If so, I cannot help feeling that it would be a blessing if they all with their priests and deacons, and monks, and all the seven orders of them, could be instantaneously prepared for heaven, and then the earth open and swallow them, like Korah and his company. The poor, oppressed, priest-ridden people would then receive the Gospel and live.

4th. Spent most of the day in the house, an unusual thing for me, as for the most part I spent my days in the open air, breathing the delightful, invigorating air of the Said, and exercising my weak lungs in talking to all who would listen. Mustapha bought a Bible and two Testaments for his two sons whom Mrs. L.

was teaching. The Mufti had purchased a Bible some time before.

In the afternoon, went, as was our custom, to call on Lord Haddo. Our sail back across the river almost made even me sentimental. There were three steamers with a long row of dahabi-yehs lying below Luxor, and their bright array of torches gleaming on the bank and reflected from the water, with the stately columns, and towering propylon of the temple of Luxor rear-ing their lofty heads, and casting their lengthened shadows in the background, and above the bright moon, and beneath the placid Nile, and all around the clustering associations of "hundred-gated Thebes." It was enough to make one far less poetical sentimentalize. But the exhilirating cup was dashed from my lips by the thought of those steamers. One of them was occupied by the brother of the King of Sweden, the other by a Neapolitan Prince, and the third by a Russian consul. All these were the guests of the Viceroy, and these steamers were given to them free, together with firmans to the shaikhs of all the villages to levy for them all necessary supplies from the peasants, and I am sorry to say all of them did not have sense enough not to avail themselves of the privilege. Others after-wards came in the same manner, and among them Mr. De Leon, our American Consul Gen-eral. Now I have no objections to the Viceroy

16*

of Egypt being hospitable, but I cannot without a flush of anger see this hospitality exercised at the expense of the eggs, and chickens, and vegetables of the poor fallaheen. Charity begins at home. At the same time other steamers of the Viceroy were taking down relays of hundreds of forced laborers for the Suez Canal. These the French Company agreed to pay 7 piastres* per day for their labor. But it paid their wages to the Viceroy, and I need not say that but little of it reached the fellaheen. It was said to be consumed in expenses, viz., in taking the men down to the works and back again, for I have been able to hear of no other expenses which the government has incurred for them.

So, instead of going up to my room to spin out in my notes long sentimental lucubrations about our moonlight sail, I merely find in them, "Delightful sail in returning from Lord Haddo's boat. Three steamers containing so and so—all Pasha's guests—*nonsense*." Yes, and it is worse than nonsense. It is OUTRAGEOUS, and "if there be treason in this, then let those who may make the most of it."

5th. Saturday. Called on the bishop to get the Scripture lessons for the morrow. He was too busy to attend to me, overseeing the slaying of a beef, for the feast which was to commence

---

* A piastre is about three cents and a half, United States money.

that night at 12 o'clock. Part of the beef was
sent very ostentatiously to the poor, and the rest
was left for him and his household to break their
fast upon, and for the entertainment of guests
who should come from distant places to keep the
feast. On such occasions the priests are put to
considerable expense, as they are expected to be
hospitable; but they can afford it. This feast,
I should mention, was their Christmas, according to their old-style calendar, to which the
Copts in common with the Greeks and the other
oriental sects still cling.

In the evening I went to the church to witness the ceremonies, and remained until 11
o'clock. I found the bishop sitting in his chair
of state, in the central nave of the church; and
never before realized how exact a copy the Coptic dress and ceremonial are of the old Egyptian
ones used in the service of the gods as portrayed
on the old temple walls. He was arrayed in a
purple robe all blazing with gold, with a tall
mitre on his head like a veritable Amun Rè. In
his right hand he held a serpent-headed sceptre,
and in his left the cross, which, with the exception of the loop on the top, is exactly like the
old symbol of life so invariably seen in the hands
of the old deities, while the people in the same
manner were kissing it, and bowing and praying
and offering incense to him. The whole made
me feel that I was in some ancient temple of the

heathen Egyptians, in which the sculptures had simply started into life.

Then too there were some things which were intensely Jewish. The officiating priests had to be blessed, and their garments crossed and breathed upon. Thus this Moses "sanctified Aaron and his garments and his sons, and his sons' garments with them." And then a whole dish of common cakes were brought to him, and after a very minute examination of them one was chosen which was "without spot or blemish" for the sacrifice of the mass. So too the old Egyptian priests turned over and over and examined the kine which were offered in sacrifice to Apis. Herodotus thus describes the process:

"One of the priests appointed for the purpose searches to see if there is a single black hair on the whole body, since in that case the beast is unclean. He examines him all over, standing on his legs, and again laid upon his back; after which he takes the tongue out of his mouth to see if it be clean in respect of the prescribed marks. He also inspects the hairs of the tail to see if they grow naturally. If the animal is pronounced clean in all these various points, the priest marks him by twisting a piece of papyrus round his horns, and attaching thereto some sealing clay, which he then stamps with his own signet-ring. After this the beast is led away; and it is forbidden under penalty of death to sacrifice an animal which has not been marked in this way."

The bishop himself performed mass, and the whole service lasted till midnight, when feasting and drinking commenced and were kept up the rest of the night.

6th. Sabbath. I need hardly say there was no service in the church to-day. They had "prayed" enough last night to suffice for this Sabbath, and besides, half the people were yet engaged in the debauch then commenced, and the other half were sleeping off its effects. It is one of the saddest proofs, as well as exhibitions of the deep corruption of the Coptic church, that obedience to the church's talmud secures impunity in the transgression of God's commands and the neglect of his ordinances. If a man only tythes mint and annise and cummin in his observance of the traditions of the elders, he may safely say Corban of all the weightier matters of the law. He may be a Sabbath-breaker, liar, thief, and profane person, indeed he may live in the open transgression of all the precepts of the moral code, and yet maintain his "good and regular standing" in the church. But if in accordance with the precept of the Apostle, "to let no man judge him in meat or drink, or in respect of an holy day or of the new moon or of the Sabbath days," he presumes to break one of the appointed fasts or transgress even the least of the precepts of the church, it is a crime to be punished by the judges, for the priests cannot forgive it.   " Thus they make void the law of God by their traditions."

But though thus relieved from public duty, it was not an idle day for me.   A few of the people were sober, and they came to me, and among them a squad of scribes from Erment came to spend the afternoon, and I need hardly say that the doings of the last evening, and of that day, gave me ample topics of discourse.   In the evening too we had a pleasant meeting with them at Monsur's room.

7th. In the forenoon went over the river for an excursion and sight-seeing with Mr. Phelps, of New York, and family.   It was a great pleasure to meet there this gentleman, and many other Christian men and women, who encouraged us in our work, and their Christian fellowship was most refreshing.   Mr. Phelps is a member of the Board of Managers of our American Bible Society, and what he saw here of our work enabled him to do us good service on returning home.

At the bishop's in the afternoon I chanced to meet together the three priests of the town; gave them a lecture on the proper discharge of their duties as pastors and teachers of the people, and urged them to come regularly to me that I might instruct them, and also urged the bishop to send them.   In doing this I found that the highest argument which I could bring really to bear upon their minds was a selfish one. I told them that they now saw that the people were determined to be enlightened—that all these Bibles and books, which they had bought and were reading, must have their legitimate effect—that the times of the old ignorance were now past—that they could not stop, even if they would, this onward movement or obscure this light—that to attempt to do so would only be like trying to eclipse the sun by raising against it their palms, and that their only true policy was to fall in with instead of breasting the popular current, or they would soon find themselves left high and dry on the banks. They complained bitterly of the niggardly manner in which the people supported them; which I contrasted with the liberal manner in which the people deal with the clergy in our land, and assured them that when they should thus do their duty they too would be thus appreciated and bountifully dealt with.

8th. Saw the priests again and urged upon them the same subject. They agreed to meet me regularly every evening at Monsur's room, and that night we met for the first, and I commenced expounding to them 1st Timothy.

A steamer came bringing another party of the Viceroy's guests. A number of his dismissed employeés had also taken the opportunity of coming up in her to see some lands, with which

on being dismissed from the government service
they had been pensioned.   I may here state
that some months ago the Viceroy was seized
with a spasm of economy, which led him to dis-
miss hundreds of the government employeés,
many of whom holding sinecures should long
before have been dispensed with, but many others
were useful public servants, who were labori-
ously filling important public offices.   But it
was a broad sweep of " Islahh," which in western phrase means "retrenchment and reform,"
and good and bad went alike.   But so paternal
a government as we here have could not thus
throw them upon the cold charities of the world
unprovided for, and so it gave them lands for
their future support.   This was done by sending around to the shaikhs of the villages to know
what public lands were still left unoccupied connected with each village.   These were divided
into parcels of varying sizes, and then distributed by lot to the pensioners ; each one receiving a number of acres proportioned to the years
he had spent in the service.   By this arrangement some of them received very valuable properties, but the majority received what was quite
valueless, as lying either too high or too low to
render the inundation of the Nile available for
culture.   A number also received old burying-
grounds, and in some instances those which were
still in use.   One of these who had now come

found that his lot had given him the high ridge
back of the village occupied by the Christian
cemetery, and one corner of which had also been
set apart for invalid Europeans dying on the
Nile. Of course he had nothing to do but go
back to Cairo and represent his case, and in the
course of months, by a system of log-rolling and
bribing of under officials, he might succeed in
getting it changed. He amused me much by
narrating how another one similarly situated
with himself had managed. He went to the
village where the lot had cast his portion, and
on showing the paper which described it to the
shaikhs of the village, they told him that it was
the burying ground. He asked them what was
to be done, and if they could not give him another parcel of land from the lands of the village.
They told him they had no other unoccupied
land, and, besides, were there, they had no authority to make the exchange—that he must go
to headquarters at Cairo. He had no inclination
for this, and so laid his plan, and taking a room
in the village settled down apparently to rest
awhile from the fatigues of the journey. After
a few days he heard early one morning the death-
wail, and sending his servant out to inquire who
was dead, found that it was one of the shaikhs
of the village—a man held in great respect in
all the surrounding country. I should have mentioned that he was a Turk, and had been in the

17

military branch of the service, and that the Turks always carry with them a prestige of terror with the Arabs. So he said to his servant : " Make haste and hand me down my sword and pistols, and make ready eatables and drinkables. I shall go out to smell the air to-day." The servant did as he was directed, though not a little surprised on finding his master insisting on a very liberal provision of arrack being made, and was also astonished on going out to find that his master's taste led him to the gateway of the burying-ground instead of some shady nook on the banks of the Nile for his day's enjoyment. He, however, had nothing to do but obey orders, so he spread the carpet for his master, who immediately, as the phrase is, commenced " filling his head with arrack." Soon the funeral procession emerged from the village, and slowly wended its way to the burying-ground. The blind shaikhs were in advance, chanting the confession of faith, then the bier, and then the friends and neighbors and mourning women. It was a great funeral, for the deceased was a highly respected man in the village. When they came up to the gate he sprang forth like an affreet with sword in one hand and pistol in the other, which he brandished over their heads while he swore a great oath that the first man who advanced a step to enter the gate was a dead man. They of course were unarmed, and

they saw besides, that the fumes of arrack were
playing with his brain, and they feared and fell
back. Then the elders of the people came up to
him, and in a spirit of peace and conciliation
demanded a parley, when they represented to
him that this would not answer, but was a great
shame, as he and they were all brother Muslems,
and the deceased was a great man among them,
and they adjured him by the life of Mohammed,
and the head of the Viceroy, and by his own
head and beard, that he let them pass in peace
and bury their dead. But he in reply swore
by the life of all these deities, and sundry other
outlandish Turkish ones, that he would not let
them pass—that he had received the burying
ground by the allotment of fate and the munificence of the Viceroy, and that it was his, and he
must make his livelihood out of it, and that he
would only let them pass on condition that they
pay him 500 piastres; and the result was that
they were obliged to come to his terms and pay
the money, when he suffered them to pass. He
told them, moreover, that this would hereafter
be the regular price for a shaikh or great man,
but that he would allow a common man to be
buried for 300 piastres. I need only add that
the people of the village soon after had a meeting at which they decided to give him a portion of good arable land in lieu of his burying
ground.

9th. Received and answered letters from Osiout showing that the persecution of the priests against our school is still raging there.

Called on Mr. Monier, a Frenchman, who has resided here some years, and has built a fine house on the south end of the great temple of Luxor, which has in constrast with the native mud hovels a very comely appearance from the river and all the surrounding country. Went below his house to see the last court and sanctum of the temple. But alas! what a desecration was there! I found he had converted it into a pig-sty! The abomination of the Egyptians was here in the Adytum—the very holy of holies of the temple. The countenances of the old gods, usually so placid, seemed covered with angry frowns, and the scepters to tremble in their hands, while the sacred basilisks in their crowns seemed audibly to hiss, though Clement of Alexandria, had he been there, might have insisted that the pigs were as decent occupants as had ever been there. He says: "The Egyptian temples, and the propyla or gateways before them, and their courts and groves and consecrated grounds, are all superbly decorated. Their halls also are supported by innumerable pillars. Their walls glitter with precious stones and with most skillfully executed pictures. The shrines blaze with gold, and silver, and amber, and with variegated marbles from India and Ethiopia. The

Adytum, or most sacred place, is overshadowed by a curtain embroidered with gold. But when you enter this sacred enclosure and are anxious to see that which is most worthy of contemplation, inquire for the image of the divinity that dwells in the temple; perhaps a shrine-bearer or some other minister attached to the worship that is performed there, looking extremely grave and singing a hymn in Egyptian, draws aside the vail a little so that the god appears. But instead of worshiping him you burst into a hearty laugh. Instead of the god we were so anxious to see, we behold a cat, or a crocodile, or a common snake, or some such foul creature, altogether unfit to be in a temple, but only in their places in dark holes and mud. Behold the god of the Egyptians! A beast reposing on a. piece of purple tapestry!"

Ezekiel saw a similar sight in the temple of God at Jerusalem—ch. viii. 7–12. "And he brought me to the door of the court; and when I looked, behold a hole in the wall. Then said he unto me, Son of man, dig now in the wall; and when I had digged in the wall, behold a door. And he said unto me, Go in and behold the wicked abominations that they do here. So I went in and saw, and behold every form of creeping things, and abominable beasts, and all the idols of the house of Israel portrayed upon the wall round about. And there stood before

17*

them seventy men of the ancients of the house
of Israel, and in the midst of them stood Jaaza-
niah, the son of Shaphan, with every man his
censer in his hand, and a thick cloud of incense
went up. Then said he unto me, Son of man,
hast thou seen what the ancients of the house of
Israel do in the dark, every man in the chambers
of his imagery? for they say the Lord seeth us
not; the Lord hath forsaken the earth."

This passage shows that the Israelites of Ezekiel's time had made a large importation of
Egyptian idolatry. The picture which he saw
in vision is most faithful to the originals. The
"dark chambers in connection with the temples
with secret doors leading to them, the creeping
things and abominable beasts, and idols portrayed upon the walls round about in these
chambers of imagery; the ancients of the house
of Israel, with every man his censer in his hand,
so that a thick cloud of incense went up"—an
artist might almost draw an Egyptian temple
from the description. For my part I must frown
with Ezekiel on beholding, as I here daily must,
these abominations in the temple of God; but
I laughed heartily with old Clement at the
French idea of the pigs in the Adytum of the
old heathen temple, and will leave enthusiastic
Egyptologers to frown. I had done enough of
this at this same drove of pigs for the depredations which I had seen they were allowed to

make on the unfenced and unhedged crops of
the poor fellaheen, as well as the unnecessary
offence of their presence to the prejudices of the
Muslems. The fields in Egypt are only separated
by "landmarks" as in old Jewish times, and so
the peasants had no protection against them except to guard their crops by night and by day.
Had they belonged to a native, there would
have been a legal remedy; but Mr. M. was a
Frenchman, and we Franks are privileged persons in Egypt. I must, however, do Mr. M. the
justice to say that I do not know that he was
aware of the nuisance his pigs were to the
neighbors, as he was seldom there. He had
given two of his pigs to the bishop, and these
were not treated with the same immunity; for
one day on calling on his reverence, I found him
in a towering passion, and he had just fulmigated
an episcopal thunderbolt of excommunication
against any and every one of his flock who
should purchase meat from the butcher of the
town, who was a Muslem. I found on inquiry
that the pigs had got out of the enclosure of the
bishop and entered the field of the butcher, and
done some damage to his crops, when he had
gone by night and poisoned them both. So the
poor Christians had no alternative left them but to
enter upon a second Lent, unless, indeed, they might
choose to eat poisoned pork; and the butcher had
to shut up shop as far as his Christian custom-

ers were concerned, and of course he was soon
brought penitent enough to the episcopal con-
fessional, and very cheerfully performed the prescribed penance, when the episcopal bull was
recalled and chained, and the Christians ate meat
again.   This incident tempts me as usual to go
into a long digression describing like puttings
forth of the episcopal prerogative and the happy
consequences in securing the authority of the
Church; but I will spare my readers. One bishop
I know who has left a whole village under the
ban unto this day because he found one morning
that the saddle cloth of his ass had taken French
leave during the night.

An instructive incident occurred this afternoon.   I was sitting in the porch beside Mustapha, when a very venerable old man, a religious
shaikh from Gournou on the other side of the
river, came up. Mustapha, who would not readily
be charged by any one with being a very superstitious Muslem, received him with great reverence, and after kissing his hand bade him be
seated on a chair which stood near. The old
man declined, when Mustapha adjured him to
take it and be seated.   The other answered,
"Am I a man to sit on a chair? a chair is not
for the like of me," and squatted on the ground.
Mustapha invited him to stay and eat, but this
he also declined, when Mustapha said, "Then
pray a fatihah (opening chapter of the Koran)

for me." When the old man arose, and, holding his open hands before his face as if reading from a book, as is the custom of the Muslems in many of their prayers, he repeated the chapter. Mustapha then gave him a present, and he left his blessing and departed. The incident showed the reverence in which such characters are held by the people, and the efficacy which they attach to the repetition of the Fatihah.

The bishop to-day seemed very discontented and cross. The evening exercise with the priests seemed to prosper and promise, and the people at once hailed it as a hope for something better than dead Coptic prayers and masses in their church services; but the bishop seemed to think that in this also I had stolen a march upon him.

CHAPTER VIII.

10*th*. THOUGHT it would do his reverence good
to take him for a call on Mr. Phelps and party,
and sent him word accordingly. He sent back
a short answer that he was not well and could
not go, and at noon Monsur came and told me
that he had called him up from school and given
him a very sharp talking to. So in the afternoon
I went to call on him. I went with the expectation of a scene, and was not disappointed.
When he saw me enter the room he averted his
countenance, and, indeed, turned his back squarely
upon me, with his face to the wall. I asked
him what the matter was, and he answered me
curtly that he "did not know us Americans—
that he knew the English, and they were his
friends." I, however, had no idea of allowing
him thus to cut my acquaintance, and so I entered
and took my seat beside him, and commenced
tugging at his sleeve and expostulating with
him. All I could get from him for a long time
was that the English were his friends, and that

Mr. and Mrs. Leider were the right kind of missionaries; that he had long known them, and they had always befriended him, but that ever since his acquaintance with us all had gone wrong with him. I knew he had sufficient reasons, special as well as general, for such a conclusion, but I soon found that the occasion of the present pout was the loss of a pole from the sakia in his garden, and I forthwith set myself to comfort him to the best of my ability. I think I have never before been called to quote the consolatory passages of our holy religion on so trivial an occasion, and after a time I succeeded. He again turned his face full and pleasant upon me, and I rejoiced once more in the light of his countenance. Poor man! transporting myself for a moment to his shoes, and trying to look at things as he must view them, I could not but feel that my course had been a very trying one to him, and as he had now melted down so nicely, I too grew soft, and relaxed my hard-pressed grasp and gave him a second £ (I had given him one soon after coming) on school-rent account. This, for the time, made him forget the affair of Antonius, and that of Fadil Pasha, and all the rest of his grievances, and so I seized the opportunity to introduce another subject which had lately been on my mind. He had spoken of his friends the Leiders. Mrs. L. had some time before sent him a couple pictures, the one

I think a baptismal scene, and the other a picture of some English beauty, intending, I suppose, that he should hang them in his room to give it an air of taste and cheerfulness; but he had supposed that they were for the church, and so had suspended them there among the staring pictures of the Virgin and saints by native artists, and I noticed that when travelers visited the church he took special pride in pointing out these pictures to them, and telling that they were from Mrs. Leider. I now told him that I was sure she had no idea of his applying them to such a use; that we Protestants are all very much opposed to the use of pictures in the church, and that the next thing he would hear would be that some one of these travelers had gone to Cairo and reported to Mrs. L., or gone to England and informed the public there, that Protestant missionaries in Egypt were furnishing Coptic churches with pictures for worship, when he would soon have Mrs. L. down upon him with her full weight, and he would repent his putting the pictures in the church. This all took him aback. He thanked me for interfering, and promised to take down the pictures. After a good deal more of talk, I left him in a much more amiable frame of mind than when I came, and entertaining better opinions of American missionaries.

Next went down to Lord Haddo's boat, and

found him in spirit for some rifle practice. He had a couple fine rifles, and putting up a mark far away on the shore, we tried our hand. In his weakness he was forced to rest his piece on the skylight of the dahabiyeh, while I held mine at arm's length; and we fired with a result which afterwards brought the rifle up to me, with a neat note, stating that I had deserved it and must keep it as a memento of our pleasant winter's work together. May English lords and American plebians never have occasion for other rifle practice than the like of this.

11*th*. The bishop called and was "as good as pie." I asked him if he had yet taken down the pictures. He said, no, but he intended doing it that afternoon. I said, While you are about it, make a clean sweep of it and take down all the pictures. He insisted that the people would not stand that, and I told him that he knew that the men had already abandoned the worship of them, and that as for the women, who were accustomed to improve the opportunity after the men left the church to have a good turn at beating their breasts and offering their prayers before them, they also would soon be reconciled to the change, and then all would thank him for taking the lead in a great reform. He, however, could not be convinced of this, and was beginning to regard me again as an American innovator, when the subject was turned by Mustapha, who,

18

sitting by, asked what we were whispering
about, when I told him, "Oh, nothing, only I
am trying to pour new wine into old bottles,"
at which the bishop laughed heartily. Mustapha
asked for further explanation, and the bishop
was pleased that I did not seem inclined farther
to expose him. But it was now Mustapha's turn
to try the episcopal liberality, or rather want
of it, more severely than even I had done. I
learned soon after landing there that these two
worthies had long lived at swords' points—that
they were in fact the recognized heads of the
two opposing factions of the village. The line
of division between these was for the most part
the one which in most places separates Christian from Muslem, but I found here the two
clans overlapping each other. Some of the
Christians adhered to Mustapha's party, while a
few of the Muslems hated Mustapha and favored
the bishop. It was a great trial to the bishop
at first that I took quarters in Mustapha's house,
and he long insisted that we should come up
and chum with him, in his single available room
above the church. But I feared that so close
a contact would soon breed familiarity and dis-
gust, and then Mustapha's room was the best,
and, indeed, the only habitable one in the village.
Besides, I thought it policy to keep in with both
parties, and I afterwards found that I was able
very nicely to play off on my boards bishop

against Aga. The two were striving to keep in
my good-books, and, in appearance at least, were
most friendly with each other. The people
were astonished to see Mustapha calling on the
bishop and being entertained by him as if he
were an old friend, and to see him on the other
hand holding the bishop's stirrup while mount-
ing his pony at his door. In the mean time I
rode the bishop's pony when I needed recreation,
and had my dinner cooked in Mustapha's kitchen
when hungry.

But to return to our conference. Mustapha
now proposed to the bishop, and urged very
strongly, that the Muslem boys should be permitted to attend our school at the church. This
proposition was the result of a good deal of talk
and reasoning on the subject which I had had
with him day by day, and with the other leading
Muslems of the place, and I was delighted to
find that he had at length so far thrown aside
the old Muslem bigotry as to make it; but how
was I astonished and disgusted when the bishop
responded with a most emphatic "Only your
boys." I knew in general how strong and
mutual the feelings of dislike between the two
sects are, but I was not prepared for such an
exhibition of *Christian* bigotry and exclusiveness, and it was so decided that I saw that there
was no need of taking up an argument against
it. Indeed, I was stupefied, and could have said

nothing had I wished, and so the subject was immediately dropped. The next day, of course, I took the bishop to task for it, when I was no less astonished to find that his opposition was not simply the result of the general antipathy between the sects, but, said he, "If the Muslems come to the church they will witness our rites and ceremonies and make sport of them." Alas for Christianity when her adherents have to be ashamed of her rites!

In talking that evening with Mustapha, I was surprised to find that he believed in the lying miracles of St. Pachomius. But so it is. The more I study practically and in their modern developments the two religions, the more I see that they stand on common grounds, and acknowledge common principles, and consequently respect one another's superstitions, and the true reason of the bitter enmity between them is *party* spirit, and that for the most part *political* party spirit. The one has its saints, and the other its santons—the one its Lent, and the other its Ramadan—the one its hadj to Mecca, and the other its pilgrimage to Jerusalem—the one its Ave Maria and our Father, and the other its fatihah—the one says, "In the name of the Father, and Son, and Holy Ghost," and the other testifies that there is no deity but Allah, and that Mohammed is the prophet of Allah; and the real controversy between them is the one

arising from the fact that the one is the ruling
and the other the subject race. And such, too,
one must conclude on reading ancient church
history, was the true issue between Copts and
Greeks in those hard-fought battles on the floors
of the councils of Ephesus and Chalcedon, and
the subsequent councils. The Greeks were
the "melchite" or *kingly* church, basking in the
favor of the Greek emperors at Constantinople,
and the spirit which made Dioscorus rave like a
madman was not the famous "odium theologi-
cum," but the natural jealousy of a subject and
depressed race. Monophysite and Monothelite
shibboleths were mere decoy ducks—banners
which were unfurled to catch the eye of the
multitude while they fought the battle—and
when the Copts were finally beaten under these,
they welcomed the Muslems as their allies, and
in so doing took to their bosoms a viper which
has stung them to this day.

This, together with the interview of the day
with the bishop, opened the way for a long and
very satisfactory conversation with Mustapha
and the Mufti. The latter is a very fine man.
He neither smokes nor drinks coffee—a *rara
avis* in Arabdom—and is a very good Arabic
scholar.

To-day word came from England that Lord
Aberdeen had closed his long and eventful career. The intelligence was brought from Cairo

by a Sir Robert Wilmot, whose servant had no
more sense, on reaching Luxor, than to go directly to Lord Haddo's boat and bluntly tell
him that his father was dead. It was not unexpected, but still it was a sad blow to him, in his
weak and shattered state, *thus* to receive the
news. His own letters had been delayed and
came the next day. Lady H. came ashore, and
I went with her to Sir Robert's boat, when we
found that the tidings were doubtless correct;
but had the servant possessed a little of the
Arab etiquette in such matters, he would have
kept quiet, and suffered the news to come by
regular course of mail.

Thus the longest and brightest earthly career
must have its close. The dying-messages which
came gave precious evidence that the busy life
had been succeeded by the heavenly rest. In
reviewing that life, we cannot help feeling that
its great error was the not comprehending the
old Scotch covenanting spirit which had its resurrection in the notable " ten year's conflict "
which resulted in the disruption of the Church
of Scotland. Perhaps his too long association
with English politics and church ideas disquali-
fied him for that intimate sympathy with the
Scotch character which was called for in that
crisis. But it is human to err, and, after all,
God has brought good out of that great evil.
The Free Church was too brilliant a jewel to be

retained in its sombre setting of "moderatism," as a mere ornament to the breast of patronage. May it long blaze in the mediatoral crown of King Jesus.

Hereafter we must call our friends Lord and Lady Aberdeen, and would that we could oftener see an earl and a countess of the realm engaged in so noble a work as that in which they so nobly and zealously lent a helping hand that winter. I have seen people at home in our democratic America who scout at aristocracy, and think that titled people must necessarily be proud, and yet, though doubtless very good Christian people in their way, they are above distributing tracts, and many other humble methods of serving Christ. They must do what they do in a certain conventional style, and with that eclat and circumstance which destroy the power of Christian effort. Would that such ones could have seen this earl, too weak to walk, riding through an Arab village, selling Testaments to the astonished natives who crowded around him; and his good lady, day after day keeping our book-accounts, filling our colportenring bags, and selling penny tracts, and administering to the ailments and bodily wants of the little dirty, sore-eyed Arab boys who crowded down to their boat. Such, be they titled or not, are heaven's aristocracy, for they are not too proud to serve the King of Heaven, even in the humblest capacity.

We had on the Nile that winter another English, earl who made himself notable in another
way.   He had a punt covered with canvas, and
which on the water, looked at a distance like a
crocodile.   In the prow of this he had mounted
a small cannon, and, stretching his long length
in the bottom together with an English sailor
who steered and paddled in the stern, he would
drop down behind a flock of geese or ducks,
and then, when near enough, let fly at them,
often killing forty or fifty at a shot.   This was
not sport, but carnage, and after his return to
England I saw it duly reported in the papers
how many thousands of ducks, geese, pelicans,
cranes, etc., he had killed.   I had the pleasure
of dining with him one evening, and found him
brimful and overflowing with the one subject.
He seemed, for the time, at least, a man of but
one idea, and some wag gave him the euphonious
title of Lord Goosey-Gander.

12th. Received a large package of letters
from America over which we spent a delightful
forenoon.   Reports of secession and impending
war were becoming louder and stronger, and
had we not been too busy to think much of it,
it would have been a sore trial to be so far out
of the regular channels of the news of the day.

To-day an American party left who gave me
some countenance in my want of enthusiasm
about antiquities.   They spent only a day and

a half at Thebes, and voted the Nile and her
dahabiyes, Egypt and her ruins, a bore.   I find
that our American friends generally, though most
of them will not suffer themselves to give expression to the sentiment, think the Nile boat
too slow. a coach for their go-a-headitiveness.
If they could go up in steamers, and thus do the
Nile in a fortnight, they would enjoy it.   But
where, then, would be the romance?

To-day an Arab, who said he was agent for
some Pasha from Tripoli, told a funny story.
This Pasha having gorged himself from the body
politic, as the Pashas, like leeches, usually do,
instead of going to Constantinople that salt might
be thrown upon his tail, and then suffer himself to be stripped of his ill-gotten gain, as is
the custom, slipped off to America, and there
invested his money, and some time after sent his
agent there to collect it.   He, on arriving, found
that he could not collect the money without the
bond or a power of attorney, and so he came
back, biting his fingers.   This man offered Mustapha half the interest to intercede for him in
the matter, and Mustapha wished me to put him
in track of doing it; but what business has a
Muslem to loan money on interest when it is
contrary to their religion, and sending his men
there without anything to show for the money?
Truly, *this* is putting new wine in old bottles.

14*th. Sabbath.* Preached this morning on Luke

ii. 1–14. This proved to be my last sermon in
the bishop's church. As we had not had service
last Sabbath, at the close I reminded the people
of the afternoon service, and in the afternoon
went there and found the church closed, and
that the bishop and priest had left notice that
there would be no service, and then had gone
out "to smell the air." Still a number of the
people had collected at the church door, and I
told them that I would meet them in the evening
at Monsur's. Whether the bishop had had anything to do with it or not I cannot say, but I
saw that the meeting with the priests was beginning to flag in interest, and determined no
longer to restrict it to them. In the evening a
dozen came, and with them Antonius, I fear
more as a spy than a learner. In the room of
Monsur's host, on the opposite side of the hall,
was a company who, when sent for to come to
worship, said they did not wish to come. Their
loud voices disturbed us a good deal in our worship, and on coming out I noticed in passing the
window, that priest John was among them, and
that they were playing dice with the arrack-
glasses in their midst! O tempora! O mores!
Such, then, were the results of my lectures on
Timothy to the priests, in which they had often
expressed themselves so deeply interested. I
was confirmed in my determination to limit our
evening meetings no longer to the priests.

15*th*. Met with a number of persons in the street, to whom I preached the Word, especially to a company gathered in front of Monsur's house. I found the developments of yesterday had put the people all on the tiptoe of excitement and expectation as to what would come next, and not at all disposed to justify their bishop in his course. In the evening about twenty persons were present, and I lectured to them on Rom. ii. How applicable is the truth of this chapter now to a dead Christian as it was when penned to the dead Jewish Church. When I came to the end, I paraphrased by substituting the words Christian and baptism in the place of "Jew" and "circumcision," which seemed to come home to them with peculiar power. For he is not a *Christian* who is one outwardly, neither is that *baptism* which is outward in the flesh; but he is a Christian who is one inwardly, and baptism is that of the heart, in the spirit, and not in the letter, whose praise is not of men but of God. In the midst of the discussion I noticed one man who was leaning back behind his neighbor, and I thought he must be sleepy, for I had been very long, though usually one can hardly be too long with the Copts; but soon his neighbor changed his position a little, so that the light fell upon his face, and I saw the tears were running down his cheeks. It was to me, in the midst of all the discouragements and trials

which the tortuous ways of the bishop had inflicted upon me, a token for good. I had long
been beating the flinty rock, and could it be true
that at length the waters were beginning to flow
out? Gibbon well compares the Coptic Church
to a dried and ghastly mummy. Could it be
that these dried bones and leathern muscles and
sinews, withered and parched for ages, were yet
to live. O Lord, Thou knowest!

16*th*. Found the bishop cold and stiff. Fadil
Pasha was bearing hard on some of his relations,
and it was evident that in this as in his other
troubles, he was giving up all hope of compassing
his ends through me. His demeanor seemed to
show that he had definitely made up his mind to
a new course of action, viz., secret war to be
covered by a polite exterior in his intercourse
with me. There was one respect which I have
not yet mentioned, in which his acquaintance
with me had not met his sanguine expectations.
He had evidently hoped that he would be able
to use me as an efficient mediator and dragoman
with the travelers, and that he would be able to
thrust my hand deeply into their pockets. I
may here state that the seat of his bishopric is
properly at Esneh and not Luxor, and that he
had long since removed to the latter place,
though it contained comparatively few Copts,
principally on account of the travelers. These
spend only a day at Esneh, but usually a couple

weeks at Luxor, and he had received from them, especially while building his church, large contributions. Many who could see only the surface, and especially Church of England men, who had had their training in the High-Church School, and of course regarded him as a high dignitary in a church which is an elder sister in the Episcopacy, were disposed to fraternize and be liberal with "the good old bishop." But here he was in great need of an interpreter. Antonius knew but few words of English, and the dragomen of the travelers are mostly Muslems, who could not be expected to sympathize in such a matter, and all of them in principle bound to protect their howajah from all depredations except their own. But here it was that I signally failed him. Had he gone on in building the school-house, I could easily have raised money enough for him to build ten schools; but this failing, I could not consent to suffer myself to be carried around by him like a borrowed baby in the arms of a street beggar. When travelers with High-Church tendencies, or who hearing as much of our story as I thought they had any business in knowing, expressed a desire to make his acquaintance, I called with him on them, and then went with them to return the call; but I could not go further than this, and consequently, like most dragomen, I sometimes had to translate what he wished to say to them

19

not literally, but according to the sense—that is
my sense of what was proper to be said.   In
these interviews I am often greatly amused by
the arts of mendicancy with which he plies them.
First when he calls upon them the watch is
pulled out and flourished every five minutes, and
as it can speak, it easily introduces its story and
ticks most eloquently in praise of its generous
donor.   Then, when the call is returned, the two
telescopes are brought out, and first the long
one is put to the eye of the poor short-sighted
dupe, and it enables him to see far away over
the propylon of Karnak, and over long reaches
of river and plain, a stranger coming bearing
like gifts, and then the short one is brought into
requisition, which brings him still nearer and
within gun-shot range, when the double-barreled
fowling piece of Salame the servant, (also a
present to him,) is brought out, which easily
brings him down, and he is bagged, lawful game.
But this year the game seemed to fly too high,
and for some inexplicable reason, episcopal
cloaks, silver communion vessels, and other like
presents were not forthcoming as freely as was
expected, and after a while the conclusion was
come to that I was not a missionary of the good
old stamp who used to send boat-loads of books to
be distributed, (gratuitously, of course,) among
the people; and one Sabbath I heard that our
English service in the dahabiyeh had been a very

barren one, as to practical results, because it had brought after it no "surrah" (parcel) the proceeds of a collection for his reverence.

In this connection I cannot help telling of a most recherché dinner which I one evening had with his reverence. A certain Mr. ——— attended morning service in the Church one Sabbath. He was an Englishman, and evidently of the High-Church school—at least so I gathered from the fact that his mind seemed much more full of reverence for this old apostolical Coptic Church, with its regular succession of bishops, priests, sacraments, etc., than with joy at the novel and hopeful fact of a Protestant missionary preaching in a Coptic church. Indeed, it almost seemed to me that he regarded my part of the performance in the light of an intrusion into the regular and settled order of things. However that may be, he kindly invited the bishop and his pro-tempore curate to dine with him the next evening, which invitation we were very happy to accept. When the occasion came the curate, of course, had to act as dragoman, and many were the kind and pretty sayings which Mr. and Mrs. ——— had to trouble him with translating for "his reverence," and "his lord-ship the bishop." Unfortunately his lordship was fasting, and so he could touch scarcely any of the rich viands which had been prepared. As soon as the soup came on, his first question

was whether it contained any "zefr," (grease,)
and Mrs. ——— said she thought it was purely
a vegetable soup.   So I told him that he might
eat, and, as he seemed yet to be doubtful, I assured him that there was not the least particle
of grease in it, and that I would be responsible
if in partaking of it he broke fast.   We all then
went at our soup, but soon Mrs. ——— and I
both found a small cube·of meat in our plates.
We exchanged significant glances, but said
nothing, and as it happened there was none in
his plate he ate the soup, grease and all, without
greasing or otherwise defiling his conscience.   I
suppose I must hold myself answerable for that
sin, if sin it be.   Then came on the more solid
food, course after course — turkeys, chickens,
meat, in rich and savory succession ; but he could
touch none of them.   He could only eat dry
bread and some vegetables which we assured
him *must* be clean, though even they had the
smell of the prohibited zefr on them.   I fear
they had been in the pot with the meat that
they were so savory.   But in the drinkables the
bishop indemnified himself.   In them there was
no zefr, and so he had no scruples in freely partaking, and by the time he had taken two tum-
blers of ale, and half a dozen (I cannot be positive as to the exact number, but think this within
the mark) glasses of sherry and another kind
of wine of which I have forgotten the name, he

was gloriously eloquent. He sat cross-legged on the settee of the dahabiyeh, and I sat opposite him, and so all his eloquence poured itself upon me. I can now see him, his voice raised high, and his arms flourishing. "Khowajah L———, you are the light of our country. Before you came we were in darkness; but the sun has arisen upon us. You are the St. Paul of our land; you have brought us the true gospel. You are St. John, the beloved disciple. You are—you are—" I never before received, and think I never again shall, such high eulogy. Then came the dessert with the spiced cordial in small but mighty glasses, and now our friend was at home. The little glasses, (and the cordial was even an improvement on arrack,) the nuts, and the empty stomach, all were exact in accordance with the most approved style of Arab drinking. But I soon thought it necessary to tread on Mr. ———'s toe, and thus give him a hint to hold his hand. I have told as much of this story as is funny, and will also hold my hand.

17*th* I had had a great deal of hard work and anxiety lately, and felt that a little recreation would not be amiss, and so arranged to go with a Mr. R. to the eastern mountains for a hunt for hyenas and wolves which the people said often came down to the plain. I also wished to attend that night the "feast of the baptism" at the old convent of St. Pachomius in the border of the desert. Monsur and he and I started in the afternoon, taking our beds and provisions with us. After three hours' ride on our donkeys we came to the hills where we soon started a couple of wolves, but as we did not know their lairs, and they could see us and flee before we could get within bullet range of them, we soon gave them up and returned to the convent. It was now sunset, and the people were collecting from the neighboring villages to the convent which except on feast occasions is deserted. We took our lunch outside under a tree and then went in where the priests kindly received us, and we spread our beds beside the central altar and sat down upon them. Soon the people began to say that it was time to commence services, when one of the priests arose and immediately commenced at the top of his voice to repeat the Coptic prayers, introductory to the mass. One of those present cried out to him, "Turn your face to the Lady," when he squared himself before the altar of the virgin, the central one in the church. He was soon joined in the responses by the loud voices of two bellowing deacons—a fitting bass for the high tenor of the clanging cimbals, which they vehemently beat together, and the work of the night was fairly under way. At such a debut, my young friend, who had been brought up a Quaker, opened wide his eyes, and I rallied him by saying that in Quaker and Copt the extremes had met. That night they went through with three long masses, besides the services special to the occasion which I shall presently describe. The principal of these were the blessing of the water and the baptism (if baptism it may be called) of all present. The church is a new one, built on the site of the old convent, and the baptistery or font in which it is customary at this feast to immerse all the males, not being yet built, they instead took two jars of water holding three or four gallons each, and after praying over them about an hour, the officiating priest occasionally stirring the water with a stick, as if stirring in the holiness which his prayers imparted (so we used to stir the corn meal into the boiling water to make hasty pudding), he then applied it to the persons of all the males present. This was done by dipping a small cloth into the water, and then applying it to the insteps, wrists, and foreheads of the congregation who one by one came forward for the purpose.

This to us was novel; but the baptism of two children, to which they next proceeded in another part of the church, was pitiful. It was performed in the women's department of the church, for the fathers did not appear in the service, the women presenting the children, and these of course could not enter the holy of holies, nor even the men's department, without defiling it (although the people generally were sitting there beside and around the altar, smoking and talking as if in a khan.) I have never before or since witnessed the rite administered as it then was. It was reduplicated. The first time it was mostly in Arabic. That part of it was very impressive and affecting in which the mother, taking the child and facing the west, renounced, in the name of the child, the devil and his works and service, and then turning to the east embraced the Saviour and his righteousness and service. Three times the priest asked her, "Do you embrace Christ for this child?" and three times she emphatically answered, "I do." (There are traces of this ceremony in the English baptismal service.) The priest then sprinkled water on the child, and I thought the ceremony was completed. But the two children were then taken to another part of the church, where was a font large enough for their immersion, and another priest completed the ceremony this time all in Coptic. The children were stripped naked, and with long repetitions of prayers they were three times immersed in the font, and then the priest commenced the process of anointing them with holy oil, which he did by dipping his thumb into the oil, and then commencing at the wrist of the child, tracing it along all its members and joints. The church was so cold that we needed our heavy shawls around us to keep warm, and the priest was an old trembling man, and very awkward in his manipulations, and as the poor things lay there on a garment on the ground, blue and screaming, until utterly exhausted they could cry no longer, I became so indignant that I could hardly restrain myself from interfering. I could no longer wonder that (as the Copts say is the case) the children are often killed by the process. This done, the priest proceeded in the same clumsy manner to dress the children in their new white clothes, when he handed them to the mothers, who seemed to take them with a feeling like that of Zipporah, when she said, "surely a bloody husband art thou to me because of the circumcision."

At length, about 4 o'clock in the morning, I grew sleepy and very weary of the everlasting shouting and the din of cimbals. People who are not in the secret may wonder how they find materials for such long and almost endless prayers, but the wonder will cease when they learn that one word will sometimes last an hour. For instance, hallelujah, which is a favorite word with them, they commence hah, hah, hah, for the first quarter hour, and then le, le, le, for the next, and so on to the end of the word, and then the chorus joins in with a magnificent *hallelujah*, repeated several times.

As I lay down to sleep it was with feelings sad and gloomy enough at this sad exhibition of the perversion of our holy religion, and this feeling was deepened by the gloom of the church around, whose broad aisles, now covered with sleeping figures, were very partially lighted by only one tiny flickering lamp, and that senseless shout now hoarse and grating was still going up. But as I raised my eyes I beheld through a small hole in the arched roof a bright star quietly twinkling in the zenith and casting its ray of light into that gloom. It was to me a star of hope sending even there its ray of promise, and I fell asleep praying that the Sun of Righteousness might soon appear to dispel all that thick darkness.

When the sound of prayer ceased, I and the others awoke, and it was soon broad daylight. The priests then brought food and we all ate, when I told them that it was now my turn to officiate. Monsur had read for them the Arabic passages of the Scriptures which came up in the course of the services through the night, at which they were greatly pleased, as he read them much better than the deacons could, and so now I told them that they had all had their turns and I must have mine. So after washing and taking a cup of coffee, as they usually do after eating, they all sat down again on the floor, and I took out my Testament and read the first part of the third chapter of John, and gave them a sermon on the baptism of the spirit, and the new birth. We then parted and went each one to his home.

18*th.* Found on reaching Luxor that the bishop had been talking with Mustapha about the school, and I thought that when he came to his greatest enemy to consult on the subject, it was high time to remove it from the church. He had also told Monsur just before starting, the day before, that ever since the school had been in the church the curse had been upon him, and he had been in trouble. I asked Mustapha if he could direct us to a room that we could rent, and he immediately said that he had one in the other end of the village to which we were welcome. He rejoiced in the opportunity of thus strengthening the bonds by which we were bound, and secretly vexing his great enemy; and so going to see the room, and finding it would answer, I gave orders to have it whitewashed and prepared for the school. I felt that it was useless having any more scenes with the bishop, and determined quietly to dissolve the partnership. Still he did not know of this purpose of removing the school, and it was left for him to be guilty of the first act of open breach, which he was on the following Sabbath.

19*th.* Called on him for the text for the morrow, and he referred me to the areef to give it to me. We were both about equally cool, and our interview was a short one.

20*th.* *Sabbath.* Went to the church and took my place beside him in my usual seat. He feign-

ed not to see me, and was deeply in earnest in
the business in hand. He made the responses
with great fervor, and as an extra, he treated
the people to a homily from St. Chrysostom.
This he had entered into the programme by way
of substitute for my sermon. When the sermon
was over he blessed and dismissed the people,
who, astonished at this procedure, grumbled and
whispered among themselves, when finally one
cried out that those who wished to hear me
preach should remain. To this I answered that
I would not preach in any man's church without
his consent and immediately left. In this answer
I followed my first impulse, and it was doubtless
the course which most men, at least most Americans, would have taken, but I afterwards repented it. It would have been better had I taken it
for granted that that was the church of Christ
and not of the bishop, and that I had a right to
preach the Gospel in it if the people wished it,
and then and there to have had a battle and a
division of the house. At all events I went home
with the comfort, that like Paul I could preach
in my own hired house, and that people would
come to hear me there. We had lately been
talking of a visit to Esneh, which is the great
centre of the Copts of the bishopric, and this
evening Antonius was dispatched there, which
was ominous. It seemed that the war was to
be carried into Africa.

21st. To-day the bishop made it with Monsur an absolute condition of the continuance of the school in the church that Tadrus (who the readers will recollect threw the paper charm into the Nile) and the Muslem boys should not be permitted longer to attend. Mustapha saw him, and he told him that he was ready to see me if I would call and make peace with him. But I felt that war was now much better than the hollow peace which I had so often patched up with him, and so declined.

Many of the people were forward in showing their sympathy with me in the quarrel. One of the leading men, who indeed was the main stay of the church, showed his by sending us a large basket of bread.

22d. This day was a very busy one in preparations for a feast which Mustapha proposed giving to the travelers who were there. It came off in the evening, and a grand affair it was. There were nineteen guests, of whom about an equal number were English and Americans. The feast from first to last was "à la Arab," except the champagne, which in a Muslem feast was a Frank innovation. First came the soup, then a lamb stuffed with raisins, nuts and rice, and roasted whole, then the two turkeys, chickens, pigeons, and all the et ceteras. Some of the guests, not knowing what they were to expect, came in white kids, but when they came

into the dining-room and found that they had to
sit on the floor and eat with their fingers, they
at first looked aghast, but they took off the kids
and rolled up their sleeves, and when once they
got into the spirit of the occasion they all seemed
to enjoy it very much. Mustapha, our host,
stood by like Abraham with his three guests
while we ate, and he seemed greatly to enjoy
the wry faces which we made when we burned
our fingers in carving the sheep and fowls with
our hands, and we in turn enjoyed his attempts
at being hospitable and facetious in his broken
English. One of the guests, a Mr. Douglass,
asked me about our mission work, and on returning to his boat sent up a kind note with a
contribution of £10. We had before received a
number of liberal donations from the travelers
in aid of our work. I never asked any one for
help. My position was such at Mustapha's, who
was both English and American consular agent,
and who often needed me to help in his post
office business, that I could hardly avoid becoming acquainted with all who came. They naturally asked about my business there, when I
gave them an account of our work, and then
those who chose to offer pecuniary aid did so.
I must admit in this connection that the English
seemed more liberal in this matter than the
Americans; although the dragomen always prefer going with American parties, as they say the

Americans are more lavish with their money. I think we Americans are more sectarian than the English are; at least we seemed better trained to do through our own church or board what we do. It is true the English have that remnant of the popish dogma of infallibility which they have concentrated as a "caput mortuum" in that little emphatic THE, as *the* church, *the* clergy, etc., but still they seem to be readier than we are to lend a helping hand to a good work wherever they find it.

23*d*. The bishop sent to have me call, or to say that he would call on me. I sent word back that I would be at leisure and in my room after an hour, and happy to see him, but, as I expected, he did not come.

24*th*. The new school-room being now ready we to-day moved the school there. I went down to see things properly arranged and settled, and had hardly got there when his reverence came puffing up the stairs. Mustapha was with me, and we took him into a little side room, when he asked why we had been in such a hurry to leave the church. I told him it was to get out of his way and to remove the curse from his house. I need not attempt to describe the long conversation which followed. At the end of it he begged my pardon for what had happened, and promised to walk straight in the future; but he besought me no longer to preach against the dogmas of the church. I told him I could not consent to teach anything except what I found in the Bible, and that if in the Bible there was anything opposed to the doctrines of the church I could not help it. He seemed now when it was too late heartily sorry that he had teazed us until he forced us to remove the school from the church. Especially when I told him that this would look pretty in the eyes of his English friends to see a Christian school removed from the church to a Muslem house. I told him, however, what I had before told the people, that had we only continued to pay Antonius $4 per month, he would for that sum have sold the whole Christian community of the place into our hands as Protestants—that it was very cheap, as it only amounted to about two and a half cents per head for each month, but that even at that low rate it was against our principles to buy souls.

25th to Feb. 3d. Nothing of note occurred during this week. The school was flourishing in its new quarters. A few of the Christian boys had left, and a few Muslems came and took their places. The latter, however, did not make good their promise to send all their children in case we would remove the school from the church. This matter is after all in a great measure in the hands of the schoolmasters, both Christian and Muslem. The parents generally exercise but little authority over the children. They go to school when they choose, and their old teachers usually have them under their control. Had we taken the Muslem areef into our employment we would have secured all the Muslem children. But this would have involved the dismissal of the Christian one, as we had not work enough for them both, together with Monsur—and with him would have gone the Christian boys. As it was, the bishop was doing all he could to get him away, but he clung to his seventy piastres and would not leave us.

Still, independently of the bishop's influence, the number of pupils in the school had fallen off from forty to twenty. This was caused by the fact that it was now the height of the season for the travelers. Many of the children had to run after the donkeys, in taking the visitors around to see the ruins, and others had to go day by day down to the dahabiyehs to offer for sale the scarabæi and little antiquities which they and their friends had collected during the summer. The Viceroy claims for himself all the antiquities which are found, and he constantly keeps a large number of forced laborers taken from the neighboring villages at work digging for them among the tombs on the other side of the river. These of course have many opportunities of hiding in their clothes small articles that they find, and then in winter they stealthily offer them for sale. Besides this there is a large business carried on

20*

in manufacturing scarabæi with their penknives,
like our friend Antonius, which in winter are
gobbled up at enormous prices by the flock of
geese which every winter comes from the North.
For the travelers who choose to give prices varying from $1 to $2.50 for a bit of stone carved
into the shape of a beetle, it matters little
whether the carving was done last summer or
four thousand years ago, provided they do not
know the difference. But for the boys, and indeed the whole population of Luxor, this is a
ruinous business. All Luxor, from Mustapha and
the bishop down to the smallest urchin that can
hang on to the tail of a donkey, depends for the
most part on the travelers for a livelihood, and
whether they be donkey-boys who learn to mouth
great English oaths, and charge Englishmen two
prices for the use of their animals, or guides who
take them to see sights which they can as well
see alone, and filch from the boys part of their
earnings, or antiquity-mongers who palm on
them false antiquities, or charge ten prices for
true ones, the whole business is most demoral-
izing. It gives a distaste for all regular and
settled work, and eats out all habits of thrift and
industry. The children cannot compose their
minds and settle down to hard study ; and as for
the men, all Luxor is not able to support a garden patch to furnish sojourners with garden
vegetables, and we have all winter been forced

to bring a precarious supply from other villages
and from Cairo. In winter it is all excitement
and eager scrambling for the bright coins which
are so profusely scattered by the inexperienced
travelers; and in summer I suspect they spend
most of their time in counting over their gains,
and in desultory searchings among the tombs,
and endless bargaining among themselves for a
stock in trade for the next season. I constantly
notice that the Luxorites are far behind their
neighbors of other villages in thrift and industry, and begin to suspect that we have made a
mistake in making this one of our first stations
in Upper Egypt.

This week Lord Aberdeen made an excursion
to Negadeh and Ghous, where he sold books for
800 piastres. Father Makhiel, when they returned, was in ecstacies about a man named
Fam Stephanus whom they had found in Ghous.
He said he had spent a day and a night with
him in most interesting spiritual converse—that
he had got far beyond the A B C of controversy about images, confession, etc., and that
they spent the time in discussing the high mysteries of religion, and in investigating and explaining difficult passages of Scripture. I afterwards became acquainted with this man, and
found that in intelligent piety he justified Makhiel's high encomiums.

CHAPTER IX.

4th. Left with Lord Aberdeen for our long-talked of excursion to Esneh. We had but just spread our sails when far in the north we saw a couple dahabiyehs with American flags coming. We had already received word by mail from Cairo that the brethren there had sent us with an American party a few boxes of books, and so we turned back and were not disappointed in finding them. All winter our trouble was to get sufficient books to meet the demand which we everywhere found, and our stock had now become low, so now we started again feeling rich. Just above Luxor the river is very tortuous in its course for several miles, and this together with the hindrance to the north winds of the high western hills opposite Luxor, almost always leaves a vessel becalmed for several hours when the men must track. After thus toiling along for some distance we found ourselves at 3 P. M. opposite a small village called Maris. Going up on the bank we found a goatherd who told us that there were a few Christians in the village, which was about four miles distant; so, taking Father Makhiel, we filled our bags with books and started off for it. When we reached the village we sought out the house of the shaikh, as they said they had neither church nor priest, and threw on him the responsibility of calling together the Christians, who soon came and bought a number of books. Then after giving them a word of exhortation to read the books with diligence, and thus make up for their lack of spiritual privileges, we proceeded to Erment, where we also sold well.

5th. This morning the big dahabiyeh came, and, after purchasing some necessaries and selling some books, we again set sail, and with a fine wind we reached Esneh at 3 P. M. I went up to the town and called on the Kummus Ibrahim, and our old friend Khaleel, who returned with me to the boat to pay their respects to his lordship.

This finished, we took a hasty glance at the temple which antiquarians say is a very ancient one, but it has now been mostly torn down to furnish building stones for the neighboring factory. It was now sunset, and the dahabiyeh was far ahead of us, so we got a couple of boys with donkeys who agreed to take us to the factory, we promising them in turn each a copy of the Psalms on our arrival. We reached there

at 8 o'clock, almost frozen with our chilly ride,
after our warm walk with our heavy back-load
of books, and our warmer discussion in the close
room of the shaikh. We were also ravenously
hungry, as a light lunch furnished by the hospitality of the shaikh was all the dinner we had
had, and the dahabiyeh was not yet, there, and
would not likely come before morning, so we
had to cast about us for food and lodging. I
spied on the shore the boat of Mr. Harris, one
of our English merchants from Alexandria, with
whom I presumed I could get a night's lodging;
but first we went into the sugar factory, which,
as it was now the crushing season, was in full
operation night and day, in the hot fumes of
which our chills soon left us, and we allayed
the sharp cravings of hunger by a delightful
draught of the rich cane juice. We then went
to the house of the chief scribe of the factory,
who hearing our story at once invited us to
spend the night with him, but the remembrance
of past experiences of Coptic fleas, and other
worse vermin, led me to accept the invitation
only for Makhiel, while I went down to Mr.
Harris's boat. Miss Harris soon extemporized
an abundant supper, and then arranged upon -
the lounge what she termed a shake-down for
the night's rest. Then as it was time for her to
retire, I went up again to the Copts, knowing
that they as usual would be in for a long " sa-

hara," and the evening is the only time when one can usually get at the scribes, as they are closely kept at their work seven days in the week. I found them just sitting down to a bountiful meal, which in the meantime they had prepared for Makhiel, and of course was forced to join them, though I had already made ample amends for the privations of the past day. But an Arab meal never makes it necessary for one not hungry to feign eating long, and it was soon through with. Then came the richer repast— the feast of reason and the flow of soul. John Marcus (our old friend mentioned in the former part of these notes), and a number of the neighbors were present, and also a priest from a distant place, who was a relative of our host. They fell in with most of the doctrinal statements which we made, but excused themselves from corresponding practice by saying that they were not freemen and their own masters, that they were in such abject slavery to the Viceroy and to Mustapha Pasha, who is the proprietor of the factory, that they were unable to do as they wished. In the single item of working on the Sabbath, which they are all forced to do, I was forced to admit the justice of their plea. But even here I urged them to take a stand in accordance with the demands of their religion and the dictates of their consciences. But this is a very hard case. The Copts have almost a monopoly of the account and book-keeping of the government; and being trained to this business from early youth, if dismissed from the service they are fit for nothing else, and starvation stares them in the face. They formerly were not obliged to work on the Sabbath, and it is provoking to think that an English employé of the government was instrumental in imposing upon them this yoke; and now it seems impossible for them to shake it off, except by a general strike throughout the country, and for this they have not yet as a community sufficient moral principle or concert of action. One, or a few individuals who should take a stand on the subject, would be punished by the government, which cannot be expected to understand or enter into their scruples, as refractory persons, besides the want into which, should they succeed, they would involve themselves and families. This state of things is one of the most serious obstacles to success among this large and most influential class of the Coptic community.

Still, in general, I could urge upon them that the slavery of Said and Mustapha Pasha was as nothing compared with the heavy spiritual yoke under which they had voluntarily thrust their necks—that the finger of a priest was thicker than the loins of a Pasha—that if the Pasha should force them to confess their sins to priests who were miserable sinners like themselves, and to work out their salvation by seven months of most austere fasting in a year, and drive them off every month or two to the convents in the mountains, to spend the long cold night in screaming hah, hah, hah, and to pay tithes, and heavy perquisites besides, to a priesthood which labored not for their spiritual edification; this would indeed be a bondage heavier than that of the children of Israel under their forefathers— that it was only because they had first rendered themselves most abject spiritual slaves, vile in spirit and emasculated in all their powers, that effeminate Muslems, whose bodily and mental powers had evaporated between the debauchery of the harem and the steam and suffocation of the hot bath were able thus to rule it over them; and that if they would only first arise and shake off the self-imposed yoke of priestly bondage, I could be security that they would not long be under the other. This outburst was not very palatable to the priest who was present, but all the rest said Amen to it. It was now after midnight, and I left. John Marcus went down with me on his way to his own house, and told me that at my last visit there I had forever settled for him the doctrine of justification by faith alone.

6th. This morning Lord Aberdeen proposed a measure which proved a very efficient one for facilitating our work. He had brought with

him a very fine tent, and this we pitched in the
grove below the town, and spreading in it mats
and carpets, and taking to it a box of books, we
were prepared to receive buyers, and to accommodate a small audience for hearing the Word.
Here Makhiel and I labored forenoon and afternoon and evening with a constancy which left
me neither time nor strength for keeping up my
notes. We found that we were seldom left without
an audience. Khaleel, Keddes, and a few others,
were almost constant attendants, and they formed
a nucleus around which the constant stream of
passers-by eddied, most of them only remaining
an hour or so, and then passing on to their
business. As too we had now set up house, the
custom of the country required of us to observe
the rites of hospitality, and so we kept one of
the boatmen with us to fill the pipes and boil the
coffee, and thus, what with books, and preaching, and refreshments, our tent soon became a
favorite resort.

There is here a large settlement of Berbers or
Nubians, and their children purchased a great
many penny tracts. One of our tracts was
called "The Rest of the Weary," and the latter
word, by changing one letter of it, they, in
their crooked pronunciation of the Arabic, had
changed to "Serpent," and so we had a rush of
them for "The Rest of Serpent." May it give
many of them rest from "that old serpent which

is the Devil and Satan; " who deceived our first parents and has since gone about destroying their progeny! Makhiel held his hand hard upon the tracts, and would seldom sell them one until they had taken a Bible or a Testament. He said, "These tracts are sweet but evanescent; you read them once or twice and then, like a bacat (bouquet) of flowers, they wither and fade in your hands; but this book is like a bit of musk in a trunk. As often as you open it, it diffuses its fragrance, and it retains it unimpaired for years."

9*th*. We removed our tent to a new place on the other side of the town, so that all its people might have an opportunity to come to us. I was rejoiced to find that the mission of Antonius to this place had proved a failure. Ibrahim, the Cummus, or head priest, was one of our most constant attendants at the tent, and to-day (Saturday) he invited me to come and preach to-morrow in the church. He is a good, simple-minded man, and, I find, no admirer of the Bishop.

10*th*. *Sabbath*. The people of Esneh have the reputation of being the most religious in Egypt, and I found the services at the church much fuller and longer than at Luxor. When I asked the reason of this they told me that the bishop had there curtailed them for his own convenience Perhaps his curtailed mass is the one which in after times, in the days of sporting Lords and complaisant priests, was known in England as the "hunting mass." I was happy to find also that instead of only one Scripture lesson in Arabic they had several. These the Kummus pointed out to me yesterday, and I choose among them John viii. 51–59 for my text. It gave me a fine opportunity for bringing out two points most important for them, as they were for the Jews in the days of the Saviour: First, That the keeping of Christ's sayings is the true test of discipleship to Him, and second, that religion is not a hereditary thing, and as the Jews were not permitted to presume that they were God's people because they were Abraham's seed, so they also should not put their trust in the fact of the Evangelist Mark having been the founder of their Church, and they descended by regular succession from the saints and martyrs of olden times.

After service, the Kummus took us to his house, where breakfast was brought to us, and then we remained till noon, explaining the Word to a company that still clung to us, and who brought forward many difficult passages to be cleared up. Then Khaleel and Keddes accompanied us to the dahabiyeh, and spent the rest of the day with us. Their earnestness and insatiable avidity for the truth astonished me, and before they left I took them aside into one of the cabins and had prayer with them. During prayer I noticed Khaleel held his hand before his face like a Muslem, which confirmed an impression which the discussion into which he had occasionally led us through the week, had made on my mind, that he had been tainted with Muslem views of truth. He seemed to embrace every opportunity to lead us into discussions of the doctrines of the Trinity and the sonship and atonement of Christ. It is no wonder that such a corrupted form of Christianity as we here have, often drives earnest minds elsewhere to seek for the jewel of truth. I had also noticed that Christians and Muslems seemed to live on very amicable terms. One day a Muslem funeral passing through the streets, I noticed in the procession quite a number of Christians, and they told me that Muslems also attended their funerals. This I have never seen elsewhere.

11th. Sedhum (already mentioned in the former part of these notes) came to-day from Edfou and immediately left business and joined our regular congregation. Poor Kiddes was still clinging to his fasting and other superstitious rites of the church, of the fallacy of which, as I have already narrated, I failed to convince him on my last visit. On coming here last week the subject was again renewed, and I soon found that the only way to convince him was to give

21*

him the full Scripture testimony on the subject,
and so taking my Concordance, I made out a
full list of all the passages of Scripture in which
fasting is mentioned, arranging them so as to
show the Scriptural times, methods, and ends of
fasting. This paper I gave him, and told him
to take his Bible and review the whole subject,
and then act accordingly. To-day he came down
to the dahabiyeh before we went up to the tent,
and Makhiel and the dragoman were just sitting
down on the deck to their breakfast of fried
eggs, when I told him " Kiddes, take hold and
welcome." He quietly answered, " I have had
my breakfast to-day." He had taken the great
stand. The Bible had convinced him, and he
had broken fast, and henceforth he is no longer
a Copt, but a Protestant.

12th. Keddes came this morning with one of
the blind areefs. While this one was sipping
his coffee Keddes beckoned to me to follow him
outside the tent, when he told me that he had
last night had a terrible contest with him until
after midnight, on the subject of the new stand
he had taken. I think I have already remarked
that the blind areefs are usually in Scriptural
knowledge the most intelligent men in the community. In all controversies and doubtful points
they are the oracles, and their decisions carry
with them great weight. They teach the children and live upon the benefactions of the peo-

ple, and I have usually found it expedient to propitiate their favor by a present of a copy of the Psalms, and in some cases a Testament or Bible. This man, Kiddes told me, came to him exhorting him to beware of false prophets, which Kiddes answered by telling him and those with him to beware of him, and not excommunicate him as they threatened, or he would take back the idols which he had given to all the churches from Esneh to Assouan, and hang them up around the rooms of his house by way of ornament. (He in his blind devotion had some time before made a large donation of pictures to these churches, which now he heartily repented.) He told them moreover that if these pictures had had virtue in them, and his fastings merit, they should have preserved him from the loss of seventeen purses (about $280) which had lately been stolen from him in Cairo. But Kiddes did not depend alone upon his hard arguments and sturdy obstinacy to carry him safely through this wordy ordeal, for, reminding me that I had by mistake passed over this areef in my gift of copies of the Psalms to the areefs, he had that morning presented him one as from me, and had now dragged him down, though very reluctant to come, on the plea that I wished to see him, and that it would be impolite not to call. This I felt had all been very keenly managed, and offered to repay him for the copy of the Psalms which he had presented in my name. But he said "No, I used to buy pictures for the churches, now I think I can afford to grant a book." We now slipped into the tent again where we found Makhiel entertaining the areef and the others who had come. He, not having been aware of our departure nor our return, must have concluded by this time that the strange preacher whom he had pictured to himself as a wolf in sheep's clothing, was a very quiet man. But I had now learned my man, and could deal my blows where they would tell. It was not a difficult matter to drag in the passage about the false teachers who were as wolves in sheeps' clothing, when I took occasion to explain at length who they were and what their characteristics, to whom the Saviour applied those epithets. The 24th chapter of Matthew served me for a full length portrait of them, and it was evident before I was done that all present, even the areef, could see in the picture a strong family likeness to the chief priests and scribes in their own midst, and that they need no longer apply the description to us foreigners. This served me for the Gospel "lesson" for the forenoon service, and then for the Epistle I took the first chapter of 1st Corinthians, which so well describes the sin of sectarianism and party spirit.

In the afternoon Sedhum asked me for a few charges of powder to add to the stock which he had already provided for the occasion of the baptism of his child, which he expected soon to celebrate at a convent of Pachomius, back of Edfou. This gave me another text, and I asked him why he should go a journey of two days to have his child baptized at a place accounted holy, while that God whose ordinance it is, is the Omnipresent One. And it also gave an opportunity to explain the ordinance at length and show how they had corrupted it. He promised to present his own child in baptism instead of having the mother or a godmother do it, and to strive afterwards to train it up "in the nurture and admonition of the Lord."

The use of firearms in religious ceremonies and rejoicings in the East is very common. Swords are also often used. I once attended a feast of the Virgin at her noted convent at Sadainiah above Damascus, where the whole week was spent by the assembled crowds in sword exercises in the church and in repeating poetry. The manner in which the latter was performed was an illustration of the manner in which the Psalms of David should be sung in our churches. There were several poets present, and sometimes one of these, forming the people into a large circle, would take his place in the centre, and then giving them a chorus, like that in the 136th Psalm, he would each time improvise a sentence, and then they in full orchestra

would break in with the chorus which he had
given them. How magnificent it would sound
to have that Psalm thus sung in our churches.
The choir that now squeaks out Watts' dogger-
els away off in the gallery to come down before
the people and chant the separate verses, and
then the whole congregation in full chorus to
join in the glorious refrain, " For his mercy endureth forever." Or that sublime 107th Psalm
in which after longer periods the chorus still
recurs, " Oh that men would praise the Lord for
his goodness, and for his wonderful works to the
children of men." A number of the Psalms were
evidently intended thus to be sung. In some
of them the chorus seems only to be given in the
first verse, and then not repeated after each verse
or period. Such for example appears to be the
first verse of the 118th Psalm: " Oh give thanks
unto the Lord for He is good, because his mercy
endureth forever." Then at Sadainiah, they had
another system which answered to the parallel-
ism of the Psalms, which one must notice is the
structure of most of them. Two poets took their
places in the ring, and improvised sentences in
response to each other, the second each time
bringing a parallel to the sentence of the first,
either repeating in different words or explaining
or amplifying his sentiment. While doing this the
circle about them would slowly and compactly
move around keeping time with the chanting

and with the musical instruments with their feet
and hands, while the sword exercises were going on just without the ring. The whole brought
to mind very vividly the 149th Psalm: "Praise
ye the Lord, sing unto the Lord *a new* song and
his praise in *the congregation of the saints*. . . .
Let them praise his name *in the dance*. Let them
sing praises to him *with the timbrel and harp*. . . .
Let the high praises of God be *in their mouth and
a two-edged sword in their hand*." Thus David
could "sing of mercy and of judgment," and
thus to this day the Arabs wreath the sword
with the olive branch. Thus, Paul too, could call
upon men "to behold the *goodness* and SEVER-
ITY of God," and could cry out, "Oh the depth
of the riches both of the wisdom and knowledge
of God. How *unsearchable are his judgments*,
and his ways past finding out." But in these
days the sentimentality of modern poetasters
has voted David a heathen, because he penned
the 109th Psalm, and even Paul, in some of his
views, an old fogy. But "nevertheless the
foundation of God standeth sure," and on the
reverse faces of his seal are these mottoes, "The
Lord knoweth them that are his—and let every
one that nameth the name of Christ depart from
all iniquity."

David and his harp following the flocks of
Jesse were brought still more forcibly to my
mind when they offered to bring me a shepherd

who they said could improvise poetry the evening long, but they failed to find him and so I missed that treat.

I may remark while on the subject that I have sometimes heard the psalms which are in parallelisms sung in the Coptic churches by two companies of singers, the one old men and the other boys, whose voices were pitched an octave higher, and the effect was delightful. Every one I think will agree that the reading of the Psalms in the English Episcopal service, in which the people respond to the clerk, is the most edifying part of the service. But even this is not enough. The whole congregation should be divided into two parties and then they should be chanted, not read.

But this hard week's work must be brought to a close, as Lord Aberdeen wished to proceed to Assouan. Our plan had been that after his visit here he should proceed on his journey, and I return on horseback, or by some chance boat. He, delighted by our success here, and the manifest interest of the people, wished to keep me with him in the trip to Assouan and back, but I did not think it right to leave Mrs. L. so long alone in the midst of the small-pox at Luxor. He then proposed that we should return for her and all go together, but I could not entertain this idea, for I saw that even with me alone his mind was much engrossed with the care of mak-

ing everything pleasant and comfortable, and I
feared that with us both his hospitality would
in his enfeebled state prove too much for his
nerves. So it was concluded that I should return,
and as there were no dahabiyehs coming down,
in which I could get a chance, and in an open
native boat there was a risk of being forced to
sleep out, he sent up to the Bey and had a horse
brought, but when I mounted and tried the saddle, preparatory to the journey on the morrow,
I found the pain in my side so severe that I could
not ride, so he concluded to take me back to
Luxor and then return.

That evening was to be our last in Esneh, and
Kiddes had made arrangements for making a
feast for me and some of our new-made friends.
When he announced this at sunset I was dis-
mayed and said, "Kiddes, you see the state I
am in. I have talked all day, indeed the whole
week, and am now too weak to stand or walk."
He answered, "We will carry you." To this,
seeing how great a disappointment to them a
refusal would be, I assented; and so clasping my
arms around the necks of Kiddes and Sedhum,
and they theirs around my back, they dragged
me up to the house. Besides our old acquaintances, I found he had got in a couple of friends
whom he had not been able to entice to the tent
to hear the new teacher, and we had but just got
seated when the Testaments were brought out

22

and I was asked to expound a chapter. This was done and then dinner was brought on, after which the Testaments were again brought out, and he asked me to give them a specimen of the manner in which they should carry on family worship in their houses. I read another chapter, with a few remarks, and then led them in prayer, the women meanwhile standing in the door passage where they could hear and not be seen. They then dragged me down again to the dahabiyeh. Noble men! I could have stayed there to spend my life with them.

13*th*. We to-day bade farewell to our friends and turned our prow towards Luxor. The wind was calm during the forenoon, and with the strong current and the oars of the men we made good progress. The Nile boatmen always sing in rowing. One of them improvising or repeating their silly ditties, and the rest shouting the chorus. The chorus to-day was

"Ya lil-asabiyeh fe homat El Medan
Sevastopol akhuthha asaker Es Sultan."
(Oh to the lions in the reach of the race-course
Sevastopol was taken by the soldiers of the Sultan.)

Such are the thanks of the "sick man" to England and France for their kind interposition to save him from the great northern bear when he came down to craunch his bones.

We met Mr. Riley, of New York, whose acquaintance we had made at Luxor, and who was afterwards very kind to us. He brought a letter from Mrs. L. containing the sad news that small-pox was in the house—that two of Mustapha's children had taken it and one of them died of it.

At Jebelein ("the two mountains," which on both sides of the valley here came down very close to the river,) the north wind became so strong that we were obliged to lie by for the rest of the day.

14th. The wind still being strong, Makhiel and I went to the west side of the river, where we had heard there was a village containing Copts. After trying the way I found it would prove too long a walk for me, and so sending him I returned and took the small boat and went down to a village on the east bank which was nearer shore; I found in it but one Christian family. The old man was weaving, and neither he nor his son, who soon came, could read. They were very illiterate. Indeed, all I could get out of them of Christian knowledge was about half of the Lord's Prayer. I was by this time hungry, and asked them if they could furnish me with a loaf. They brought me a load of "bittaws," (small Indian loaves,) and some cheese. After eating I offered to pay them, but they said, "No! would we take money for bread! that would be a shame." They said they had children; so I gave them a Testament and some tracts and they promised to have their children taught to read. By this time a couple of Muslems had come in, and so I took my Testament and read and explained the parable of the Prodigal Son. They seemed delighted with it, and the old man and his son said they had never before heard it. I then left and had proceeded about twenty minutes when one of the Muslems came running after me, wishing me to go back, saying that the whole village had now collected, and that they wished to hear that same teaching. This invitation it was very hard to decline, but the wind had now lulled, and the dahabiyeh had started, and I did not feel able to walk back, and so I had to commend him to the books I had left, and them all to the leading and enlightenment of God's word and spirit.

But I found after he left that Makhiel had not yet come down on the opposite bank, and so I stopped at another village which was near at hand. In it I found, as in many villages of the Nile, only one Copt, and he the Government accountant and tax-gatherer. He met me in the street before his door, and so we sat down there, as we often must do when the house is not large enough for a harem and reception-room. The coffee was brought out, showing that there was no lack of hospitality, and he brought a Bible. The Muslems going and coming began to sit down on each side of the street, to see who the

new-comer was, and what his business, and soon
I had a company of twenty or thirty of them.
I offered to sell them books, and on inquiring
what books I had, I told them the Holy Book
of God. The Khateeb (orator) of the Mosque,
was present, and so they referred the matter to
him. He examined my wares and dubiously
shook his head. I then quoted to him the first
verses of the "Cow" chapter of the Koran
which say, "There is no doubt in this book. It
is a direction to the pious who believe in the
mysteries of faith, who observe the appointed
times of prayer, and distribute alms out of what
we have bestowed on them, and who believe in
that revelation which hath been sent down to
thee, and that which hath been sent down to
the prophets before thee, and have firm assurance
of the life to come. These are directed by their
Lord, and they shall prosper." I then said that
their own prophet being judge, they must
believe in "that which hath been sent down to
the prophets before him," which they admitted
was the revelations of Moses and Jesus, and the
Prophets, that unless they believed them they
were not "directed by their Lord and should
not prosper, and that they could not believe
them unless they would buy and read the book.
This argument I have often used with the Muslems, and they have sometimes bought Bibles
on the strength of it. The Khateeb, however,

22*

brought up the old Muslem argument, that the
Jews and Christians had corrupted the Bible,
which led to a long discussion, in which the
company admitted that their champion was
worsted. The Christians sat amazed to see me
thus beard the lion in his den, and to hear me
quote the Koran, which the Muslems do not
allow them to read, as they say that none but
the clean must touch it.

I limped down to the boat, and now found
Makhiel waiting on the other side. On the
shore it was very hot, but on the water we
found it cooler, and I took a sound nap in the
stern of the boat, while Makhiel held over us
the umbrella, and the men rowed us down to
the dahabiyeh, which we overtook at Erment.
Here we found, as it was market-day, and many
villagers in from neighboring places, that the
men had sold a large number of books. My
long nap, and a bountiful dinner which her Lady-
ship had in readiness for me, refreshed me for
new adventures. I accordingly went up and
took my seat on the shore to see who would
come. John Markus spying me from the window of the Dewan, took the liberty of closing
his day's work as it was now near night, and
came out. We had a long talk, but, poor man,
I thought I noticed then the beginnings of what
was very marked in a subsequent visit, viz.:
that he had come to a stand, and that on the

question of Sabbath-breaking. He promised to
read constantly his Bible, and to walk according
to it and his conscience. But it is hard urging
a man to follow his conscience whose bread
depends upon his systematic commission of a
known and acknowledged sin. The one sin
known and indulged in sears the conscience and
eats out the spiritual life. One thing, at least, I
told him he could never again do. He could
no longer go as the others do to the priest and
confess, and receive absolution, and the false
peace of conscience which it brings, while he
and the priest were both aware that there was
one sin unconfessed and unrepented of—nay, dis-
tinctly proposed to the mind as a sin to be lived
in all the days of his life. I left him in a state
of pitiful anxiety and distress, and trust the
Lord may lead him in his own good way and
bring him to a wide place. We left at sunset,
and reached Luxor at eleven o'clock P. M.

CHAPTER X.

15th. I must now return to bring up the thread of Theban history. The Bishop was absent on a visit to Ghinneh, to pay his respects to Fadil Pasha. And well he might do so, for that dignitary had put forth his hand to vex him still more in the persons of his relatives, and some of them had been taken to sweep the streets of Ghinneh, with the attachment of a ball to their legs by way of rolling them. Now I understood why, after his ugly cut of me in the church, he had twice sent to me to be reconciled, and why, unable to stoop so low as to call on me, he had even come to the new schoolhouse at the neutral ground, and attempted to patch up a false reconciliation; why also he shut himself up in his room and refused to see any one, and even had no heart for public services in the church on the Sabbath. He hoped still to use me in propitiating or subduing the Pasha, and when my journey to the south cut off this hope, he took his departure for the north to see what he could do by a personal interview. On leaving, he forbade the Christian

(260)

boys attending the school any longer, and they for the moment obeyed, but, as soon as his back was turned, they returned to school. But I had come back just in time to see them scatter again. Word came, I know not how, that Fadil Pasha had expressed a determination to deal with the boys who should continue coming to the school, so all the Christian boys, except six, left. These seemed determined to brave the ire of both Bishop and Pasha. The parents of the rest came to me, and with a sorrow which was evidently unfeigned, said that they did not care for the Bishop, that they would send their children in spite of him, but that Fadil Pasha was a mighty man, and was too much for them. That they were sincere in this was evident from the fact, that up to this time they had continued sending their children in spite of the prohibition of the Bishop. I could not believe that Fadil Pasha had taken any such step, but they evidently believed it and that was enough. It thinned our poor school terribly. I tried to talk it out of their heads, but in vain. I might have traced the report up to its source and then have striven to correct it, or if true to reverse it, even if necessary by a visit in the wake of the Bishop to the Pasha, but I was heartily sick of Luxor politics—indeed, my hard labor at Esneh had left me unfit for anything but the bed. I had learned in that trip that there was yet a great deal of the land of Egypt outside of Luxor, in which labor would be much more productive. The time of our departure was also at hand, and it was evident that Monsur, weak in body and unable to cope with the wiles of the adversary, could not be left behind for the summer, and so for the few days which we were to remain I determined to let things swing. In my notes of the time I find the following entry : "This whole movement is doing good. It has brought down upon the Bishop the odium among his own people, which he so richly deserves. The school for the time suffers, but he will yet find that like old Kronos he has only swallowed a stone in swaddling clothes, and that there is a young Jupiter growing up to manly strength in the mountains, who will yet be down upon him and make him vomit up what he has swallowed."

The report of Fadil Pasha's interference to crush the school *was* true, but I did not ascertain its truth till we were on our return voyage home. I was then informed at Ghinnch and at Osiout, that the Bishop on going there had secured the interest of the Italian Catholic priest, whose influence with the Pasha through the French Consular agent was considerable ; and that one of the enemies of our cause at Osiout, had also written to a relative of his who was a favorite scribe with the Pasha, securing his influence against us. When they once got the Pasha's ear they could of course tell him anything they chose about this strange American and his doings and purposes, and there was no one present to contradict them. My curt message formerly sent to him would probably not predispose him in our favor, so we will have to admit that the Bishop at length Luxor triumphed. But it was a well-fought battle, and we Americans have since learned that an occasional defeat, even in a good cause is no disgrace. His triumph was a greater moral defeat to him than though he had been conquered. All the Copts who heard of it, even the debased Luxorites, blushed with shame to see a Christian bishop thus fight against a Christian school generously established by Christian philanthropy for the instruction of their children in the oracles of truth, and that he finally scrupled not to call to his aid a Catholic priest and a Muslem Pasha. And if any were disposed to think differently, the victory which we achieved a few months later in the case of Farris, which made the ears of all Egypt tingle, set us all right again.

17th. *Sabbath.* I was too unwell to-day to preach either in Arabic or English, though a number of dahabiyehs were in port.

18th. To-day Mustapha made a good speculation. Our American Consul-General had secured for him (I hardly know whether by *him*, here I intend to say for himself or for Mustapha,) from the Government permission to dig for antiquities, and Mustapha, with his Consular agencies and his Muslem Agaship, was able to command sufficient patronage to have, like the Viceroy, his band of laborers in the tombs, these mines of antiquity. These were willing to labor for the small pickings they were able to appropriate to themselves, while they gave the large things to Mustapha.

I will not tell how we often had to brow-beat them to make them disgorge a share at least of the scarabæi which they found; but they could not conceal in their bosoms the mummies, and to-day he had a couple of fine ones sent to a Mr. D., whose taste took that direction. They were evidently man and wife, and both cases were of very superior workmanship, though the husband's was much the finest. A bargain was soon struck for this one for fifty pounds, and Mr. D. invited a few of us to be present at the opening, which took place in Mustapha's back hall. The two beautifully carved cases which enclosed the mummies were sawn through and broken up; though had they been taken to England with the mummies in them, he would have something worth seeing for his money. The body was then unwrapped, bandage after bandage, until the ornaments were reached, and they were a few trinkets, such as he might have pur-

chased from any of the boys for a dollar. But
Mr. D. then concluded that the treasures must
be with the wife, and so he purchased the other
one for twenty pounds, and this too was unwrapped; and the result of the dusty job was
a heap of dried dust, and bones, and bitumen.
Poor Mr. D. had got the value of a dollar's worth
of antiquity for three hundred and fifty dollars—a
pretty dear whistle! People may wonder at this
and call it infatuation; but not long since a mummy was found of an Egyptian Queen, in which
golden ornaments were found to the amount of
thirty-four pounds weight; and so who knows
but that each mummy may be a queen, and men
will invest in lotteries. The Luxorites, however,
are better connoisseurs, and can better judge of
the value of one of their mummied ancestors
than the strangers can, and they themselves
open the mummies that are likely to contain
treasures. They can distinguish between a
mummy of the times of the Pharaohs and of
the Ptolemies; and it is said they sometimes
replace one of the former by one of the latter
in the cases which they sell to their Frank cus-
tomers. Of course, I do not intend to insinuate
that either Mustapha or his Gournour diggers
had done this in the present case. Mustapha
did well with his curiosities, and he had still a
statue for which he pretended to ask $1,000.
It usually stood very conspicuously in the centre

23

of the main hall. But when our Consul-General, Mr. De Leon, visited here a few weeks ago, it was removed to the harem, and I was charged not to say anything about it.

Among the notable things of Luxor is the tomb of a noted Muslem saint, called Abu El Haja, and his mulid or feast has this week kept Luxor in a perfect turmoil. This Abu El Haja must have been a redoubtable cavalier, for horse-manship was the leading feature of his feast. Many came from distant places with their fine horses, and the exercises were kept up through the week in the open space between Mustapha's house and the river.

I was surprised that they did not undertake the famous Eastern tournament of the Jereed, but they did not. The spectators, who num-bered thousands, arranged themselves in an im-mense ring, within which the exercises were performed to the sound of harsh, horse music, which was kept up by the hour. A quick start, a brisk run, and a sudden stop and wheelabout were the favorite feats of the riders. The horses were bleeding at the mouth by the savage bits with which they were thrown upon their haunches when in full run, and their sides were gashed and bleeding by the shoveled stirrups which served for both stirrup and spur. And this, together with the music, made men act as if infuriated.

Meanwhile the men might be seen here and there forming little circles and lashing themselves into fury by the Derwish exercises. In the evening the mosque of Abu El Haja and its precincts were beautifully illuminated, and feasting and revelry, dancing and torchlight processions, were the order of the programme. Many were the offerings which were made to the saint, and many the sheep that were sacrificed and eaten.*

Thus when the Israelites made their Golden Apis in the wilderness, "Aaron made proclamation and said, 'to-morrow is a feast of the Lord,' and they arose up early in the morning and offered burnt-offerings and brought peace-offerings, and the people sat down to eat and to drink and rose up to play."

I am ready to admit even to the most skeptical Egyptologer that Israel borrowed that part of their religion of the desert from Egypt. This introduces a large subject which in these days has led many believing souls into deep waters. I shall do little more than state the question. Indeed I am not qualified to do much more, for modern and not ancient Egypt has been my study.

---

* I use the word "*sacrificed*," although it is the common opinion that the Muslems have no sacrifice, because the Arabic has no other word to describe the slaying of an animal, even for the table. And in one sense it is a religious rite, partaking of the nature of a sacrifice; for unless the name of God be named upon the animal in the act of slaying, its flesh is prohibited.

In visiting the ruined temples and tombs of
Egypt, nothing at first so strikes the Christian
beholder as the marked similarity between the
Egyptian sculptures and many of the rites and
ordinances of the Jewish religion. We see the
gods usually in triplets or trinities—the ark often
carried in solemn procession, with the accompanying symbols of the deities, with sacrifices and
offerings and incense, and many other things
which Moses must either have borrowed from
the Egyptians, or they from him, or from some
earlier teachers of the religion of the Bible.

Most of our Egyptologers take the former
horn of the dilemma and make Moses little more
than an Egyptian plagiarist, and the pure crys-
tal fountain of living water which welled up at
the foot of Sinai, they have pretended by many
devious ways to trace up for its source to the
muddy waters of the Nile. It is lamentable that
so many of our antiquaries are skeptics or open
infidels, and one cannot stand before the temples and columns and towering obelisks of ancient Egypt, or with torch in hand thread the
devious mazes of the rock-hewn tombs and
behold the neatly-cut and gorgeously-painted
myths and long lines of mysterious hieroglyphics
which everywhere present themselves in such
lavish profusion, without sighing for the time
when some Christian scholar, who has the genius
and leisure, shall grasp the key which has been

found and devote his life to the unlocking of these secrets of the past.

I wish to make only two remarks which for the present should, I think, hold our faith in God's word firm and unwavering. First, the disagreement which we behold in the result of the labors of different eminent Egyptologers— the sweeping character of the conclusions which they often evidently draw from very narrow premises, and in many cases their manifest *penchant* to throw disparagement upon Bible history, should make us cautious in implicitly following them. However unlearned one may be in antiquarian lore, he cannot look into a book like that of Bunsen without feeling that he is not a safe guide. As far as we can follow him, he is evidently in the midst of a thick German fog, and one feels a chilly tremor coming over him lest, should he follow him too far, the proverb of the blind leading the blind should receive its fulfillment.

Secondly, it is probable (even admitting, which in many cases we are not yet prepared to do, that the monuments were prior to the time of Moses,) that the people who lived before Moses, and even the antediluvians, knew much more about the true religion than the mere outline given in the Pentateuch would lead a superficial reader to conclude. In the Old Testament we have so distant a view of the religion of God,

23*

which was revealed to Adam and his immediate progeny, that only the bare outlines, the skeleton as it were, of the picture is seen. In the Egyptian sculpture we have a part of that picture, filled up and mixed with much extraneous matter, brought nearer to view. Let us not suffer the nearer picture to hide from our view the more distant one. And how much more of that more distant one would we see could we apply to our eye the telescope of a juster interpretation. Our Saviour has given us a specimen of this when He so logically deduced the doctrine of the resurrection of the dead and a future state from the phrase, "I *am* the God of Abraham and of Isaac and of Jacob." Take a specimen of the application of each of the two foregoing remarks. I met at Thebes an antiquary with whom one could not long be without observing that he improved every opportunity to throw discredit upon the Mosaic narrative. He made a remark in the course of the conversation, that he had no doubt the ancient Egyptian, or language of the hyerogliphics, was the original language of the human family. I asked him what proof he had of this. He said the fact that the Egyptian is a very polished and complex language, that it therefore must have been first, and that men afterwards reduced their system of language to greater simplicity. I told him that I would draw exactly the opposite conclusion

from his premises. I then said to him, "You
will at least admit that such a man as Adam
lived, and Cain and Abel and Abraham and Ishmael, and others mentioned in sacred history."
He answered, "Oh yes, we have evidence of that
in records independent of the Bible." "Well,"
I remarked, "these names are all significant, and
in the Hebrew of the Mosaic narrative that sig-
nificance is explained in words, for the most part
verbs, which express the reason of the same.
Thus we know, from Arab records which are
independent of the Bible, that such a man as Ishmael existed. Now take his name, 'The Lord
said thou shalt call his name Ishmael, because
the Lord hath *ishmaeled* (heard) thy affliction.'
Now, does the connection here existing between
the name and the verb expressing the reason of
it, exist in this or any similar case in the old
Egyptian?" "No." "Can it exist in any translation?" "No." "Then the Hebrew is not a
translation, but the very language in use when
he was named. And so of Adam, Cain, Abel,
and the others, and if you can find your old
Egyptian beyond them you are welcome to do
so." This man had spent years in the study of
antiquity, and has the reputation of being an
able reader of hieroglyphics. We will leave
him to follow their tortuous complexities, while
we still will walk in the plain path in which our
fathers trod.

Another, a Christian man, who had read Hengstenburgh and similar works, remarked one day, that we must admit Moses borrowed much from the Egyptians. He instanced the Cherubimic figures we see so constantly amidst the sculptures. I had just then in my pocket an antique signet-ring, on which was engraved the symbol of one of the deities between the wings of a cherub. Taking it out I said: "Granting the point, which, however, it would be difficult to prove, that this stone was carved before Moses lived, you would then conclude that Moses borrowed from it, or its contemporaneous sisters on the temples, the idea of the Cherubim." Certainly." "But," I said, "the Cherubim are much older than Moses. We have them first placed at the east of the Garden of Eden when Adam was expelled. Have any of the antiquaries been through that gate and found, beyond, Egyptian Cherubim from which those were copied? So we have, in this bit of stone, on the admission which we have made, that it is older than Moses, or even on the supposition that it is a copy of those that are older, a proof of the truth of the narrative of Moses older than himself. This is an interesting subject, but we must return to Abu El Hajaj.

Sabbath, the 24*th.* This was the great day of the feast. We had service in English in one of the dahabiyehs, but it was impossible to get any Arabs together. All Luxor seemed crazy. The crowd in front and around the house was immense, and the discharge of fire-arms, with the din of music and the shouting of the multitude, deafening. We went down to Mr. Riley's boat to secure a little Sabbath quiet; had it not been Sabbath, the ceremonies of that day would have been an interesting study. The main feature in the procession was a boat rigged up as a dahabiyeh and drawn upon a rude sledge, and in it sat Mustapha's little daughter, decked out most gorgeously in flaming silks, and jewelry, and tinsel. The sight of it, together with the multitude shouting, and singing, and dancing, and beating their musical instruments, recalled similar scenes which are so frequent in the Scriptures, as well as the removals of the Ark of God, first to the house of Obededom and then to the house of David; when David and all Israel played before God with all their might, and with singing, and with harps, and with psalteries, and with timbrels, and with cymbals, and with trumpets, and when King David danced and played before the Ark.

They also had in the procession a camel bearing a Mahmal, with a new richly embroidered silk cover for the tomb of the shaikh, similar to the one which is annually sent with such ceremony to the prophet's tomb at Mecca.

We were this evening honored with the arrival

of a distinguished guest.   Before leaving Cairo
I had noticed, riding with the Viceroy in his
carriage of state, a tall, dark-skinned Arab.   This
was Ahmed Abu Sin, the shaikh of the Bedawin
in the region of Khartum, at the junction of
the White and Blue Niles.   This morning a
messenger came to Mustapha, post-haste, informing him that this dignitary was on his way up,
and would stop at his house a few days to recruit,
as he was sick.   This put Mustapha in a great
fever of excitement and preparation ; and about
sunset the dahabiyehs containing him and his
suite came.   He was sick enough with a dangerous attack of inflammation of the lungs.
(Consumption or pulmonary diseases seldom
occur in Egypt, except with the Central Afri-
cans, who are accustomed to a much warmer
climate.)   His attendants carried him up to
Mustapha's, but first took him around to the
Mosque of Abu El Hajaj, that at his tomb the
healing power of this great patron saint of
Luxor might be sought.   Fortunately, a Dr.
Douglass from Canada was in port, and he came
up and prescribed for the old man, but as he
left the next morning, I had to attend to the
administering of the medicine, usually not an
easy matter with the Arabs, who believe more
in charms and saints than in medicines.   The old
shaikh was a noble looking man, and he had in
his suite a company of noble men who seemed

devotedly attached to him. He had with him a mufti who seemed his favorite, and who was a man of mind and intelligence. He had purchased at Cairo a large box of books, to which, though not without a good deal of Muslem scruple, he made a few additions from our stock. It was for some time difficult to believe that under a black skin, and from two thousand miles up the Nile, we should find so much mental polish. He always lifted his master's head when I administered the medicine, and repeated the formulary, "In the name of God, and the Prophet, and Abu El Hajaj." A good example this for us. It would be far better for us were medicine oftener administered and taken in the name of God and in dependence upon his healing power. "The Lord killeth and maketh alive; He bringeth down to the ground and bringeth up; He maketh sore, and bindeth up; He woundeth, and his hands make whole."

25th to March 2d. This week I had a high time in discussions with the Muslems. We had two muftis, the shaikh's and our own old friend Yuseph; two cadis (judges), the one of Luxor and another from Asseirut, who had remained after the feast, and a number of other learned dignitaries, and the presence of our sick shaikh brought a constant crowd around us, so that we did not lack for an audience. The Muslem rule is never to enter into controversy with Chris-

tians, and they will seldom allow Christians with
impunity to presume to controvert their dogmas. They quote for this a passage of the Koran, which says, "Do not controvert the people
of the book (Christians and Jews) except with
that which is better;" which they usually inter-
pret as prohibiting all controversy; an interpretation which I think is founded on the persuasion
that they cannot stand their ground in a fair
controversy. It is therefore a delicate matter
to engage a company of bigoted Muslems in a
religious discussion. They seem to feel that the
only proper weapon with us, if they only dared
use it, is the sword. I led them into the discussion by placing myself into the attitude of an
inquirer. I told them that their book said that
"the religion with God is Islam," and that it
consigned us unbelievers to the torments of hell-
fire, boiling water, serpents and scorpions, and
like terrible things, which, as my soul was dear
to me, I had no desire of encountering; that I
was ready to renounce Christianity and embrace
Islam, if they would only convince me that the
former is false and the latter true, and that I
was ready to hear their arguments, and was sure
they had sufficient regard for my eternal interests to present them. They could only say that
there is no deity but Allah, and that Mohammed
was his prophet. I told them that I already believed the first article of that faith, and wished

proof for the second. They continued referring me to the Koran, and said that I must first receive it and then it would give me all necessary instruction. But I insisted that they must first bring proof that the Koran is true and divine before I could believe its teachings and be profited by them. In the Koran, Mohammed constantly testifies to himself; but we must first settle the previous question, Is his testimony true? Is it God speaking through him, or the testimony of a mere man to himself? In one word, was Mohammed a true prophet? To this they could absolutely say nothing, except that I must first believe the book and then I would learn. But I told them, why should I not then after receiving Islam relinquish it again, as I had received it, as soon as any other system should present itself to me unsupported like it by proof? This opened the whole subject of evidences, and it was fully discussed, and then we proceeded to other points. I love controversy with Muslems. There is a certain selfish gratification or pride in being able with impunity boldly to attack them, while the native Christians around dare not undertake it. It is fun to maul a man with one's naked fists, who has a drawn sword in his hand, which his religion commands him to use, and yet he dare not do it. It seems manlier than to fight the poor, weak defenseless Copts, who usually after a few passes cry for quarter. The

24

difficulty, however, is to get them fairly engaged.
Besides the obstacle which I have just mentioned, it is necessary in the outset to allow them to
preserve the dignity and prestige which is theirs
by the ruling race, until the blood is up, and
then the harder one strikes the better. I have
found it very useful in breaking the first reserve
to quote freely several passages, or short chapters from the Koran. For a Christian to do this
seems so strange a thing to them that they conclude that you must be an initiated one, and
perhaps a Muslem in disguise, and it almost invariably makes them communicative.

In argument they are much more acute than
solid, and I have found certain small arms more
effective against them than the big guns of
heavy calibre which we find in the books on the
Muslem controversy.

We also had Kiddes, from Esneh, with us
this week. Hearing that we were to leave the
first of next week, he saddled his ass, and putting on also a bag of dates as a gift to us for
the journey, he came. With him and with the
three or four from Luxor, who seemed to be
really impressed with the truth, I had many
earnest conferences this week, and strove to
have them established in the faith.

On Saturday, Abu Sin, who was now much
better and impatient to be again on his journey,
left. I fear, as is usual with the Arabs, that

Abu El Hajaj got more credit for his recovery
than Dr. Douglass' medicine and my nursing.
Still, he seemed truly grateful for the attention
he had received during his illness. He said he
would like much to see me in his own country,
and I doubt not but that should I go he would
extend to me the rites of Arab hospitality and
the protection for which the Bedouin Arabs are
so noted. I afterwards gave a company of German missionaries, who left Cairo for Abyssinia, a
letter of introduction to him, and they wrote
back that he received them with great kindness,
and was of special service to them in their further journey.

3d. To-day Lord Aberdeen came. He had
been taken in tow by a government steamer at
Assouan, so that he came sooner than we expected. At Assouan he hired for us a dahabiyeh,
in which we were to go down to Cairo in company with him, selling books by the way. Mr.
Riley, who took a deep interest in our work,
was also very kind to us, and offered to take us
down in his boat, although it was pretty strait
for three passengers. We were now provided
for, but yet he concluded for a time at least to
join our party, and well it was he did so, as the
sequel will show.

5th. We were now all preparation for our departure—"on the wing of departure," as the
Arabs would express it—and to-day the daha-

biyeh came from Assouan, and we concluded to
start the next morning. The dahabiyeh was a
pretty rough-looking affair, but it was the best
Assouan afforded, and we were accustomed to
rough it. I had hired a horse to take down
with me for the purpose of visiting the villages
more distant from the Nile. Past experience
had taught me, that though the spirit was willing
the flesh was too weak to allow me to walk from
village to village under the burning sun of Egypt
with the simple apostolical equipage of staff and
scrip. The Apostles did not have to carry the
scrip full of big Bibles.

CHAPTER XI.

6th. This morning we took our departure from Luxor. The bishop did *not* come down to the ship to bid us farewell, and give us his apostolical benediction, and his "May God make it easy for you," on our journey. He still kept himself closely shut up in his room. News of the patriarch's sudden death came a few days ago, and now he seemed to be seized with a sudden spasm of contrition, on account of his long enmity to him, and now they said they put all his sulks on the ground of mourning for him. I have no doubt, however, that he was heartily glad when he saw our backs, and came out of his retirement. The new wine had burst the old bottles. "What communion hath light with darkness?"

Many of his people, however, came down to say their partings, and pray for a prosperous journey for us home, and for a short separation. Some of them shed tears, and with none of them was our parting more affecting than with our good friend—nay, our son in the Gospel—Kiddles.

24*   (281)

At length the parting words were all said, the dahabiyehs loosed from the shore, and Mr. Riley and I mounted our ponies. On mine I had a pair of saddle-bags well stuffed with books, as we purposed taking Zeinieh and Nega El Kattab in our way. As we left, a thundering complimentary discharge of firearms saluted our ears. Mustapha led off with his cannon, and then the guns and pistols popped from different parts of the town. Our men from the boats answered them, and thus we bid adieu to Luxor and Abu El Hijaj.

On our way we passed once more through the great temple of Karnak, and took a sad parting glance at its ruined walls and towering propyla, through the mute but elegant sculptured images and scenes of which we had so often held communion with the spirits of the misty past, and then we were soon at Zeinieh. Here we sought out the house of the Christian shaikh, and we were soon surrounded by a large company of hearers. A sick child was brought in that we might prescribe for it, whose case showed such hard-hearted neglect on the part of the parents as to call out a homily on the last verse of the Old Testament: "And he shall turn the heart of the fathers to the children, and the heart of the children to their fathers, lest I come and smite the earth with a curse." The cruel neglect of parents of their children in this country, especially in sickness, is heartrending to behold. At Luxor, one day I was called up to a house where a woman had not long before lost a child with the small-pox, and she had carelessly left a second child upon a cotton bed with a lamp also standing upon it, which was upset, and the poor child was literally broiled and calcified in the burning bed. The hardness of heart which the mother manifested at the harrowing sight was pitiable. The next day the little sufferer was relieved from its torments.

Other subjects of discussion then came up, and in the midst of them what was our surprise on beholding Kiddes enter. Unable yet to give us up he had followed on his donkey. One of those present was keen for controversy. He brought up various topics, and among them transubstantiation. The Copts can hardly be said to have a settled faith on this subject. It is not a dogma of the church, and there is one passage in their favorite Chrysostom which we can always quote to them, and to which they always assent: "That as the Jewish sacrifices were types of Christ, so the Lord's Supper is a retrospective type." Still they have in their church service some expressions which seem to favor the dogma; and then many have taken it up from Catholic books which the Romish church has palmed off on them, and which they receive as orthodox without knowing the source whence they came. The general faith of the church is perhaps nearer the Consubstantiation of Luther than either our view or the Romish one. In the midst of the discussion the Muslem shaikh of the village had dropped in; and, after listening for some time with great interest, he broke in with the exclamation, "That man speaks the truth," when he joined in the discussion very warmly on my side, until Kiddes, his eyes flaming with rage, jumped up and broke out upon him with, "What business have you, who are a Muslem, with our religion? Away with you. This conversation concerns only ourselves." The Muslem answered as warmly, and for a time we all had ado enough to keep them apart. Kiddes had understood the Muslem as only wishing to revile and cast reproach upon our religion; but when the people of the village assured him that this was not so, but that the Muslem had long been an earnest reader of our Scriptures, and that he was always talking to them in the same strain in which I had done about their superstitions, Kiddes cooled down, and then stepped up to our newly-found Muslem Protestant and asked his pardon and kissed his head, and all was calm again.

When our discussion was finished, the Muslem warmly invited us to his house; and feeling that we could not decline, Kiddes and Mr. R. and I went down, and he treated us to a cup of coffee, by which time a number of the Christians had also come, and so we had another talk, when we bade him farewell, and Kiddes also, a second time, and proceeded on our journey.

In less than half an hour we reached Nega El Kattab, where we found a kummus, or arch-priest, who bore the strange name of Salaf. He seemed a simple-minded man, and sat down with us in the street; but we had not talked long before on came Kiddes jogging on his diminutive donkey. The kummus proved to be from Esneh, and an old friend of his; so he helped us on a great deal in our short interview. Then we had to have a third parting scene. I did not wish a succession of them all the way to Cairo, and so I said, "Kiddes, it is enough; we must now gallop to our boat, and you must return. God be with you." We again embraced, when we sprang upon our horses and a long gallop, or rather steeple-chase, of fifteen miles we had of it over water-courses, shadoofs, and plowed ground, and it was far in the evening before we reached the boats which had stopped opposite Negadeh to await us. But oh, what a night we spent! Bugs! bugs! bugs! crawling out of every crack and crevice, marching over the settees in squadrons, dropping from the roof; the old boat seemed alive, and on every side they came up in troops, apparently determined to dispute possession with us. But I will leave the subject, as Oriental travelers have done it ample justice. I can occasionally spend a sleepless night under such circumstances very good humoredly; but to have such an one after that day's labor was too bad.

7th. There is here (Negadeh) a very large Coptic community; but Lord Aberdeen on his late visit had supplied them with books, so that we did not now meet a great demand. We visited the school which is in connection with the church, which is the largest in Upper Egypt and the only one at which females also attend. They told us that the number of pupils was over three hundred, but there was not nearly so many present. There is here also a bishop, and he and our old friend of Luxor keep up a chronic war, the " casus belli" being that he (of Luxor) managed a few years ago, by the aid of the Governor of Ghinneh, to take away from him the two villages on the other side of the Nile and annex them to his own bishopric. Had I called on him he would probably have treated me to a sound berating of his neighbor; but though this might have been grateful to some of my feelings, I preferred on the whole to forego the pleasure.

There is here a Catholic convent and church, but the people told me that but one man with his family had been perverted.

We called on the Christian shaikh, where we

found Yakob, our old friend the scribe of the government shorneh at Luxor, who was formerly so attentive a listener, but whom I had missed after our return from Esneh. He seemed very glad to see me, and when we left he wept like a child.

In the afternoon I galloped over to Ghous, three or four miles from the river on the eastern side; made the acquaintance of Fam Stephanus, whom Makhiel had already so highly commended. He seems, indeed, as he has the reputation of being, the ablest man in Scriptural knowledge in all Upper Egypt, and he has besides a great deal of general information. He sent for the priests, two young men who came, together with a large company of the neighbors. We spent a delightful two hours, after which we had supper and I returned to the boat. The interview with this noble man made a deep impression on my mind. He and a number of others whom I have met in Upper Egypt are examples of what the Bible alone, without the living teacher, can do in raising up intelligent, devoted Christians. On the question of Protestantism he was (or rather he seemed simply to play) non-committal. He introduced into his conversation several remarks, in praise of the old apostolical orthodox Coptic church, in a style which left me in doubt whether the serious, playful, or ironical was the prompting spirit. On afterwards thinking them over, I con-

cluded that they were intended to test my sentiments and draw me out. I think he wished to
ascertain whether, with our orthodoxy in sentiment, we were as proselyting in spirit as the
Catholics are. New converts from a corrupt system usually have too much of this spirit, and perhaps Makhiel had exhibited it in his late interview with him. If this was his object with me,
he signally failed, for with such men I make it a
principle to adhere to a simple statement of
truth.

Next to the study of the Bible, he seemed to
have made ancient church history a speciality,
and was prepared to give proofs from the fathers
and the councils that the present corruptions
of the Coptic church are mostly comparatively
modern inventions—that they did not belong to
their ancient doctrine or practice. He had also
deeply studied what in modern times is called
the Calvinistic controversy, and was sound,
though not clear, in the statement of all its parts.
I have since made him two visits, and find him
improving on acquaintance. His at first apparent shyness of Protestantism has all vanished,
and the last time I was there the priest came to
me with a pitiful complaint that he no longer attended the church. For this I administered to
him a not very cutting reproof; when he answered me and the priest that he had laid down
for him the condition upon which he would at-

tend church, viz., that the Coptic mummery should be removed from it and its services made edifying. To this the priest retorted that he had agreed to do so, in case he would set apart a portion of time each day to giving him instruction in the Scriptures, so that he might become qualified properly to discharge his duties. To this the other responded that he would be happy to do so but his other duties prevented; when both joined in an earnest request that I would remain and instruct the priests, and in the meantime officiate in the church. Truly there seems an open door.

8th. To-day I went to Koft, the ancient Coptos, from which the Copts, and indeed the land of Egypt, derived their name. On the way I called at two other villages and at both preached to large companies, mostly Muslems.

I went to Koft to see a young man named Sidere, whose story is a most romantic one. This Egyptian Luther, seven months ago, took it into his head to commence reformer, and he undertook it in a truly Egyptian manner. He went to Ghinneh, and purchasing a sheet of stamped paper, such as the law requires for all petitions and legal documents, he wrote upon it in substance as follows, addressing it to Fadil Pasha. After the usual complimentary introduction, he proceeded, "In passing through the streets of Ghinneh to-day, I heard a man, (the Muezzin or

25

crier for prayer), crying from a minaret, and in
his cry he used the expression 'God and his
angels pray for the prophet.' Now I wish to
ask, with all respect, did this man use these
words on his own authority or by command?
If on his own authority, I would suggest that
he should be called to account for the utterance
of such blasphemy. If by command he used
those words, I wish to ask how can God and his
angels be represented as praying for the prophet
who was a mere creature, and is now dead, and
if they do so, to what higher God do they
pray?"

He followed this argument by a brief statement of his faith in the Lord Jesus Christ, the
Son of God, the last of the prophets, who became man by being born of the Virgin Mary,
and who alone is able to save us from our sins,
and that in him alone should be our faith and
trust.

To this document he affixed his seal, and then
sent it in to Fadil Pasha. What followed I will
relate after an explanatory remark. The expression "God and his angels pray for the
prophet," is part of the regular call to prayer of
the Muezzin, and is also frequently in the mouths
and religious services of the Muslems, but they do
not generally understand the signification in the
expression of the words "pray for," and it is,
therefore, little wonder that Sidere (a Copt) did

not understand it. The word (yassalam), the doctors say, means, when applied to men, " to pray ;" when applied to angels, " to intercede for," and when applied to God, " to bless." It has these meanings in the old Arabic, in which the phrase was first invented and used. It is now commonly used only in the first sense, and, therefore, Sidere's whole argument was based upon a misconception.

When the Pasha read this strange document, he ordered our hero to be cast into prison, and then called together the Shaikhs El-Islam, who, in Ghinneh, are neither few, nor wanting in bigotry, as this is one of the stations of the holy pilgrimage. These disagreed among themselves as to the punishment which should be inflicted upon the young man. It is said that some of them counseled his immediate execution, but others feared to take the responsibility of so extreme a measure, and wished to have the case referred to Cairo. This was finally decided upon, and at the end of two weeks Sidere was taken from prison, a wooden collar put upon his neck, and he was sent to Cairo *afoot*, under a guard of soldiers, a distance of over three hundred miles. When he reached the capital, the case was referred to the Shaikhs of the Mosque El Azhar which Mosque has connected with it the greatest university of Moslem learning in the world, and it is the province of its Shaikhs to de-

cide all knotty points of Mohammedan law and
jurisprudence. I know not what may have been
the case with the shaikhs of Ghinneh, but these
shaikhs, at least were not ignorant of the true
interpretation of the above phrase; yet they
neither condescended to use it to answer Sidere's
argument, nor to mitigate his crime, but gave
judgment that he should be executed for pre-
suming to make so impudent and shameless an
attack on the religion of Islam. But, Said Pasha,
the Viceroy, influenced by his notorious infidelity,
and perhaps, also, in a measure by a salutary fear
of what the Christian powers might say, should
they become aware of the fact of such an execution, interposed and said that the young man
should not be killed, that the time for killing men
on account of religion was past, and that they
must reconsider their "fetweh," and bring in
judgment that the young man was mad. This
they did, and the young man was sentenced to the
mad-house, and forthwith carried away thither,
though protesting all the time that he was not
mad; of which fact he strove to convince them by
saying, (accompanying the words with corresponding gestures,) "There is the north, and there
is the south; there is the east, and there is the
west. I am here in my sane mind in your midst;
I am not crazy." He spent four months in the
insane asylum, and then, probably from a fear
that his case might come to the ears of the Con-

suls, if he were not removed from Cairo, his sentence was commuted to a year in the galleys, in Ghinneh, and he was sent back there and set at hard work. But not long after, on occasion of the circumcision of Tousoon Pasha, the little son of the Viceroy, a free pardon was granted to all the criminals in Egypt, and he was free.

This is the story as I had it from his own lips. I had several times before heard it, but feared it might have been greatly magnified by the oriental love of the exaggerated and romantic; but I found only slight variations. I wished also to see him to ascertain if he was indeed an Egyptian Luther, or only a hair-brained youth, who had done this thing in mere wantonness. I found him a modest, unassuming youth, about twenty-two years of age, loth to tell his story, and, though a grain wiser from the experience he had had, yet not apparently feeling that he had either done or suffered too much for his religion. He was slender in form, and pale, and with a remarkably sweet eye and expression of countenance. I had pictured him to myself a Luther or a scapegrace. He stood before me a Joseph in Egypt. I stopped at the house of a friend of his, who, before I left, spread a nice table. It was Friday, and of course fast-day with the Copts. My host put his hand with me in the dish of eggs, fried in butter, but Sidere would eat nothing, not even the bread and vegetables

25*

which were lawful. Like the more religious
Copts, he was literally fasting till sunset. I
recommended to him one of our books " on fasting and prayer," which he purchased, together
with a testament, and I gave him the Memoir of
Asaad Es Shidiak, the proto-martyr of Protestantism in Syria. Avoiding reference to the corruptions in doctrine and ecclesiastical practice in
the Coptic church, I pointed him to the moral
desolation which on every hand he saw within
her pale, and advised him, henceforth to bend
his efforts to the reform of these, and for the
present to leave the Muslems to us and God.

The man at whose house I supped, was also a
noble specimen of a man, and he had a family of
the finest and apparently best-trained children I
have seen in Egypt. One little fellow, only six
or seven years of age, took up a book on the duties of children, which was far above his years,
and spent most of the time that we were talking
in reading it, evidently with great interest.

Returning to the river, I saw a steamer and
two extra dahabiyehs moored in the midst of
our little fleet. Lord Aberdeen, had all winter
been expecting his brother from England. The
English Consul General had agreed, when he
came, to ask the Viceroy for a steamer to take
him up, and as the Nile was becoming very
low, Lord Aberdeen now obtained permission to
retain the steamer to tow the big dahabiyeh

down to Cairo. But his brother's coming had been so long delayed that he had at length given him up. Besides the steamer, he had also taken a dahabiyeh at Cairo, which he occupied, while a Mr. R——, who is one of our first English merchants in Alexandria, had taken the opportunity for a hasty visit, with his wife, to Thebes, and occupied the steamer. Another belated dahabiyeh of travelers, had also hitched on in their train. Here was a pretty kettle of fish. Five dahabiyehs and a steamer, each one with a party on board, and each party with its own ends, plans and idiosyncracies, and all to be harmoniously reconciled. Lord Aberdeen must have the steamer to take him slowly down to Cairo, which he wished to reach by the middle of April, and we must remain with him to assist in the book distributing business, we and Mr. Riley, not wishing to be longer than the end of March at furthest. Mr. R——, who was in the steamer, wished a hasty glance at Thebes, and then back to his ledgers, and having no previous knowledge of the arrangement to detain the steamer. Some wished to go to Edfou, some to Assouan, etc. I passed and re-passed from boat to boat, making myself oil upon the troubled waters, and emery between the rough surfaces, until I had mastered the conditions of the problem, and then his Lordship and I sat down and solved it, I am happy to

say, much to the satisfaction of all parties, as
follows : the steamer to take up the three dahabiyehs, viz., the two already with her, and Mr.
Riley's, to Luxor, and Mr. Riley then to remove
himself and effects to her, and relinquish his dahabiyeh to Mr. R—— and then leaving the three
dahabiyehs to take care of themselves, return on
Monday, and overtake us at Ghinneh, where we
relinquish our *living* boat to its multitudinous
occupants, and also go into the steamer, and
thus proceed on our journey towards the big
dahabiyeh. This involved our sleeping, or
rather staying, another night in the Assouan
boat.   Last night Mr. Riley kindly gave us
lodgings in his, and to night we might have remained in the big one, but for one night's rest
we did not wish to inform his Lordship that his
kindness in bringing us a boat from Assouan
had missed of its mark.   We intended, at
Ghinneh, to break the news, and make some new
arrangement ; but the coming of the steamer
had made this unnecessary.   But our little in-
convenience was nothing compared with the
disinterested and noble sacrifice which Mr.
Riley made in giving up his dahabiyeh.   He
was an invalid, and it was a great sacrifice to
leave his neat boat, which, in all its arrangements, was better appointed than any one I had
seen on the Nile, and go into the fumes, and
smoke, and clatter of a steamer ; and besides

give up his independence and liberty, and be subject to our movements. But he made the sacrifice, and this was the keystone which held our little arch of arrangements. But for this, Mr. R——would have been forced to take our boat, which, with his young wife, would, I fear, have caused a sad eclipse of their honey-moon.

9*th*. This morning our first work was to pitch our tents, and remove ourselves and effects to them, so that we might have a couple days' thorough airing before the coming of the steamer. Then Lord Aberdeen paid our Reis a month's wages for the boat, and we sent him back to Assouan, " with our peace."

10*th*.—*Sabbath*. This forenoon Ibrahim came down to the tent, and we had a long and intensely interesting conversation with him. This is a very honest, upright young man, and earnest in his religious convictions, but still clings to some of the superstitions of the church, and this is not to be wondered at, as his father is a priest.

11*th and* 12*th*. I spent these two days mostly with Ibrahim, in his shop, selling books and conversing with those who came to purchase. I was very happy to find that he had now concluded to remain in Ghinneh, and was willing to take books back again into his shop, and continue the business, and that our Bishop's late sojourn in Ghinneh had not so set the people against us that they would not buy books. In-

deed, this love for books among the Copts, seems
to be an appetite which grows sharp by feeding.
This is the fourth book-selling visit Ghinneh has
received this winter, viz.: Brother McCague first,
then I, then Lord Aberdeen, and now we again,
and each time they seem to take more books
than the time previous. This time we have
sold fifteen hundred piastres, or about fifty dollars worth. Still, a few of the black-turbaned
aristocracy turned their faces the other way when
they passed the shop. Among these was one,
who, in passing, stopped, and looking very sar-
castically over the shoulders of the crowd which
surrounded us, said to Ibrahim, "What are you
doing here?" Ibrahim's color changed; and
then, quietly, but very decidedly, he answered,
"I am selling books; what of it?"

When he left, I asked who that man was, and
he informed me that he was his partner in business, or rather, the man who furnished him with
the capital for his stock in trade. This was a
foreboding of trouble for Ibrahim, but still before we left he took from us a new stock of
books to sell in his shop, and although we give
him twenty per cent. on his sales, it is evident
that love for the book is his chief motive in engaging in the business.

CHAPTER XII.

13*th*. We are now ready for a new start. Mr. Riley had returned from Thebes in the steamer, and we had also moved into her. As we had our own servant Abdallah with us, we might have kept up our own establishment, but Mr. R. insisted on our considering ourselves his guests, and so besides Monsur and Makhiel, Abdallah was also left at liberty for the book-selling work. These three attended to the villages on the banks of the river, while I, with the horse and saddle bags, visited those more distant. Mr. R. had also brought with him two of his favorite sailors from the dahabiyeh, one of whom assisted his cook as scullion, and the other carried books for us. His dragoman was Giovanni Zarb. A sense of gratitude for the abundant manner in which he catered to our wants, makes it duty for me to mention him. I have seen and known a great deal of dragomen and their doings. They are an able and astute class of men, which is proved by the fact that, almost invariably, parties will be found coming home from the trip saying that "Dragomen, as a class, are the greatest scoundrels in the world, but *our* dragoman is an exception," while a very slight peep of an eye, experienced in Egyptian affairs, behind the curtain, will suffice to show that *their* man *should not* be made an exception. But Giovanni *is* an exception—an exception to all the Maltese I ever met, who are most bigoted Catholics, for he reads diligently his Italian Bible, and says he will do so in spite of Pio Nono and all his ruffian priests; and an exception to the dragomen for he is an honest and industrious man. Mr. R's style and cuisene, were, throughout the winter, the envy of the travellers, though his expenses were much less than theirs; and he had besides, the luxury of a dahabiyeh all to himself, and thus avoided the danger of jarring and discord, which often arise in parties composed of uncongenial material, hastily conglomerated at Cairo. But this was Mr. R.'s second winter on the Nile, and in his former visit he had learned a thing or two.

And now the books are all arranged, the colporteuring bags made, the big dahabiyeh is fastened to our stern by a stout long cable; and again, in her wake, comes a little native boat, whose occupants have just tumbled in, viz.: a mare, (on which his Lordship daily made a short excursion,) with her colt; an ass, (kept for her milk,) with her foal; a goat, (also for the same purpose;) a cage of chickens, and a Nubian, (their curator,) sitting in the midst of them,

black as Erebus, but smiling as an Egyptian day.
This Lady Aberdeen called her " happy family ;"
and over all, for we are the Viceroy's guests,
was the crescent waving in its field of red.
Never did it wave over nobler work, though I
fear that we who were engaged in it, were not
always actuated by as firm a faith and trust in a
present God, as that implied in the war cry,
" Allah Akba," (God is most great,)with which,
under it, the Muslem warrior has so often hurled
himself upon his own and his God's enemies.
When the time for starting each day came, the
column of smoke would ascend for two hours,
to the clear sky, and then the stragglers were
called in, the " happy family" scrambled into
their boat, the piles were drawn, and cables
thrown aboard, and it was puff, puff, whist,
whist, and we were under way, the wonder and
puzzle of the gazing crowds on the shore. Then,
·when we came opposite the village at which we
wished to stop, it was a long circuit with this
long train, so that we might come to the shore
against the current, and not be driven by it all
aheap, the dahabiyeh upon the steamer, and
the happy family upon us both, and then with
our Turkish captain and crew, instructed by
English engineers, the word was " ease 'er, ease
'er; 'alfa speed, 'alfa speed; stop 'er." Then we
seized our full bags and started ashore, to find
sometimes, that the boys and young men of the
26

village, thinking we must be agents come from
the Government, for conscripts or forced laborers, had fled and concealed themselves. But,
with our flag of truce, the Bible in hand, we
brought them back, when we would soon be surrounded by purchasers. This work done, and it
often called for a good deal of bargaining, for
orientals love bargaining, and they must too
have time to do things deliberately, the next
thing in order was conversation and controversy.
The scene of our operations was sometimes the
Caffi, or open streets, and sometimes the church,
school, or government offices, where the scribes
may usually be found, or the priest's house.
Sometimes we would only spend a few hours at
a village, and sometimes a day or more, especially when there were other villages in the neighborhood, when we would scatter our forces
among them, I taking the more distant ones
with the horse. Sometimes, when the next stop
was not too distant, I went down, on the horse,
in the back country, stopping at every village,
though it might contain few or no Copts, and
when the distances were longer, the owner
took him on shore while we sailed down. Horses
were then plenty in Upper Egypt, as the Pasha
had a short time before disbanded there a cav-
alry regiment; and for owner and horse I had
to give but twenty-seven cents per day. Such
was the general character of our work. We

strove to canvass thoroughly the villages visited, and as for general results, we visited over seventy villages, and sold books in all for over twenty-five thousand piastres, equal to about eight hundred and forty dollars.

We reached Sahil Bahjura after sunset. This is the port of Bahjura and Farshoot, which are inland, and is the centre of a large Christian population. There is here a large sugar factory, belonging to one of the royal family. The engineer over the works is a Mr. Dickson, a member of Dr. Cook's church, of Belfast, Ireland. The English engineers and workmen employed by the Government and wealthy Pashas are numerous in Egypt, but Mr. Dickson is the only one I know who insists on observing the Sabbath as a day of holy rest. He deserves the more praise for this, because unlike the most of the rest, he is far removed from the public ordinances of religion. With his wife and daughter, (a young lady about seventeen years of age,) he lives there a stranger among strangers, without physician or minister, and deprived of many of the comforts of civilized life, and I was pleased to find he had acquired a high reputation among the natives for integrity and sterling uprightness of character.

14th. In arranging the books yesterday, I had put away in a corner thirty-six copies of the the Psalms in Beirut edition, which is much larger

print than the London edition, and I had intended
to reserve them for special occasions, but had not
informed Mousur of this intention, and this
morning on going out I found him on the
shore with a large company of Copts around
him, and he had already sold them all. Above
all books, the book of Psalms is in demand
among the Copts. It is the universal school
book, and most of the children commit the one
hundred and fifty Psalms, plus one additional
one, which they have picked up somewhere, I
know not whence. In after life their prayers consist mainly in repetitions of these, but most of
them never enter very deeply into the meaning.
Like parrots, they repeat them by wrote. It
forms, however, a good foundation for Christian
character, when in after life God's spirit flashes
light into the dark store-rooms of memory thus
furnished. Our supply of even London Psalms
was limited, or our sales would have been much
larger that winter. We could have sold a large
edition of the Psalms at full cost.

16th. To-day I remained within, preparing for
the morrow's services. About four P. M., I
went up on deck to "snuff the air," when seeing
a number of Copts coming around the corner of
a house upon the shore above, I cried, "Whither
bound?" They said, "To the convent to pray."
"And I with you." So I started up without
giving Mrs. L. notice of my intention. Mon-

sur, who was in the village, also joined the
company. There were among them two elderly
men, who had asses, and they immediately dismounted and bade me ride. They swore they
would not ride, and I asseverated that I would
not, and they might as well re-mount at once. I
insisted that they were old, and I young and
able to walk; and they affirmed that I was honorable, and it would be a shame for them to ride
and me to walk. We kept up this controversy
in the midst of our talk for three-quarters of an
hour. When we reached the convent I was
weary enough to be glad to ride a short distance,
after which they mounted. The convent is situated in an open plain, and consists of a high
wall enclosing a church with a few straggling
rooms, which were formerly occupied by the
monks, but now only by a family which looks
after the church. The people of several of the
neighboring villages worship here, and they were
now coming to it in straggling parties, scattered
over the plain. When we neared the convent, I
noticed that the high-water mark was several feet
from the ground, upon the walls. I asked them
how they got there to worship in high Nile.
"We wade." "And how high is the water?"
"In some places," they answered, "to the middle,
in some places to the breast, and in some places
we must tie our clothes to our heads and swim."
What think ye of that, ye fair weather Chris-

26*

tians, who are detained from church by a
passing cloud, or a wet side-walk? They told
me, however, that not so many attend during
high Nile as at other times. They either worship in their houses, or go to other villages.

When we entered it was not yet time for
service to commence; so, to avoid the litter and
fleas below, they took us to the roof, and sitting
down, with our backs against the wall, and the
beautiful plain, dotted with villages and clumps
of palm trees, now all bathed in the glory of
the setting sun, before us, we strove to make
profitable, to the audience that gathered around
us, the hour until service commenced. When the
clatter of cymbals and the loud voice of chanting below informed us that *work* had began in
the church, we went down, and though I have
heard among the Copts much loud praying and
chanting, I never heard any thing to match that
night. The orchestra was a full one, and the old
men on one side, and the boys on the other, absolutely screamed, while the crash of the loud, high-
sounding cymbals, was almost deafening. In
one of the pauses I heard some of them com-
menting upon the fact of our presence with
them in the church. They seemed pleased with
this evidence of our tolerance and brotherly
feeling, and compared it with the bigotry of the
Catholics, who they said would never attend.

17th.—Sabbath. We had Arabic service at

twelve, M., on the steamer, but the town having but few Copts besides the scribes of the factory, and most of these being yet at the convent, we had but eight present besides our own people. I preached from Rev. xxii. 17, and from the same in English, at four, P. M., in the dahabi-yeh. It is a pleasure to preach to people, Arabs or English, who hunger for the Word; and such seemed emphatically to be the case with Mr. Dickson and family.

18*th*. Priest Makhiel started for the first day's work across the river, hoping this time to reach Refr Es Sayfed and How. But his box was again emptied before he reached How. So we concluded the next morning to retrace our way there with steamer and all. During our stay here we had sold books for two thousand five hundred piastres, about eighty-four dollars.

19*th*. Went up to How, and keeping up steam, we went ashore and sold a number of books, and then sailed down to Beliane.

20*th*. To-day Mr. R. and I started to visit the ruins of Arabat El Madfanch, (the buried Ara-bat,) which the antiquarians tell us is the ancient Abydus, and some of them the still more ancient This. It is a long ride of seven miles, and as our plan was to rejoin the boats at Girgeh, and we hoped to take a number of vil-lages in our way, we put a box of books on a donkey to follow us instead of a bag on the sad-

dle. A large canal waters abundantly this section of country, and we spent the day riding
amidst the most charming pastoral scenes I have
ever witnessed. The clover, wheat, barley,
beans, peas, etc., seemed all in most luxuriant
growth, and the cattle, horses, buffaloes, and
other domestic animals, which on every side were
tethered in the rich clover fields with their keepers who attended to them, gave the whole land-
scape an air of life and animation.

We crawled into the temple which is almost
buried in sand, and while we were admiring the
rich carvings and brilliant colors, as bright as
if yesterday put on, a company of Coptic scribes,
who were enjoying a holiday, and had come like
ourselves to see the ruins, entered. They sat
down with us on the sand bank and soon said,
" O, Khowagah, by whom were all these figures
made, and for what purpose ?" I told them,
" By your forefathers, as mementoes of their and
your religion." I had before me my diagram,
and it was an easy matter to prove my proposition. " There, you see that great fellow, robed
and mitred, with staff and cross—that is the
Bishop. These others, as you see, are priests
burning incense to him, kneeling before him,
bringing offerings which, for all I know, may be
communion cakes to be examined, and one selected for the mass, etc. To all which they said,
" *True, true,* (*sahieh, sahieh,*) why did we not see

all that before." Then came the application, which in brief was, Your Christianity is much older than Christ, and is little better than baptized heathenism. A Protestant wag, when asked the question, which we must hear so often even in Egypt, " Where was your religion before Luther ?" retorted by asking, " Where was your face before it was washed this morning ?" and these monuments show where and what the Coptic religion was before it was baptized.

By the time our Q. E. D. was said, the box of books had come, and our Coptic friends purchased freely. When, after sating ourselves with admiring this beautiful ruin, we departed for a convent on a spur of the mountain to the left. The site of the ancient city was a magnificent one, lying in the lap of the mountain, and overlooking this luxuriant plain, and over the hill we could still see the road which led to the great oasis.

At the convent we found an old priest, just saying mass before the altar in the church. When he saw us over his shoulder, he abridged it to the length of a " hunting mass," after which we had a pleasant conversation with him over a cup of coffee, and left some books. We then rode to Shaikh Marzuk, the village of Botros Bey, the wealthiest Copt in Egypt. He has 2,300 acres of land, sugar and indigo factories, seventy slaves, and flocks and herds almost without num-

ber. He has a fine family of sons, and one of
them was taken by the Government as a con-
script, and it had cost him more than $300, as
here in America, to secure for him exemption.
So to secure himself from any further trouble
of the kind, he had procured a Russian consular
agency for Osiout. The office, of course, was a
purely nominal one, as he is a non-resident, but
it answers the purpose intended. It secures
Russian protection for himself and family. I
think he must have received favorable accounts
about us from Wasef, our consular agent in Osiout, who is a relation of his, for he received us
with distinguished favor. He lived in a house
which, in comparison with Egyptian houses generally, may be called a palace. The large reception
room was quickly spread with the richest Persian
carpets, and it was soon evident that a great feast
was in process of preparation. This was more
than we had anticipated. A traveler in Luxor,
to whom he had shown a favor, had authorized
us to present him a Bible, and as my horse was
beginning to show the effects of hard riding in a
lameness, I had been directed to him as a man
from whom I could probably purchase one, and
we only wished to stop to attend to these two
matters of business, and to satisfy our curiosity
as to this Coptic Dives, and if possible speak a
word of truth and pass on. But we saw that
we were in for the afternoon, and could only

strive to make it as profitable as possible. He
listened with respect to my expositions of truth,
but his heart was evidently in his possessions,
and not very deeply engaged in the matter of
religion. We, however, were pleased to find
among his other enterprises and improvements,
that he was building a church. When I made
known my wish to him to purchase a horse, he
immediately called one of his slaves, and, whispering in his ear, he sent him to the fields for
one. I proposed that we should go to the field
and see his horses, of which he said he had four
hundred and twenty, and there we might choose
such an one as would suit; but he said, "No;
we will bring you one that will suit." The slave
soon returned with a splendid Arab blood horse,
and when he had him show off his paces before
us as we sat before the door, it was enough to
make the teeth of a lover of good horses water.
He asked whether he pleased me. I said, "O,
yes, such a horse would please any one; but he
is a better horse than I need for my purpose."
He said, "If he suits you, take him. He is
yours." I saw at once that this expression was
not, as usual in Arabdom, a mere preface to a
long course of higgling and bantering, but that
it was an earnest *bona fide* gift of the horse, and
I began to cast about for a way of gracefully
backing out of my proposition to buy a horse.
It is the custom of the Arabs once a year to take

the shoes off their horses and turn them out to clover for a month or six weeks, during which time they never use them; and indeed they become so fat and soft that they are unfit for use. So I said, " I am sorry to find that I have come just when you horses are all out to grass. I wish a horse for present use to ride down to Cairo, going from village to village, and one day of such riding as I do would ruin this horse. I will have still to cling to the old one, although he limps a little." But he immediately shut this door against me thus: " Very well, I will keep him till he has done with clover, and then I will send him down with one of the boys to Cairo. In what street do you live in Cairo?" I was again taken aback, and the perspiration began to flow freely, so that Mr. R., who sat by and could not understand the conversation, noticed and wondered at my embarrassment. It was a great relief to be able to resort to an English explanation to him by way of recovering my equilibrium, and preparing another speech. I could not think of accepting the horse, and he must be declined in a manner which could not be considered a breach of our short but warm friendship. I was finally able to compose myself sufficiently to tell him that I was exceedingly obliged to him for his generous offer, but that I only wished a common horse for present use, and had intended to sell him on reaching Cairo; that

there I had no use for a horse, and we missionaries could not afford to keep one as a mere luxury. This ended the matter, and I felt greatly
relieved. The Arabs generally are adepts in the
art of "bating with a sprat to catch a mack-
erel," but he seemed to have no such game in
his mind. The offer seemed evidently a hearty
and disinterested one.

It was after dark before our grand dinner was
prepared, and then we had a long night ride to
Girgeh. Our host sent with us a guide, and
when about half way down we passed through
a village in which he informed us there were
many Copts. Our conscience began to smite us
that we had passed the afternoon to so little
profit, and we concluded that we would adhere
more closely to the Saviour's rule, to "salute no
man by the way."

21st. Intending, as far as possible, to make
amends for last night's omissions we sent Monsur back to Bardis, the village we had been
forced to pass through, but he met with no success. The priest forbade the people from buying, which was the first time we had met with
any active opposition from the priests to our
book-selling work. At Girgeh also, we sold but
few books, although it is a large town. Giovanni heard the Copts saying in the town that the
priests had prohibited their buying, but on inquiring we found that it was a Catholic priest.

27

We next went down to Asseirab, where is a wealthy Moslem family, called the "Sons of Hamsa." There are several brothers of them, and I had heard that the eldest of them named Muhammed, was an infidel to the Muslem faith, and a man of singular character, but great ability, and having a letter of introduction to him, we called. He had many questions to ask, and many of them were very shrewd ones, and he cordially fell in with some of my arguments against Islam, but I fear a covert alliance with the bottle is at the root of his infidelity to the faith of his fathers. He took us to see a chicken hatching establishment which he has, and as it was the first one we had seen, we found it a great curiosity. There are two long rows of ovens with a passage between them. On the floor of each of these ovens several hundred eggs are placed, and they are heated by a long funnel in front, in which pulverized charcoal is placed, so mixed with earth as to burn slowly and keep the ovens at an even temperature. He opened several of the ovens for us, and one of them in which the chickens were just hatched. It was a funny sight to see several hundred chickens so pure and clean, chirping and running to and fro in all the delight of release from their long imprisonment, while some of the more tardy ones were just picking through the shell; others had split it and were struggling for deliverance while some like little turtles were running about with half a shell on their backs. These establishments are an Egyptian institution. The peasants bring to them their eggs and exchange two eggs for a chicken, and take them home to their wives to cluck to them and rear them by hand. The mild climate and equable temperature of Egypt are admirably adapted to rearing poultry. The men who attended the establishment were Copts, and they purchased three Testaments.

CHAPTER XIII

Souhaj.—This place has recently been made the capital of the district in the place of Girgeh. When the scribes learned what our errand was they came down, keen to buy. The first man purchased for seventy piastres, and in less than an hour we sold books for $30. There was but little higgling about prices. Even when it was attempted, it seemed more from habit than a desire or hope of obtaining the books cheaper. When one would attempt it the others would interpose, saying, that it was no use, that they knew us to be men of "*one word;*" that the binding of the books was worth more than the prices we asked, and that we brought the books to them as a present, and only asked the expense of transportation. Thus, frequently we find them comparing the prices of our books with what, with them, would be the cost of transcribing and binding them, and of course they consider them very cheap, even when we sell at full cost price.

Sabbath, 24th. This morning a priest with a number of people came down to buy books. We told them that we did not sell on the Sabbath, but that on the morrow we would let them have all they wished. I then, seeing the people pass to and fro on the shore and thinking that from them we might gather an audience, asked them up to some shade trees where we took our seats in the dust beside the road. The rebuff and reproof which the priest had received in the matter of the books, seemed at once to turn all his milk into curds, and he did not wish to remain, but by way of propitiating, and engaging him, I gave him the Testament; and asked him to read to us. He opened at the 18th chapter of Luke and read two chapters, when I took the book and explained the passages in the chapters read, which seemed fitting to their circumstances. By this time enough of the passers-by had joined us to form a good audience. At 4 p. m., we had English service for our little company, and after it three men, who had been with us in the morning, returned and we had a long conversation with them.

25*th*. Stopped to-day opposite Tahta, going ashore with our box of books we had great trouble to find a beast of burden to carry them. We finally succeeded in impressing a sorry-looking woe-begone donkey which was as guiltless of saddle, bridle, or halter as on the day of its birth. But "necessity is the mother of invention." We plucked up a bundle of green wheat, and making it serve as a pack saddle, and then

27*

fetching an end of the rope from the boat we
tied it around the animal's neck. By this I led
him, or rather dragged him, while Monsur and
one of the boatmen supported the box on either
side. It was a group for a painter. My rig
was far from being after the most approved
style of clerical costume, and I bore a staff six
feet long to assist in walking, and as a safe-
guard against dogs, for Oriental dogs are often
as intolerant as Muslems of strangers, who may
disturb them in their road-side naps. We too
were disposed to be as facetious as our appearance was comical. We met many people coming down the landing, and they stared at the
strange cavalcade. We stopped each man as
he came along, and if he wore a light colored
turban we asked him, "Do you fast Ramadan
or the 'holy forty' (lent)." If he said "Ramadan," we said, "Then go in peace, we only have
some Christian books to sell." If he said
"The 'holy forty,'" we next interrogated him,
"Are you a Copt or 'Tabia' ('adherent')?"
There are many Catholics in Tahta, and the
Catholics in Egypt are called "adherents" of
the Pope. If he said "a Tabia," we said "We have
nothing to do with you. We have Bibles to
sell, but your priests will not let you read the
Bible. But we also bring you word that the Pope
is dead; Garibaldi has just killed him." If he
said "a Copt," we answered, "You are just the

man we want to see. We have some Bibles and other religious books here, and sell them very cheap. All we want is the cost of transportation, and as they surveyed our method of transportation, they concluded that that could not be much, so we threw up the cover and exposed our books. Thus we went up to Sahil Tahta, a distance of half an hour. Here we sought out the church, and entering found the people at mass. The priest before the altar stole glances at us over his shoulder, and the boys and most of the people turned their faces full upon us, and their backs to the altar. After standing awhile we concluded that we had not time to see them through, and that we would go on to Tahta itself, and stop here on our return. But when we left there was a general stampede of the congregation, and so we entered upon our business at once, and those without taking some of the new books inside, the few who remained within also came out, and I think the priest was left entirely alone to finish his mass.

We next proceeded to Tahta, which is some distance further on, and a rich time we had of it, going through the streets and crying our wares like sellers of radishes, and several rich encounters we had with the Catholics, who not content with not purchasing themselves, strove to persuade the Copts not to purchase. We sold a good many books, and having supplied the market returned to the boat.

In the evening we came down to Timneh, and the next day, the 26th, we canvassed it, and the neighboring villages. In one of these we were told there were Copts, but not one that could read, and so we were minded to pass them over. But his Lordship was determined as far as possible to offer "*the book*" to all the Christians of Egypt; and so as the rest of us were engaged we sent our servant Abdallah to this village.

We despatched Father Makhiel, Abdallah and one of the men with a box to Abutij, and the other villages en route for Osiout, and we started for it and reached it about noon, the

27*th*. We went up to the town and found Faris in high spirits on account of the favorable turn which our affairs had there taken. He is a bold, fearless man, and besides his triumph over the Copts, he had ventured to attack the Muslems, and had beaten in public discussion their chosen champions. This made the timid Copts glory in him, and even faint-hearted Bukhtor, reassured by his success, had returned to duty, and had left four days previous with a bag of books for Benoud, his native village.   •

Our school, however, was not yet succeeding; but it was a consolation to know that the Patriarch's school has also failed, although the teacher whom he sent had now been on the ground three months. The Areefs were evidently the cause of the failure. They wanted neither the Patriarch nor us to take there a modernized schoolmaster to establish a new-fangled school. Their little earnings were at stake, and so the poor children must still have psalms not comprehended, and incomprehensible Coptic prayers beaten into them at the soles of their feet. That this was the sole cause of the present opposition, and that the priestly ban against us had been broken, was evident from the fact that of late the people had again commenced purchasing books, and so we spent the

28th in putting the book department on a more efficient footing. We made accounts of the past sales, hired a shop in the most frequented street of the town at the trifling rent of one dollar per month, and left for it a new supply of books. These book shops, opening upon a public street where passers by are tempted to drop in, to purchase and talk, we have found among our most useful ways of disseminating the good seed. In the streets of an Oriental town, we do not see people as at home rushing through the streets as if they were in pursuit of a thief, or carrying the mail, or running for the doctor. They know how to preserve the " *otium cum dignitate*," and are seldom in too great a hurry to stop for a cup of coffee and pipe, or a friendly conversation. And if an able and sociable man, who has what the Arab proverb calls a "pliable side" in intercourse with others, is put into one of these shops, he soon attracts around him crowds.

In the evening Faris brought for a friendly call a man who through the winter had been the leader of the opposition, and who had also written the letter to Ghenneh which was so influential, in aid of the Bishop, in securing Fadil Pasha to his interest. It was wonderful how Faris had been able to bring this man over to our interests.

He also told me of the case of a Coptic woman, who had some years before been seduced by a Muslem, and who now wished to return to her old faith, and said the Copts were very anxious he should undertake her defense with the Government, and asked what he should do. I told him that if in a friendly way he could do any thing with the Government to secure her in her return to the faith of her fathers, he might do so, but that he must be very careful not to compromise himself nor implicate us with the authorities. He, however, went beyond his letter of instructions, and four months after it resulted in an affair which almost cost him his life, but which made us politically the first men in Egypt.

We left at noon, and at sunset reached Hawatke, and the next morning we divided our forces between it and Egawe, and in both places we found many who manifested their desire for the Word of God by purchasing.

29th. We went down to Manfaloot. About three hours ride back of this place, at the foot of the western hills, is a convent, called Mahar-rak, which is the most flourishing institution of the kind in Egypt. It has large landed possessions in the valley, and contains about three hundred monks. I told Makhiel that I purposed going to the convent, and wished him to go along and help me deal with his brother monks. He answered in astonishment, " *Me!* If you take *me,* you will neither sell books, nor get a mouthful to eat after the long ride, and they will make you sleep outside on the ground." He then went on to explain that he had been instrumental in the enlightenment of one Abd-El-Masieh (servant of Christ), of whose story I had already heard. This man is one of God's "hidden ones" in Egypt. He was a studious, earnest man, who spent much of his time in searching the Scriptures. Some years ago, while on a visit to Cairo, Makhiel made his acquaintance, and spent several days in conference with him, which resulted in his being put upon the Protestant track.

He went back to the convent, and employed himself in studying the Scriptures with his new light, and writing annotations upon them, and it is now said that he has a large volume of them, and that the book is decidedly Protestant. That he might the better make himself acquainted with the whole contents of the Word of God, he has with his own hand copied the entire Bible, and in the mean time, by way of recreation, he read the old church manuscripts in the convent of which he was librarian, and whenever he found in them any thing opposed to the Scriptures, he tore out the leaves, and, cutting them into shreds with his scissors, gave them to the winds from the window of the library. Such leaven could not but work in that mass of three hundred monks, and one day Abd-El-Malak (servant of the angel), the Abbot, awoke from his cups to find that heresy was at work in his monkish family. Abd-El-Masieh and his adherents were arraigned and tried, and the result was that twenty-four of them were stripped of their monkish robes and turned out into the world, some of them stark naked, so that they were forced to use bricks instead of fig-leaves, until they could find some friendly Muslem or Christian to give them a garment.

When I heard that Makhiel had been identified with that movement, I concluded to leave him at home and take Monsur instead; and I thought, besides, that a little eclat and circumstance would not be amiss with these purse-proud monks. Since the disabling of the horse, I had usually preferred the humbler equipment of an ass, with large saddle-bags, or a box, for

the books, but this time I went to his lorship and
told him of the convent and my desire to visit
it, and that if he pleased I would order the captain of the steamer to take them down to a
place called Abu-Zeid, where I would meet them
the next day. He agreed to this, and then made
the proposition which I was fishing for, viz., to
send up to the Governor for horses to take us.
I said, " Oh, your lordship, that is not necessary ;
I think we will be able to find donkeys in the
street." He insisted, and immediately the dragoman was despatched to the Governor to make
known our wants. The son of this dignitary,
who is also the Nazir, soon made his appearance
at the steamer to inquire where we wished to go
and how many horses we needed. We said we
wished to go to the convent, and would need
two horses and a guide. He said, " Upon my
head and eye ;" and leaving, he soon returned
with his father's horse and his own for me and
Monsur, and a splendid white Meccan donkey
(which in Egypt are more valued than horses)
for himself, besides a great crowd of horses,
donkeys, and attendants. The Governor's horse
was a splendid Arab charger, all done up in blue
silk velvet heavily studded with gold.

> " Blue was the charger's broidered rein,
> Blue ribbons deck'd his arching mane,
> The knightly housing's ample fold
> Was velvet blue and trapped with gold."

28

This horse the Nazir pointed out for me, and I
at once concluded that he was none too good for
me. The second one was but little inferior to
him, and Monsur looked at him aghast, and absolutely refused to mount him. So I had to
apologize for him, and he selected one of the
donkeys, and putting the large, well-stuffed saddle-bags across him he mounted astride them.
Mr. Riley usually accompanied us on these excursions, and I urged him much to take the second horse, but Bro. R. was an Episcopalian, and
that chanced to be Good Friday, so thinking of
the Saviour's entry into Jerusalem the day previous on an ass, and his sad journey through the
" *via dolorosa* " that day, he preferred remaining
at home to keeping the feast. What troubled me
more was that the Nazir insisted on doing us the
honor of going along with us. We did not
think that his presence would assist us any, and
besides it was now 3 P. M., and " the world was
Ramadan, and consequently we had to suppose
him fasting from day-break that morning, and
now not feeling like taking a three hour's journey on an empty stomach, but rather sighing for
the sun to make a sudden leap to the horizon
when all good Muslems may break fast. He had
brought the chief Government scribe, who was a
Copt, to introduce us to the monks, and that
was enough, and I entreated him to remain, but
he was incorrigible, and insisted that it would
be a shame to allow us to go alone.

Finally the cavalcade was ready for starting, and an imposing one it was. I counted the attendants, who, like Elijah before the chariot (I think it was the horse) of Ahab, had girded their loins and were running before, and found them just twenty-four. (Absolem had fifty.) There were pipe-bearers with their neatly bagged pipes, and great pouches of tobacco in their bosoms; grooms with the red cloth over their shoulders, and watchmen with their long staves; and they ran in two rows, keeping the road between them; the leaders flourishing their staves by which they sent the flocks and herds that were coming down the road scampering into the wheat fields, while the peasants who were coming, if mounted, immediately dismounted, and all men, women, and children stood aside reverently bowing their heads, and crossing their hands over their breasts. Thus we proceeded to the first village on the road where we were duly received by the Shaikh; the Persian carpets were spread under an awning in front of his house, the ground for some distance around was sprinkled, and the coffee and pipes were brought. These the Nazir at first declined, more, I think, to keep up an appearance of consistency than from conscientious scruples. But then I also refused to partake, and reminded him of their law, "No fast upon a journey," when he partook. Thus it was at the second village, and at the third, when it was sunset; and I, more earnestly than at the other villages, renewed my injunctions that he should go no further. But he was still minded to see us through, when I said, " It is now your time to eat, and you shall not go on; I have sworn." I did not swear though, for that expression is a very common one, and only means that one *will* swear if the other does not yield the point in dispute, and it is usually immediately given up; for an oath is yet for confirmation, an end of strife. So we went on without him. When we reached the convent and pounded at the heavy gate, a monk came and timidly asked who was there, when our *friend* the scribe slipped in and had a parley with them, when the gate was thrown wide open and we entered. The black robed brethren were at once flying hither and thither. It was Father Paul here, and Father George there, in most excited tones, and soon I was seated cross-legged upon the high " dewan" in the corner of honor of the large reception room, with Boulos, the brother of Abd El Malak, who in the dotage of the latter is acting Abbot, beside me; while I magnificently sipped the coffee and smoked the long pipe. It was soon evident that preparations were making for a sacrifice and a great feast, but I told Monsur to inform them that it was my pleasure to have a light supper, and that I wished as many of the monks as convenient to come together, as

I had a word to say to them. Soon there was
a great circle of them standing around respect-
fully crossing their hands before them, and it
was with great ado that we could get them to
sit down on the floor. I then asked for a Bible,
and they brought an immense manuscript folio
containing a part of it, and I spent till eleven
o'clock in reading and expounding to them.
They had but just left us that we might retire,
when a great rap was heard on the gate, and the
confusion which ensued showed that the Nazir
had followed us after taking his late dinner.
Monsur and I, fearing that we might be kept up
two hours longer, hastily wrapped ourselves in
the comforters and stretched ourselves on the
dewan to sleep and put out the light. Soon we
heard them at the door whispering: "They have
gone to sleep we cannot disturb them." It did
not at the time occur to us that there might not
be another decent reception room in the convent;
but thus it must have been, for the next morning
we found that the kind Nazir had again left that
night, and gone back to the village which was
about an hour distant. The next morning the
lamb was slain, and we had a substantial breakfast, considering that we were in a Coptic convent; and then we brought out our bag of books,
and in a very short time the monks gathered
around and they were all sold, and many more
would have been taken had we had them with

28*

us. They literally stripped us, Meshakah's books and all, and soon we bid them adieu, rejoicing that we had again been able to place the leaven in that mass of human corruption, and to leave the living and life-giving Word in the midst of that spiritual *death*. (When the Coptic monks take the vow, part of the ceremony is to dress them in their grave-clothes, to signify that thenceforth they are to be as if dead and buried to the world. Most of them *are* dead to God and holiness !)

Several months afterward Brother Hogg again visited the convent, when he found that the leaven was working with power, and Father Boulos (Paul) told him that it was no use for them any longer to resist it, that they who were advanced in years must be left to die in the old way, but that all the rising generation were following the New Way.

On our way we picked up the Nazir at the village, where I fear, from his seedy appearance, that he had not had as comfortable quarters as we had in the convent, and we had many regrets to offer. We reached the river in safety, and soon the boats came along and picked us up.

April 1st. Stopped at Rhoda, where Ismail Pasha, the present Viceroy, had a large sugar factory, and an immense building in process of erection for another. Besides our sales of Bibles to the Copts, two Muslems here bought Testaments.

Minyeh. We found here that our stock of Bibles was nearly exhausted. I had all along had great ado to convince Lord Aberdeen that we could sell all our Bibles at our own prices. *His* object was to put the Bible into the hands of all the Copts in Egypt, and to do this he was prepared to make and did make a large pecuniary outlay. *Our* object was also to supply the demand for the book, but at the same time to put the book-business in Egypt on a proper and satisfactory footing, and to maintain and further establish our reputation as men of one price.

We here made the acquaintance of a man named Ibrahim (I have forgotten the rest of his name) author of "Egypt's Princes." He had formerly been a very bigoted Copt, but on a visit which he made to Cairo some time before, he had met our good Father Makhiel, and *he*, together with the books he had taken with him, had enlightened him. I found him to be not only a man enlightened in religion, but what is unusual among the Copts, a man of a good deal of literary taste, so that he purchased copies of all the new books we had on poetry and literature, as well as those on religion. The next morning before leaving, I called on him and the other Coptic scribes at the Divan. As he was head scribe, he was setting in the chief place, while the others, fifteen or twenty in number, were sitting around behind their small desks and big account books. He was smoking, which was an unusual sight, as it was fast-day, and prayers were not yet through. He handed me the pipe and called for coffee, while the others looked dubiously on. In the mean time I distributed specimens of our books for them to examine, when in came a tall, stalwart priest. He took the seat pointed out to him, and then looking at the pipe which I had passed back to our friend, and the coffee-cups, he opened conversation by saying: "The Muslems are fasting Ramadan, and the Christians are fasting, and what are you doing?" Quietly applying the amber to his lips, he took a deliberate inhalation, and said: "I am smoking my pipe," and then passed it back to me. A Testament was just lying beside the priest, and I asked him to do me the favor to pass it. He did so, and turning to Col. ii. 16, I handed it back and asked him to read. He read the verse, when I, taking my puff, said, " Paul says, ' Let no man judge you in meat or drink,' etc., and whence do you derive your authority to judge us?" A suppressed titter burst from those sitting around, and our friend the priest picked himself up and walked out, without even leaving his " salaam."

We found here a friend from Cairo, who had opened a dry goods shop, and as he seemed

willing to add a few books to his stock in trade
we left with him a quantity of kinds that we
had in abundance.

2*d*. This morning, after we had steam up, and
were just about casting off from the shore,
Makhiel came running down with word that a
man named Hannah Egawell, from Cairo, was in
the town sick, and wanted medicine. This man
is one of the Council (Presbytery) of Twelve
connected with the Patriarchate at Cairo, and a
man of great weight and influence. He had
been a Government scribe, and had received a
pension of land back of Minyeh, and I found
that on riding out to see it yesterday, which
was a hot day, he had been sun-struck. He was
suffering greatly, and in great fear and excitement lest he should die there, away from his
home and friends. His complexion and eyes
showed that he had a superabundance of bile,
and I sent up to him a heavy dose of blue pill and
oil. He clung to us, and piteously besought us
to take him with us in the steamer, so that he
might die at Cairo, but to remove him then
could not be thought of. The medicine proved
just the thing for him, for a few days after he
had so far recovered that he could be carried to
his Dahabiyeh in which he overtook us at Benisouef. That little circumstance created for us
an influential friend in the high places of the
Coptic Church. He still clings to it that our

faith and medicine saved him, and seems never to weary with telling how we took the pains after steam was up, and we all ready for starting, to go and see him. Whenever now in Cairo, he is taken sick, he sends at once for me, and if the doctor must come, he will not have him, except "at my hand." He is a pious and intelligent man but very superstitious.

Just before evening we reached Calosineth, and took a hasty turn through the streets with our books, but met with no success. The next day, the 3d, was a market day. Most of the large towns of Egypt have a weekly market, when the peasants from the neighboring smaller villages come together to buy and sell, bringing with them whatever they have for sale. We have found these markets an admirable institution for our book-selling craft. Their great draw back is that many of them are held on the Sabbath, which is a great temptation to the Christians to Sabbath profanation.

The next day we sold well at Sharubiyeh, and another village, and afterward repented much that we did not go to Sharone, which is some distance back in the country, in which there is a strong Protestant element. Indeed the priests and the people have since, by common consent, removed the pictures which formerly they worshiped, from the church, and instituted other reforms.

We then went down to Benisouef where we found the "Ibis" awaiting us. Mr. Riley and I now both wished to reach Cairo as soon as possible; he to avoid the hot winds of the Khamseen (*fifty*, so called, because, commencing about the first of April, they prevail for fifty days), and I, if possible, to overtake and see Brother McCague before his departure for America, and to take his place in the mission at Cairo. We had therefore sent word to the brethren at Cairo to have the "Ibis" sent to meet us here. We were now the more ready to hasten home, as between Benisouef and Cairo there are not many villages, and in them but few Copts. The district, however, of the Fayoum remained, in which there is a large Coptic population. It is a day's journey back of Benisouef, and is the region of the Labyrinth, and the artificial Lake Moeris, both so famed in days of old. It is still watered by Bahr Yuseph, which formerly fed Lake Moeris, and is the garden of Egypt, as Egypt is of the world.

Besides my reasons for reaching Cairo as soon as possible, I was much worn with the labors of the trip, and did not feel able to undertake this excursion, but his Lordship was determined that it too should be supplied, and so we rigged out Monsur with a load of books and dispatched him thither.

I must tell something of the effects of that

load of books, as they were subsequently developed. Among the purchasers was Priest
Makar, the nephew of the Bishop of the Fayoum. Providence put into his hands Mashakah's book, and he had not read far in it before
he said to himself: "It cannot be that this man
quotes the Scriptures correctly. The Bible is not
thus against us." He took the book to the
church and compared passage with passage in
the manuscript copies of the Scriptures there.
He found that there were only verbal variations,
and that even in these, it was evident that
Mashakah had the better reading. He then returned to Mashakah with new zest, and mastered the argument, making an abstract of the
passages of the Scriptures, which were against
them. He thus quietly satisfied his own mind,
and then commenced to act accordingly. His
first overt act was on the occasion of the baptism
of a child, when he proceeded to perform the
ceremony in Arabic, instead of Coptic. The
startled people sprang up in the church and cried,
"What do you mean? Where is your Coptic?
Have you forgotten your Coptic." He quietly
quoted Paul, "that five words with the understanding were better than ten thousand words
in an unknown tongue," when they allowed
him to proceed. This opened the whole subject, and for fourteen successive days priest and
people met in the church, and read Mashakah's

book, and comparing his quotations from the Scriptures with their own manuscript copies, and thoroughly sifting the whole controversy.

There was already in the place a small Protestant nucleus. Many years ago Messrs. Leider and Kruse of the English mission, had taken them the Bible, and five years before Bro. Barnett and I had made them another flying visit, and taken them another importation of the truth. Of the results of the reading of the copies of the Scriptures thus introduced, we know little, except that two men had become convinced of the corruption of the Church, and had indeed seceded from her, and been excommunicated. They have since worshiped in their own houses after a form invented by themselves, with the light of the Scriptures. One of these men has since visited us at Cairo, and we found him a very intelligent, earnest-minded man, but with strange notions on some points, and the other is reported to be even superior to him.

The Bishop is an old inefficient man, who, report says, is principally noted for the facility with which he grants illegal divorces to those who have been unhappily matched, *for a consideration.* He therefore could not be supposed able to cope with this new state of things, and besides one of the leaders in the movement was his own nephew, the Priest Makar. Two other nephews in his house were deeply imbued with

29

the new doctrine, and the three managed the
old man.   Finally, those who were still zealous
for the " traditions of the fathers" wrote to the
Patriarch at Cairo, petitioning him to interpose
with a Coptic bull, for the crushing of this new
sect, and stating that there were in Madinet El
Fayoum sixty families of Protestants.   We think
their fears greatly magnified, and that there
could not have been so many, but such was
their statement.   The Patriarch thinking that
Makar must be the soul of the movement, and
that they could manage him if they could only
get him to Cairo, sent an order for him to come
at once, and it was talked that he had even
made application to the Government to have him
brought in chains.   But that was after the affair
of Faris, and it had been settled that that sort
of dealing would not answer with Protestants and
so it was not attempted.   He refused to come, but
finally as we wished to see him that we might
hear the whole story, and further instruct him in
the truth, we sent for him.   We found him a
not particularly bright, but an earnest, and decided man ; much such a character as Kiddes of
Esneh.   We exhorted him, as far as in him lay,
to follow after the things which pertain to peace
in his intercourse with the Patriarch and his
brother priests.   In accordance with this advice,
he allowed himself soon after to be taken to the
Patriarch's cathedral in Cairo.   When once

there they beset him to engage in the services, but he refused. Finally, they forced a censer into his hand, and holding his hand clasped upon the chain, they dragged him up to the Patriarch, and waved his hand; so that he thus, by passive consent at least, burned incense before this earthly god. He was led to this act of compliance by their earnest representations that should he not do it, his Holiness would be highly offended, and that it would be a great shame to him not to offer him this small tribute.

But the act was no sooner performed than contrition seized him. He thought of his martyr ancestors, so many of whom cheerfully gave up their lives rather than throw a pinch of incense upon a heathen altar. He rushed to the house where he was staying with his cousins, and they afterwards told me that he locked himself up in a room where he remained two days and two nights without food, while they from without could hear him weeping and praying for forgiveness. He will never again, even by compliance, burn incense to the Patriarch.

Some time after this, Makhiel, one of the elders of our church at Cairo and a blind man, who in the days of his youth had been a Government scribe, received from the Government a pension of land in the Fayoum. He wished to go and *see* his land and to make arrangements with the peasants for having it productive. This Makhiel has for years been an efficient evangelist in Cairo. He is a good man and has an extensive knowledge of the Scriptures. His custom was to hold a meeting, which for several years was in the house of Mr. Leider, of the English mission, in which one of those present would read a chapter or two, and then Makhiel would explain the passages read. In this way, a blind man—or rather, as the Arabs describe such, one whose eyes are of the heart—has been the means of giving light to many of the spiritually blind of Cairo.

As he was about leaving for the Fayoum, with his sister, who is also almost as blind, we told him that if he could make himself useful in further instructing in the way of truth those new-fledged Protestants, we would be pleased if he should remain there some time. He had not been there long before word was sent to us that the people of the Fayoum were much pleased with his expositions of Scripture, and wished him to remain. He remained there several months, and recent word from Cairo shows that he found there an open door for the Gospel.

We spent two days pleasantly and profitably at Benisouef, and took steps for the establishment of a school, of which an account will be found in the next chapter, and then—

April 7th. Mr. Riley and we removed to the "Ibis" and hoisted over her again the stars and stripes, and on the 9th we reached Cairo. The Khamseen winds commenced the next day.

29*

CHAPTER XIV.

ABRAHAM LINCOLN, President of the United States of America, to His Highness MOHAMMED SAID PACHA, Viceroy of Egypt and its Dependencies, etc., etc., etc. :

GREAT AND GOOD FRIEND—I have received from Mr. Thayer, Consul General of the United States at Alexandria, a full account of the liberal, enlightened, and energetic proceedings which, on his complaint, you have adopted, in bringing to speedy and condign punishment the parties, subjects of your Highness in Upper Egypt, who were concerned in an act of cruel persecution against Faris, an agent of certain Christian missionaries in Upper Egypt.

I pray your Highness to be assured that these proceedings, at once so prompt and so just, will be regarded as a new and unmistakable proof equally of your Highness' friendship for the United States, and of the firmness, integrity, and wisdom with which the Government of your Highness is conducted.

(342)

Wishing you great prosperity and success, I am your good friend,

ABRAHAM LINCOLN.

Washington, October 9, 1861.

By the President:

WILLIAM H. SEWARD, *Secretary of State.*

THE VICEROY TO THE PRESIDENT.

To the Honorable ABRAHAM LINCOLN, President of the United States of America:

HONORABLE SIR AND FRIEND—Mr. Thayer, Consul General of the United States at Alexandria, has presented me the letter you were pleased to write me, expressing your feelings of satisfaction for the punishment which I have inflicted on some individuals guilty of evil and cruel treatment towards an agent of certain Christian missionaries in Upper Egypt. Mr. Thayer, who I am happy to say, entertains with me the most friendly relations, had already expressed to me the feelings of your Government.

In this case, honorable sir and friend, I have only executed the rule which I have always endeavored to follow, in protecting in an equal way and without consideration of creed, all those who, either by inclination or for the fulfillment of a duty, sojourn in the country submitted to my administration.

I am profoundly sensible of the friendly manner in which you express your sentiments both to myself and to my Government, and I pray you, honorable sir and friend, to accept with this offering of my thanks, my sincere wishes for the success, perpetuity, and integrity of the American Union, which, I hope, under your able presidency, will soon see an end of the trials with which the Almighty has been pleased to afflict it.

Your most devoted friend,

MOHAMMED SAID.

Alexandria, November 21, 1861.

The foregoing are copies of the letter sent by our President to his Highness, the Viceroy of Egypt, thanking him for his prompt and vigorous action in punishing the perpetrators of the outrage upon our man Faris at Osiout, and the Viceroy's answer, for the sending of which for publication, our Consul has received the necessary permission. It is a document which deserves publication, even to the ends of Christendom. It is a firman of religious toleration, and it is clear and explicit, and not as such documents have too often been, equivocal in its terms and dubious in meaning, and what is best of all it is a " word" after a " blow." The saying, " A word and a blow," will not answer here, where people have become accustomed to thousands of words without any corresponding action.

But I will give a few facts in connection with

that case, showing its effects. When the Viceroy gave the sentence, he was on the eve of de-
parting for the capital to visit the new Sultan.
Before leaving, he stated to Mr. Thayer that
some of the men sentenced, and especially El
Kashif, were men of such influence in the country that he feared evil might result from their
long imprisonment, and requesting him, as a
special favor, in the course of a month or so, to
ask for their pardon. The Viceroy returned
after a month, and soon after Mr. Thayer asked
him to release the men from imprisonment and
pardon them, which was done. In the meantime we had been receiving letters from Faris,
showing that the most happy effects had followed
the execution of the sentence of the Viceroy,
but which led us to fear that the new popularity,
and, indeed, power which Faris had acquired in
Osiout might prove a snare to him, and that he
might compromise himself and us; and as he
was also writing very urgently for one of us to
come and assist in the work which had now received a great impulse, the brethren decided
that I should go.

Oct. 9th, 1861. Left Old Cairo at 10½ A. M., in
"Ibis," bound for Osiout. Company, Mrs. L.
and baby, and Miss D. still suffering from her
recent severe attack of illness, and hoping for
renewed vigor from the more balmy breezes of
the Said. A strong north wind has all day

driven us careering over the turbid waves and headlong torrent of the Nile. The Nile! but truly this is no longer our old friend the placid, thought-inspiring Nile, quietly wending his way between the dark brown banks, with a rich store of freighted wealth. It is as if the land of Egypt were liquified, and, boiling in its rocky basin of the Arabian and Syrian hills, were pouring itself in thick, dark, turbid waves into the briny deep. It is said that the Nilometer records show that in a century there has not been such an inundation, and we have all day witnessed sad proofs how unprepared the country was for such a flood. Dykes, canals, gardens, fields, hamlets, and villages are all being swept away by the desolating element; and many lives have been lost. This afternoon we passed three corpses thrown upon a low bank. Two of them were in ghastly embrace; the clasp it may be of desperate self-preservation, now stiffened in death—the embrace we will trust it was of two loving hearts, united in life and tenderly clinging to each other as they met their fate. It is most pitiful to behold the half-famished flocks and herds, with groups of homeless, desolate men, women, and children clinging to the remnant of their dissolving villages, or (these being already swept away) clustering upon little knolls and patches of rising ground gazing in stupid horror and dread apprehension upon the encroaching, all-devouring flood. Thus, of old, God sent his deluge to sweep away a sinful race. May this deluge prove a purifying baptism to sin-polluted Egypt.

The scene, as I took my evening promenade upon the deck was at once beautiful and sublime:

> " Heaven's ethereal bow,
> Spanning with bright arch the glittering hills below."

The setting sun tinging those hills with purple while bathing in lurid light the vast inclosed expanse—the groves of tall palms, their feet bathed in the flood, but rearing far aloft their Corinthian heads and golden clusters — the deep green clumps of accacias opening up far-reaching vistas of the watery waste; now gleaming in the slanting rays of the setting sun—the villages with their tall minarets, like huge hulks dismantled and drifting o'er the flood—the vast fields totally submerged, or covered with the tufted tops of cane and Indian corn still struggling for supremacy—and here and there the now silent and ruined sakias, or shadoof posts standing in pairs like sad sentinels over the wide-spread ruin. These, together with the many lateen-sailed craft, like great white-winged birds gliding hither and thither, or hovering like angels of light over the dark watery waste, are elements of distant enchantment, combined with present surrounding desolation, dismay, and death which would have repaid the poet Campbell for a pilgrimage to Egypt before prefixing his matchless frontispiece to his "Pleasures of Hope."

Mrs. L., Miss Dales (who was just recovering from a severe attack of illness, and very much needed the change), and I, prepared to depart, and we left Cairo on Wednesday, the 9th October, in our favorite "Ibis." The "Ibis" gave us, as usual, a swift passage, and on Saturday, the 12th, we reached Osiout. As our arrival was unexpected, I immediately went up to ascertain the "statu quo" of affairs. I found Faris with his house full—pupils, parents, patients, people from Osiout and the surrounding villages, seeking his interference in all sorts of political, priestly, and family troubles — in short, he was evidently "master of the position," and the centre of a powerful influence, which was quite a contrast to his former state, when for weeks, and even months, while under the priestly ban, he could scarcely find a man to return his salutation. We remained ten days, and were happy to find that he had shown as much prudence and tact in prosperity, as he had fortitude and endurance in adversity.

I can describe but a small part of what took place during those ten days. I will only attempt to state a few facts, showing the new direction which the popular current has taken.

In the first place, Faris had been instrumental in saving another woman from the meshes of Islam. It was, even more clearly than the other, a case in which the woman had been forced against her will to marry a Muslem, or rather, he laid claim to her as his betrothed, for the marriage had not yet been consummated.

Another case will be sufficient to show his political influence. The Nile was unusually high this year. In many places it did immense damage to the country and crops, and the people were doing all they could in building up the dykes to keep out the overflowing flood, which, at many points, was even sweeping away the villages. In a village near Osiout, the Sheikh, (Muslem,) called out the people for this purpose, and he very wantonly had them take away the dirt from around the church to put upon the dyke, in a way which left the church exposed to be undermined and ruined by the waters. The priest went over and entered his complaint with Faris. The latter finally consented to go and see. He took with him a number of influential Copts from Osiout, and went to the house of a friend near the Sheikh's house. The villagers crowded in, and among them a spy from the Sheikh. Faris seeing this, began to talk largely. He said that the Sheikh thought he could do any thing because he was wealthy and had some land; "but," he added, "we will see what will

30

happen to him. El Kashif also had land, and
his wives had since needed it to cast upon their
heads," etc., etc. The spy left, and the sheikh
soon came and kissed Faris' hands and head and
begged for quarter. Faris told him that he must
take back the earth which he had removed from
the foundations of the church, which he promised to do, and it was done.

As to the prisoners, the telegraphic wires had
been broken by the flood, and so the pardon
had been delayed nearly two weeks; and, on
reaching there, I was much surprised to find
that it had only reached a few hours before, and
the prisoners had been released only that afternoon. The whole town was in an excitement
of wonder, and especially when they heard that
the pardon had been granted at our request.
This they could not understand. They crowded
around us, Christians and Muslems, and asked
how it was. The Muslems were full of joy.
Some of the Christians slily hinted that we
should have left them to finish their year. I
told them that, after having given them an ex-
example of the justice of the Gospel, we wished
also to show them its clemency and mercy; and
to the Muslems I said: "The Koran imprisoned
you, and the Gospel set you free." The day
after our arrival, El Kashif sent word that he
wished to call on us. I sent back that I did not
receive calls on Sabbath, and, besides, that I had

no particular desire to see him, after what he had done. The next day, however, I heard things concerning him, which convinced me that he was truly penitent of what he had done, and, on the repetition of his request to be permitted to call, I consented. He came, and with him and after him about fifty of the chief of the Copts. After getting as many of them seated as we could, and the usual complimentary pipes and coffee, I handed him my copy of the Koran. He looked at it, and said: "The Koran—and a fine copy it is." I said: "Yes; proceed now." He answered: "How? With what?" I said, quoting a passage from the book he held: "Produce your proof, if ye be true." He was confused, and endeavored to avoid the issue. I said: "No, but you must bring your proofs for this religion, for which you have shown yourself so valiant. You have tried the sword with us, and found that it would not work. That time is past; but we are ready to hear proofs, and, if conclusive, to receive your religion." He still declined. Then I said: "I find some difficulties in this book, of which I wish your solution." I stated a couple, when he, finding the matter was turning against him, turned it off in a pleasant way, saying, "I am not the man for this; you will have to send for El Ghouse." (El Ghouse was one of the culprits, and a most fanatical man against the Christians, as well as obnoxious to the Muslems, he having made an attempt to get up a fifth sect in Islam. I am sorry to say that this man escaped the punishment which he so justly deserved. His name was mentioned in Faris' letters, but not amongst the thirteen at the head of the Kadi's letter, and so he was overlooked, which all classes at Osiout lamented.) I said: "Then why did you what you did? You certainly see that such an outrage was against both the laws of religion and humanity." He answered: "It was a temptation of the devil." This closed the matter, and our subsequent conversation was very agreeable. Indeed, he seemed an amiable sort of man, and all the Christians bore witness to the truth of his assertion, that he and his family had always before shown themselves friendly to them. I had a word ready for them also. (The Arabs always divide the whole of a thing into twenty-four parts, for the denominator of their fractions, as we do into ten in our decimals.) I told them that twenty out of the twenty-four shares of the guilt of the outrage upon Faris belonged to them —that we had come to them with brotherly love in our hearts and the Bible in our hands, and that they, from the first, unlike the people of all Upper Egypt, had met us with coolness and jealousy and excommunications, and that thus their treatment of Faris and our cause had emboldened the Muslems to do what they had done. This charge was too true to be denied, but they promised for the future to do better.

El Kashif, on leaving, invited us to call and take coffee with him the next day, and at ten o'clock the next morning, he sent his donkeys and servants to take us up. The ladies could not go, so I went alone, little anticipating the reception which had been prepared. He had invited a number of the leading Copts, together with Faris and our other adherents—and, when the time came, a grand dinner was brought on the carpet, opening with a sheep, roasted whole, and followed by turkeys, chickens, etc., to the extent of some thirty courses. Faris and I sat one on each side of him, and he took particular pains to show his good will to Faris; among other things, saying, that if ever any thing else happened to him, we must hold him responsible. The day was mostly spent in discussion of the truths of Christianity, and, I trust, to us profitably.

Faris had been able to re-open the school, which contained, when we were there, fifteen boys, and we hear that it is since growing. This, notwithstanding that some of the priests are still doing all they can against it, but not now openly, as before. The Bishop is very favorable to our cause, but he is a simple-minded old man, who has not much influence.

We brought Faris with us. His wife and

30*

child were in Khums, and he was longing to see them. Poor fellow, he was much more severely beaten, than even his letters gave us to understand. It is a great wonder how he escaped with his life—and it would hardly have been possible, but that he was a very strong, vigorous man. As it was, he received a severe blow on the back with a club, which, we fear, has affected his right lung, as he has ever since had a severe pain in it, and all the way down, and until he left here, he coughed terribly.

CAIRO, *Dec.* 20*th*, 1861. We left Osiout on Tuesday, and as we had left Monsur at Cairo to officiate at our Sabbath services with the intention of only being absent two Sabbaths, we wished to reach there by Saturday evening, so that our time was limited, and we could only stop at the "Benders," or large towns.

We made our first halt at Manfalout. Here in our journey down last Winter, Father Makhiel found an enlightened priest named Botros. I did not then see him, as I immediately, on reaching the town, had started up to Deir El Muharrak, the largest Coptic convent in Egypt, about three hours back of the town in the mountains.

Faris and I, after some difficulty, and a long walk through the town, found the house of Botros, and were happy to find him at home. He knew not at first who we were, nor did we take

the pains to inform him. The conversation soon
turned upon the subject of image-worship. He
expressed himself clearly, but at first cautiously,
on the Protestant side of the controversy, in
which, of course, I united with him. Faris, however, took it into his head to take, for the time,
the opposite side of the question, and urged the
usual arguments in favor of the images. Such
as, that the devotions paid them were not religious worship, but the due honors which we owe
the saints thus represented ; that they are not
paid to the wood, and canvas, and paint com-
posing the images and pictures, but to the beings
represented ; that the pictures may be useful,
historically, to the ignorant, who cannot read—
all which our friend Botros met very aptly with
the usual Protestant refutations, but at length
cut short the discussion by saying, very warmly,
" I cannot and will not worship wood ; my heart
revolts at the idea, and that is enough." But I
asked, " How do you when you go to officiate in
the church ?" He answered, " I pass straight by
the images to the altar, and do not notice them."
" And the people ?" " Some of them still worship them, and others follow my example."
"And confession ? Do you confess the people ?"
" No, I do not. The people come to me, and wish
me to do it ; but I tell them that the Apostle tells
us ' that we must confess our faults *one to another*,'
by which he means our sins against *one* another ;

but that our sins against God we must confess to Him." "And transubstantiation?" Again sound. And thus we took him through the category of disputed doctrines. "And whence did you obtain these new doctrines?" From Abd El Masieh, and from Meshakah's book." He added, "Some of the people tell me I should leave this book, and cling to the Bible alone; but I tell them that they cannot show me one point in which the little book opposes the big one, and that, therefore, the little one is the daughter of the big one."

He took us to the church, where we were soon surrounded by a large concourse of people, and there, surrounded by the stiff, staring pictures of saints and angels, we took the opportunity of showing them that the pictures were historically false, blundering and ridiculous in execution— a temptation to the ignorant, and a stumbling-block to the Muslems and others outside the pale of the church, and that they should be removed. One picture was a representation of the judgment scene, and contained the scales in which the good and bad deeds of the departed souls were being balanced, which we told them was a Muslem idea, and opposed to the doctrine of salvation by grace through the atonement of the Saviour, and not by works; and that in the gospel, where it is said that our good deeds will be brought forward in the judgment, it is not

with the intention of counterbalancing with them
our evil works, but only as evidences of our love
to the Saviour.

He then "accompanied us to the ship," where,
giving him some medicine for a sick brother
whom he had seen in the house; a little farther
instruction to establish him in the present truth,
and a couple of books, other daughters of the
big one, with whom he had not yet made acquaintance, we left.   We told him we were intending, if possible, to form a class of enlightened and inquiring priests in Cairo, for the study
of the Scriptures.   He said that whenever we
should send for him for this purpose, he would
hold himself in readiness to come.

We found our friend again in the divan.   As
there were some Muslems present, before whom
we could not talk freely, books and pens were
put aside, and he and a few friends retired with
us to a side room, where we enjoyed, I trust, a
profitable hour.   They asked about the Faris
affair, of which they had heard many reports, and
when told "This is Faris," they caught their
breath and looked at him almost with the reverence with which they would regard one risen
from the dead.   They seemed scarcely to know
how to express their gratitude to us for our action in the matter, and confirmed the reports
which we had heard in other places respecting
the wide prevalence of the spirit of fanaticism of

the Muslems against the Christians at the accession of Abd El Aziz, of which we have had such a sad exhibition at Osiout. They said emphatically, that the decision which we had obtained was not for Faris alone, but for our common Christianity.

They pressed us strongly to spend the night, and we were very sorry not to be able to do so; but the north wind, which had thus far baffled and retarded our progress down, had taken a lull, and it was yet morning, and we felt that we must go. They urged us strongly for a school.

Our third and last stop was at Benisouef. Here is a man, by name Fanoos Gabrian, of whom Brother M'Cague truly wrote, in his notes of his first trip, "One of a thousand." But to go back even further. A few days ago Fanoos related to me the following: Between five and six years ago, our shopman, Awid, was sitting on the bank of the Nile, at Benisouef, awaiting an opportunity in some passing boat to come down to Cairo. Fanoos (then a stranger to him) happening to pass, called to him and asked if he could assist him in the matter. A few earnest words from Awid arrested the attention of Fanoos, and he said, " I will secure you a passage down, but not until you have come up to my house and spent the night." Awid did so, and it was the beginning of a friendship which has lasted to this day, and promises the happiest results. Those few words were the handful of corn on the mountain top, whose fruit, we trust, shall yet wave like Lebanon. Subsequently, he was accustomed annually to make a visit to Cairo, where he also became acquainted with Brother M'Cague, and he used, in returning, to purchase and take with him a quantity of books for gratuitous distribution. I may here state that he is a wealthy man, the present head of the first Christian family of that whole section of country. He is the owner of a large village called Beni Bakhit, with its lands, which is an hour back of Benisouef. Last year I met him there. But I must now go back to introduce you to another character. Makhiel Ibrahim, some twenty years ago, was a pupil in the school of the Church Missionary Society here, then under the care of Messrs. Kruse and Leider. They took great pains with Makhiel, even to the extent of hiring a Muslem teacher to give him lessons in Arabic, grammar, etc. He turned out to be a good scholar; but, alas! he blasted all the high hopes which were entertained for him by drunkenness. Thoroughly Protestant in sentiment, upright, amiable, and estimable in character, bating his one bad habit, I found he was pitied, but beloved, by all who knew him. The day we reached there happened to be a feast day, and Makhiel soon came aboard, as we would say, "three sheets in the wind." He was, of course, most eloquent in his praise of Protestantism. Speaking of his old friend, the Church Missionary Society, he said, "It was the daystar for our land, but it set; and now the American Mission—the sun—has arisen, which shall enlighten all Egypt." But, poor fellow, he received a sad fall from his high horse. In leaving the boat, he fell from the plank into the water and upon the stones, badly cutting his face and head. As he sat on the shore, now perfectly sobered and wiping the blood from his face, he was a most pitiable spectacle. The next day he came back in his right mind, and insisted on repenting ("at my hand," as he expressed it,) and opening a school for us. Thirteen of the leading Copts of the place also came down and pleaded. for him; and though I could not have much confidence in his promise of reformation, I could not withhold sanction of the experiment, especially when they proposed supporting Makhiel, and said they only wished the influence of our name, and some school books which Lord Aberdeen gave them. After we left, however, the Copts verified the proverb of too many cooks spoiling the broth. They did not agree as to the details of the movement, and poor Makhiel returned to his cups. He had however, I believe, but one good spree when he resorted to a novel method of curing himself. The New York Society for reforming inebriates, should, I think, take note of it. He caught a large fish from the river, and cutting off its tail, he squeezed its blood into his arrack bowl and drank off the mixture. It made him deadly sick for several days, since which time (at the date of our last visit, five months,) he had not tasted, nor been able even to endure the smell of his formerly loved arrak. All testified (which was evident from his changed appearance) that he was now a reformed man, and all urged that the school should now be opened. Fanoos was not in town, being unwell in his village; but anxious not to subject the movement to its former mishaps from divided counsels, as to the school-room, I went to the street at once with Makhiel and hired one.

In the evening we rode out with a large company of Copts to Beni Bakhit to see Fanoos. The gallop over the plain was a delightful one. Our friend had been suffering from a slight attack of cold, and was better and able to receive us. The fatted lamb was killed, and we spent a very pleasant evening with the sole drawback of the presence of the hated arrack, of which the guests had brought a bottle with them. Fanoos never touches it, nor does he (noted as he is for hospitality) furnish it for his guests. Though confirmed drunkards, in our sense of the word, are seldom met among the Copts, this custom of arrack-drinking in their evening sociables, after their day's work is done, is fearfully prevalent.

The matter of the school was freely discussed.

31

They decided that the house which I had taken from a Muslem would not answer, as near it was a café, which was a centre of dissipation and evil; but that they would procure a Christian house, and have the Muslem return me the money (which has since been done). Fanoos promised to procure school-rooms, and they said that, in the mean time, the school should be kept in the church.

We spent the night there, all sleeping on the floor of the guest room, which we quite covered; and the next morning we returned to town. By last accounts the school contained thirty-five children, and Makhiel was giving great satisfaction to all. Fanoos has been here the last two weeks. Before leaving home, he set apart, for school premises, a lot of ground containing 400 pics (the pic is about twenty-seven inches) of land, and he purchased a large quantity of bricks, lime, and other building materials, and the last few days here he has been purchasing timber for rafters, doors, windows, etc. I have been helping him with his plan, and a fine one it is. He proposes building a large school-room, and three smaller rooms and a kitchen—two for recitation rooms, and one for a guest room when we go to see him. He also takes with him one of our school-boys (who has been in the school here five years) for assistant teacher, principally for English, and his wages are to be paid by the people there. Truly, this man *is* "one of a thousand." Would that each village in Egypt had one such man.

I asked Awid about the narrative above narrated, of his first acquaintance with Fanoos. He told the story in the same manner, only he gave me the following characteristic addition: He said that he had gone there with and at the invitation of a Coptic friend here, to visit some friends in a village back of Benisouef. While there, he advocated Protestant doctrines so freely and decidedly, that at length they told him, one evening, that he must be silent on the subject or leave. He said, "Very well, I will think over it to-night." The next morning he arose early and hired a boy and donkey, and rode into Benisouef, where he was sitting friendless and alone on the bank of the river when Fanoos came along.

CHAPTER XV.

In a journal of a trip up the Nile in October, 1862, I find the following account of Bashoi and of Makhiel, which may interest the reader. The size of the volume will not permit me to insert the journal entire:

During the regimé of Faris at Osiout, he fell in with a monk named Bashoi, from a village on the opposite side of the river, who had seceded from the Coptic to the Popish Church, and taken the whole Coptic community of the place with him. Faris so far instructed him in the truth as to bring him and his people back to the Coptic church—the half-way house to Protestantism. But Bashoi did not stop there. He subsequently came to Cairo, said he was a Protestant, and wished to enter our school. We told him the school was open and bade him walk in. He was not long in the school before some of our Protestants preached to him the gospel of matrimony, and nothing would do but that he must take to himself a wife. We strove earnestly to persuade him to relinquish this purpose for the present, and diligently give his whole mind to his studies for a year or two,

(364)

when we would hope to send him back to his village prepared to labor effectively for the spiritual good of his people, and with a help-meet with him. Thus, the subject was put off for a couple of months, and we think he would have followed our advice, but his officious friends were urging him on in the matter, and finally they found for him a Coptic girl who had agreed to marry him. (These matters are arranged by third parties in Egypt, and a man seldom sees his intended until after she has become his wife.) The girl and her friends were told all about him, except that he was a monk. But before the matter could be consummated, the Copts got wind of the affair, and threats of excommunication were immediately held over the girl and her family, which broke off the whole matter.

Some time afterwards I was in bed sick, one Saturday forenoon, when they came to me saying, "Come, now, we have a bride for Bashoi. She is a Greek widow, and we have told her that he is a Coptic monk, and she is willing to marry him, and we have her all ready at our house, and can bring her here in ten minutes. Up, now, and marry them, before something else happens to prevent." I arose, put on my dressing-gown and slippers, and in a short time they were man and wife. We then told him: "You know on what conditions you have taken this step against our advice. We now understand

what was the extent and scope of your Protestantism. Thus far we have helped you; but now,
as we told you, your education in our school is
finished. Take now your wife and go to your
village, and support her by your honest labor,
and the blessing of God go with you."

He left, and, as we knew would be the case,
the affair was soon noised abroad, and an ecclesiastical thunderbolt was fulminated and sent
after him. He went to his father's house; and
the house, and much of its furniture, and some
land, were the fruits of his own mass-saying industry in former years. But when the priestly
ban against him reached the village, his father
turned him into the streets. All his former people turned against him, and even instigated the
Muslims to revile and stone him whenever he
passed through the streets. He went over to
Wasef, our American consular agent in Osiout;
and Wasef should have acted energetically in
the case, which, with the memory of the affair
of Faris, would probably soon have quelled this
petty persecution. But while Wasef was personally very kind to him, and gave him and his
wife a passage in one of his boats to Cairo, he
could not bring himself to the point of facing and
putting down the Episcopal bull. He doubtless
could have done so had he wished, and perhaps
it was too much to expect from him.

This is all of the story of Bashoi that is necessary for our present narrative, but my readers will doubtless wish to hear the sequel of his story :

He and his wife came down to Cairo, more dead than alive. We met him with : " Well, what next ? Did we not tell you before that they would persecute, excommunicate, and strip you of every thing, and if possible, even kill you ? And that if you would marry, we would perform the ceremony for the general effect of the act on the Coptic church, but that as to yourself our responsibility would there end." " Oh, yes !" he bitterly answered, " you told me all, and you were a true prophet. But what can I now do ?" Poor man ! he wept like a child. Besides the persecutions which had befallen him, he had found that in his blindfold leap he had not married a Greek, but a Tartar, which made it much worse for him. We could not help pitying him, and finally said, " What can we possibly do for you ?" He said, " Only let me stay here, under your protection, and have a crust of bread and cup of water, and I will do any thing. I will take care of the donkey, or sweep the school-rooms, or any thing you say." We wondered whether the priestly dignity had really come down to this, and we took him at his word : " Sweep the school-rooms, you shall ; and your wages shall be four dollars per month." *He did it*, and meantime he went into some of the classes in the school, and the longer he remained the more he convinced us that he was a man of mind and piety, and that his Protestantism had not been simply in obedience to the gospel of matrimony. He bore, too, the burden of an ill-assorted match, and instructed and prayed with his wife in a manner none but a truly Christian man could do; so that soon a manifest improvement was apparent in her. After a time we found him qualified to teach a class in the school, then another class, and soon he commenced writing sermons—one of which he brought to us every few days for correction—and in them he showed a very extensive knowledge of the Scriptures. Indeed, his first sermons were almost entirely from the Scriptures, and to the point, too, which is wonderful, when were member that they have no Concordance in Arabic; and when corrected on this point, and told to bring more of his own, he answered that he dared not, but that whex he spake from the Scriptures he knew he was right.

When our blind Makhiel went to the Fayoum, we opened for Bashoi a room for a nightly meeting in the heart of the Coptic quarter, in which, and in labor in the streets, he has shown himself laborious and faithful, and now he regularly preaches the Word. Thus the matter of his marriage has turned out well. It was the first case of the kind, and as the marriage of Luther

with his Catharine made Europe tremble, so this
convulsed the Coptic church. It broke the spell.
Another, as has been already narrated, has followed the example, and soon we trust the daughters of the Copts will no longer say of a union
with a priest or a monk, " Would a girl marry
her father ?"

The story of Makhiel is even more interesting
than that of Bashoi :

Makhiel, when a youth about fifteen years of
age, was induced to devote himself to the monkish life, and he left Beleine, his native town, and
went to the Convent of the Virgin, also called
the Syrian Convent, in Nitria. This district, it
is said, contained in the fourth and fifth centuries
of our era, about twenty thousand monks. It is
situated in the Delta, south-west from Alexandria, and thirteen hours of hard riding over a
barren desert west of Wordan. There are now
there only four convents, and in each of them
twenty or thirty monks. These monks are now
for the most part illiterate men, who spend their
time in the empty routine of Coptic prayers, and
in attending to their temporal affairs, and in
quarrelling with one another. A number of
them who have come to us confess that they
spend most of their time in wordy war, which
sometimes comes to blows and even blood.
Young Makhiel went there with a desire and
determination to learn to read. He found that

the monk whose duty it was **to** grind the flour
for the fraternity, knew how to read, and by
taking his turn occasionally on the mill, he
bribed him to teach him the letters, when he
commenced with him the Psalms, of which he
learned to read, and memorized nine. **He** then
went on helping himself with the rest, and finally
committed the one hundred and fifty-*one* Psalms
(for **the** Copts have an extra one, which they
have brought I know not whence). In the
mean time, as he had a very inquisitive mind, **he**
read pretty deeply the old manuscripts, of which
the convent has a large collection. Among these
he found one which he read and re-read, which,
with his knowledge of the Psalms, laid the foun-
dation of his Christian character. This book, of
which the abbot **of** that convent gave me a copy,
which is five hundred and **seventy** years old, is
evidently a translation, but by whom or where
it was written, it **is difficult** to conclude. It **is**
called the " Book of the Spiritual Shaikh," and
bating some mysticism, and that the sense **of**
much of it has been lost in translation and trans-
scribing, it is in much the style of Rutherford's
letters. While thus engaged, a wider and richer
field of study was opened to Makhiel in a copy
of the entire Bible. A monk who had been to
Cairo **brought one** which he had obtained from
the English Mission there. As soon as Makhiel
saw **it,** he said, " I must have it." The other,

however, would not give it to him except for twelve piastres. Makhiel had no money, but he had a pair of new shoes which had been sent him from home, and, taking them off, he threw them to him and said, " There, take those and give me the book!" He now read the Bible constantly, but for a long time to come he was still very superstitious. He has told me how he used often to spend nearly the whole night in praying and repeating Psalms before the picture of the Virgin, bowing before her to the earth, sometimes hundreds of times in succession, until his knees were calloused by it, and that he used to imagine that the picture smiled benignantly upon him, as if pleased with his devotion. Some time after he made a visit to Cairo, where he became acquainted with a Copt who had been partially enlightened, who introduced him to Mr. Krusi of the English Mission, which led to a correspondence after his return to the convent. Afterwards (I cannot give dates, for the Arabs seldom take account of them, and I merely give the outline of his life as I received it from him), when a new Abuna or Bishop was appointed to the Abyssinian church by the Patriarch of Cairo, he being a young man, Makhiel was sent with him as his *factotum*. He spent seven years in Abyssinia, and thoroughly mastered the Ethiopic, and were our Church prepared to drive the wedge of light which has been entered at

Egypt, still further into the African continent—
that great triangle of thick darkness—a new missionary should be sent for the purpose from
America, and, taking Makhiel with him, should
establish a mission in that most interesting
country.   He was in Abyssinia during the time
of the political revolution in that land, which
resulted in the establishment of the throne of
Theodore, the present king.   He was a chief
actor in those scenes of craft and bloodshed, and
his narrative of the events of that yet unwritten
chapter of modern history is intensely interesting.   But he was yet, though partially enlightened, in the bondage of superstition.   When Dr.
Krapf, about a year ago visited Cairo, the two
met and recalled a reminiscence of a former
meeting on the hills of Abyssinia.   When the
Doctor went there, Makhiel said to himself,
What would this stranger do?   Would he
bring to us a new religion?   He stirred up the
native priests against him, and then took a company of them and went to him with a picture of
the Virgin, Makhiel said to him, " Worship this."
Dr. Krapf shrugged his shoulders, and said,
" No, I will not enter into the religion of Satan."
Said the other, " You *must* bow to this, or you
must leave this land."   He, of course, was inflex-
ible, and was forced to leave.

Finally, the Abuna took a position in politics, in which Makhiel could not follow him,

and the result was, that he was cast into
prison, where he remained several months, when
he was sent barefoot over the mountains of
Abyssinia, a journey of seventeen days, to Aden,
at the entrance of the Red Sea.   He then took
boat and sailed up to Suez, and so to Cairo.   He
here came more frequently into contact with the
Protestants, and especially with blind Makhiel,
of whom account has already been given.   Finally, he began boldly to give expression to Protestant sentiments.   This was brought under the
notice of the church authorities; and one night
the Bishop of Cairo had him inveigled into a
house where he was thrown upon his face into
the mud in the court, and cruelly beaten, but he
would not recant.   His excommunication followed, and he was left to wander through the
streets of Cairo, disconsolate and alone, without
any one to return his salutations or minister to
him, and without any means of support.   It was
at this time, over seven years ago, that he came
to our missionaries in Cairo.   They would have
given him employment, by which he might earn
a livelihood; but, while intelligent enough, they
found him unable to write; nor could he make
himself useful in conversing with the people, for
the excommunication cut him off from them, and
even most of our Protestants looked upon him
with suspicion.   He was a burden upon their
charities as he had no means of support, and he

32

could not be supported by the mission without a remuneration of actual work. In this state of things the brethren sent him to Alexandria, with the hope that the prejudice there might not be so strong against him, and that we might be able usefully to employ him. I had at the time the sheets of the new translation of the Testament, which was then being published in Beirut. Putting these in covers, I gave the volume to him, and said, "This will be something new for the people; put this under your arm, and wherever in the streets or shops you find a man willing to listen, read to him." He entered upon this work with zeal, and the Syrians and Greeks, of whom the population of Alexandria is largely composed, did not share in the Coptic prejudice against him. He also spent a portion of each day with me, receiving regular instructions in theology. For a long time, like most new converts, his mind was far too prone to controversy, and in these encounters his hot, impetuous blood often got the better of him. By frequent admonitions, and long and earnest efforts of self-control, he gradually overcame this disposition, and learned that it is the truth, and not controversy which edifies. He also showed himself a man of prayer. He lived with a friend in whose house he had no closet, and early every morning it was his custom to go down to the sea-shore and take his morning bath, and then, in a nook, behind the

wall of the city, spend the first hour or two of
the day in reading his Bible, meditation and
prayer. He then went forth into the streets and
highways, his heart hot within him to tell what
he had learned of the love of the Saviour. Thus
he continued for nearly three years, until Lord
Aberdeen came, when we sent him with Lord
A. to Upper Egypt as colporteur.

When he returned from Upper Egypt, we
allowed him to commence exercising his gifts in
the public, formal preaching of the Word, and in
this work he has since been engaged. The exi-
gencies of our Egyptian mission requiring that
he and Brother Watson should be left alone at
Alexandria, he, for more than a year, while
Brother Watson was yet unable to preach in
Arabic, took the sole charge of the Arabic service in that place. He is an able preacher. He is
mighty in the Scriptures, being familiar with the
whole volume of Divine truth; and often, in
hearing him preach, have we wished that more
of us, who have been called to be stewards of
the mysteries of God, could, like him, be more
restricted to the fountain of truth and light—
the oracles of the living God. His extensive
reading of native books and authorities have
also made him at home in the department of
ancient church history, and especially the history of the Coptic church. May his bow long
abide in strength!

CHAPTER XVI.

AWID, our bookseller at Cairo, having left a few days previous in our new boat, the " Morning Star," on her first colporteuring trip, I left Cairo on Tuesday, May 5th, to join him at Semanoud. Reached Tanta at noon, where I took the branch railway to Semanoud, on the Damietta branch of the Nile.

We soon reached Semanoud, and after washing off the dust of travel in a delicious cold bath, I was ready for work. Two young men soon came aboard. The one asked for the " Makamat of Naseef," a literary work of the great Arab grammarian, and when he found that we had not this, nothing could induce him to purchase any of our religious books, although he was evidently free from all priestly shackles in the matter. And when Awid strove to explain to him the uses and advantages of the " Reference Testament," he was " as one beating the air." The other asked only for religious books, of which he took a number. This difference led me to suspect a difference in nationality which

(376)

was not indicated by the appearance of the two lads, when I asked the former from what part of Syria he hailed, and he answered Beirut. The other was a Copt; and this difference in the religious tendencies of the two nations we constantly remark. Syria and Egypt are both awaking from a sleep of semi-barbarism of ages. But the civilization which Syria is putting on is French and infidel. Egypt's is Anglo-Saxon and Protestant.

Just beside our boat a Muslim was repairing a grain-boat, between whom and his wife Awid had overheard, a couple of days previous, the following conversation. The wife said: "Oh, my husband, the book (Kuran) says that the 'mumaneen' and the 'mumanat' (male and female believers) are after death to inhabit Paradise, but it says that each one of you male believers is to have seventy houris, and does it not say what we women are to have? Are there no male houris, and if so, how many are we to have?" He answered her, "Hold your tongue. It says nothing about your having any." But she answered, "Are we not even to have our own husbands there, after we have toiled and borne with them in this world? that is not just." He answered this by cursing her very soundly for her inquisitive impertinence; and the next day he divorced her with the treble divorce. (The law of the Kuran is that a man may divorce

32*

his wife twice and take her back again, but that
the third time he cannot take her back until she
has married another man and been divorced.
To save trouble, a man often says, "I divorce
thee with the treble divorce," when the thing is
ended.   Though not unfrequently, on repenting,
he persuades or hires some other man to marry
and then immediately divorce her, when he again
marries her.)

As Awid had been four days in Semanoud and
finished the bookselling work, we dropped down
by night to Mansoura (the Victorious).   This
town is on the east side of the Nile, and it, as
well as Semanoud, has become a large and flourishing place since the immense expansion of the
cotton interest the last two years, as this is the
centre of the best cotton district in the country.

I found that Awid had invented a new and
very useful contrivance for facilitating our work.
Before leaving Cairo he had written the following notice. of which he had made the boys of the
school write a large number of copies :

"Notice.—The boat 'Morning Star,' has arrived, having on board a quantity of religious and
literary books, which are for sale at low prices.
Let all, therefore, who wish books, come without
delay and take what they need, for the reading
of these books is most important and necessary,
since they bring consolation to the heart, and

especially the Holy Book of God, which he has given us by inspiration through holy men and prophets, and which is profitable for the present life and for that to come. Therefore, our Glorious Lord has commanded us to search the Scriptures, and the Apostle, in his First Epistle to the Corinthians, v. 21, has said, 'Prove all things: hold fast that which is good.'"

On arriving we sent out a large number of these, and by the time we had finished breakfast the first bevy of black-turbaned corps were seen coming. They took books to the value of ten dollars—a propitious opening. Others followed until noon. After dinner Awid took the bag and went through the streets, and I remained and attended to those who came to the boat.

One of the least to be desired, but still most natural results of the new cotton prosperity in Egypt, has been *a great revival of the slave trade.* The cotton crop is a heavy one, requiring much more and heavier work than the ordinary grain crop, of the country. Its cultivation was introduced into the country by Mohammed Ali, who, having procured and distributed the seed, stimulated its production in his own arbitrary way, by passing laws requiring each district to produce a certain amount of cotton annually. The land produced it so abundantly, and of such good staple, that it was a profitable crop, even when the South was a competitor in the market. And now, since King Cotton has removed his throne from Dixie to Egypt and India, he has distributed his favors so bountifully that no more laws enforcing the cultivation of cotton have been needed. I recently heard of one man who last year sowed two hundred and fifty acres of cotton, from the produce of which he has already sold cotton for fifteen thousand dollars, and he had still a quantity on hand; and a friend told me yesterday of a neighbor of his, whose sister was accustomed to come daily to his house to beg a piece of bread as her brother could not support her, he having only five acres of land. This brother was seen a few days since driving before him, through the streets, a male and female slave which he had just purchased, and when asked how he could afford it, he answered, "I sowed my five acres with cotton this year."

But the great obstacle to cotton-growing has been, and is, the scarcity of hands. The conscription for the army, and forced labor for the Suez Canal and the Government works, make heavy drafts upon the working population. Fully one-third of the available muscle of the land is at present thus employed, while it is lamentable to behold the wheat crop everywhere perishing on the ground for want of hands to reap it. This state of things has created a great demand for slave labor in Egypt. But slavery is against

the law ; for England and France, in former
years, when it suited them to quote even " base
Egypt" to the United States as an anti-slave
power, obtained from the Sultan and the Egyptian Government an ordinance abolishing slavery.
Still, this law being imposed by foreign pressure,
and not sustained by the public sentiment of the
country, was in a great measure a dead letter.
True, the public slave-markets in the large cities
were abolished: but the " Jelábis," or Central
African merchants, still clandestinely brought
down, with their cargoes of ivory and ostrich
feathers, a few slaves; and the Government
winked at the trade, except so far as particular
officials found it to be to their interest to confiscate
to themselves these cargoes, or levy black-mail
upon the owners.   And besides, the Government
was the great slave-merchant of the country;
for it was constantly stealing and bringing down
from the upper country slaves, who were distributed to its favorites or enrolled in the black
regiment of the army.   And then, too, according to the law of the Kuran, which allows four
wives to each believer, besides as many concu-
bines "as his hands may possess," wealthy and
lecherous Muslims must have their female slaves
for the harem, and thus the trade was carried on.
Meanwhile the representatives of the European
powers that had, procured the passage of the
law were too anxious to preserve the " entente

cordiale" and the "integrity of the Turkish Empire" to make any very strong protests against the system, and thus it was continued. Now the European abolitionists view slavery through spectacles brought from Richmond, and there being, in addition, the increased demand above mentioned, caused by the great expansion of cotton culture, the supply is found keeping pace with the demand, and the result is a great revival of the slave trade.

I may, however, remark, while on the subject, that slavery is not there the cruel bondage, the odious institution which it is in our Southern States. It is alleviated by various considerations :

First. We have there none of that senseless "prejudice of color," or "caste of race," so prevalent in America, both South and North. Whether it be a white Mamaluke from the North, who is bought and sold as a chattel, or a black Dongolian (so black and shiny, and with such an entire absence of the red or pale in the palms and lips that he seems "dyed in the wool," black, through and through), it is all the same—"a man is a man for a' that." And in the female branch of the trade, whether it be a Caucasian beauty or (like Miriam, who was sent to the harem of Mohammed to stay his conquering sword and propitiate his favor) an Abyssinian maid, Anglo-Saxon in feature, but dusky in color, and all reeking in castor-oil, and all the more valued from having been converted—*stolen* —from a nominally Christian country, it is all the same—" a woman is a woman for a' that."

Second. Slavery is rendered a lighter yoke, from the fact that slaves have not been for the most part field-hands, crushed to the earth under the cumbrous wheels of King Cotton, nor any other great grinding demand of base avarice; but, like Abraham's three hundred and eighteen, they have been the domestic and body servants of the rich and great, and, as such, are often petted and trusted by their masters, and, as a consequence, acquire influence, and are respected by those around.

Third. We have here no fugitive slave law. Slavery, as has been said, is against the law of the land; and consequently, if a slave is not well treated, and chooses to walk off, he need have no fears of blood-hounds, nor even take passage by the " Underground Railway." The master has no redress, except it be through some corrupt Government official, whom he must bribe so heavily that, in most cases, he may better buy a new man. This latter feature takes the sting out of slavery, and almost makes it no slavery at all. It is probably the principal cause of the cheapness of the article. Two years ago a good slave could be purchased for from forty to sixty dollars. Now the price has risen to about one hundred dollars; and even yet, though the foreign pressure is removed, the Government continues a fitful and dubiously disinterested opposition to the trade.

9*th*. Awid having dispatched the books and returned, he took animals and a box of books and set out for Radaniyeh and Selamon, two villages about two and a half hours back in the country.

We next proceeded to Selamon, which is about twenty minutes further on and across a deep canal, which is navigable for good-sized craft. This canal leaves the Nile only a short distance this side of Cairo, and flows to the sea. It has on its banks many villages, and must, as soon as may be, be threaded by the "Morning Star."

When we reached the village we went to the church and asked for the priest. We found him in a small upper room connected with the church, very busily engaged correcting a manuscript copy of the memoir of St. George. We told him that we had Bibles and books for sale, and asked if any of his people needed any. He said he thought not, as they already had many books, and asked us if we had the book upon which he was laboring. We took a cup of coffee with him, and then went out with our box into the town to the Christian quarter, and seeking a shady street we sat down and exposed our

wares, at the same time sending off the boys,
who by this time had collected around us, to inform the people.   They soon came in good numbers, and we were happy to find that they were
of a different mind from their priest as to their
need of books.   We spent the day selling and talking to them, and sold them to the amount of two
hundred and ten piastres.   Once our business came
to a dead-lock in this wise : A boy who had bought
book brought it back, and quietly showed a passage in it to an old man—evidently the oracle
of the village—who dubiously shook his head,
and whispered something.   Others then drew up
and read over their shoulders, when, without saying any thing, the boy brought the book back
and demanded his money.   The rest dropped
the books which they were examining, and the
sale was stopped.   I saw a crisis had come, and
asked the boy what was the matter with the
book ?   After some reluctance he showed me
the passage, which was to the effect that the
Virgin Mary, like the rest of mankind, was a
sinner, and in strong terms he reprobated so
heretical a doctrine.   I turned, in the Testament
which I held in my hand, to Luke i. 46, and had
him read it aloud to all : "And Mary said, My
soul doth magnify the Lord, and my spirit hath
rejoiced in God *my Saviour ;*" and then asked
him from what he was her Saviour if not from
sin, and how, at his age, he came to be so wise

33

above what is written? All, even the oracle, bowed with a submission, which is peculiarly Coptic, to the authority of the Word of God, and the work went on again. This is only **an** example of the manner in which in these book-selling **and** street-preaching excursions **we** are called upon to meet opinions of all shades and hues. The whole debatable ground lying between them and us must usually **be** gone over, and a full account of one such day's work would fill a volume.

Our evening ride back over the open plain was delightful after our long day's work in the hot, dusty street. The country here is more beautiful than in Upper Egypt. Though the picture here lacks the frame-work of the Lybian and Arabian hills, which there so heightens the effect, we have here the sublimity of apparently endless expansion, and the eye is relieved by shade trees much more thickly scattered over the surface. Here, too, is wanting the "shadoof" with its saddening idea of crushing **toil,** and the sakias are in groups on the shady banks **of the** canal; and their concert of creaking wheels and flowing waters, enlivened by the cheerful crack of the whips of the drivers, and their lively songs, inspiriting the laboring beasts, is much better than their solitary groan in the Said. Camels, **with** towering sacks of the precious cotton balancing on each side, were wend-

ing their way with stately, measured step to the
market, while all around the new cotton crop
was just sprouting from the carefully-leveled and
ridged fields. Happy Egypt, in these days of
America's distress!

11*th*. In the night we dropped down to the
landing-place opposite Damiane; and in the
morning, before it was yet light, were awakened
by the vociferous screams and quarrels of the
pilgrims, who, the day before, and during the
night, had reached this stage of the journey, and
were now preparing for the land-journey of
three hours to the convent. Such a scene of noise
and confusion as is the first morning of starting
of an Eastern caravan, when all the bargains are
to be made and the loads proportioned and arranged, cannot be described nor imagined; it
must be seen. We, too, secured our animals,
and a little after sunrise were all in motion—
and a picturesque cavalcade we were—camels,
horses, mules and asses, about sixty in number,
and laden with towering loads of tents, boxes,
beds, and all the paraphernalia of kitchen furniture, and surmounted by a motley crowd, men
and women, boys and girls, and tender infants—
white, black and copper-colored, and all, released from the toils and confinement of the
town, and, with the great feast in prospect, in
high and exuberant spirits.

The convent soon loomed up before us, yet

eight or ten miles distant, appearing with its
white walls like a marble castle standing in the
midst of a wide-spread lake formed by the de-
ceitful waters of the mirage. I have never seen
this phenomenon so perfect as during those few
days on this plain. It seemed quite impossible
to believe it a pure illusion, and I often found
myself half determined to start off for a bath and
a sail. We tried to stir up our weary animals,
but neither they nor their drivers had a mind to
leave the caravan. Finally we reached our des-
tination, and found our man with the tent and
boxes of books awaiting us. We immediately
commenced setting up the former, but were
much vexed to find that, notwithstanding our
strict charges to our friends at Alexandria to
send it to us all right, one of its sides was wanting, and so we were left to broil by day and
freeze by night, like Jacob with the flocks of
Laban—a process which, after three days, made
it necessary for me to leave in the midst of the
feast.

After arranging as well as we could our temporary habitation, we went up to see the Sitt
and the Reis, or head of the convent, our old
friend, Father Makar. This Makar I had met
a year previous at the convent of the saint whose
name he bears, in the Nitron Lakes. But how
changed! Then, he was a poor monk, barefooted, and with a homespun zaboot. Now, he

has shoes and stockings, and dons an expansive cloth cloak over a silk tunic, and flourishes a long staff. Then, he was glad to walk with me six hours over the desert to the other convent for a few piastres; now, he has come here to swallow his thousands. Then, I found him in our long walk a very attentive and interested listener to the doctrines of Protestantism, and especially to the gospel of matrimony, which is usually the only gospel which brings glad tidings to the monks. Now, he is cold and stiff and distant. But Father Makhiel, who was then the Abbot of his convent, and he his factotum, has since been made Patriarch and occupies the throne of St. Mark, and as his most tried and trusty man has sent him here as Reis of the convent to work this rich mine of wealth.

The convent is a high inclosure about one hundred paces square, surmounted by numerous small domes which form the roof; and it is accounted one of the wonders of the Sitt that no man can count them—that is to say, no two men can agree as to the number; one making them one hundred and fifty, and another more or less. In this inclosure is, first, a small open court, then a good-sized church with numerous other smaller chapels, and the rooms of the monks, of whom only three now remain here. Every thing is dirty and untidy and out of repair, as it must needs be to be Coptic.

33*

To the left of the dark passage leading into the church is a small room about twelve feet square, surmounted by a dome, and lighted by two apertures about a foot square, one opening to the north and the other to the east. Here are witnessed those miracles of the Sitt, which draw together these crowds of people from all parts of Egypt. The northern aperture opens upon a low roof several feet below it, and ten or fifteen feet wide, and in front of this are several upper rooms which, during the feast, are let to visitors. These, passing to and fro, cast their inverted shadows upon the sides of the dome within on the principle of the *camera obscura*, while the expectant worshipers within, who constantly crowd the room almost to suffocation, invoke, with loud cries and upstretched hands, at each appearance of the apparitions, their favorite saints: " O Sitt Damiane, defender of the two seas and the two lands, preserve the children and save them!" " O Mary, most blessed Mother of God, regard us!" " O Saint George, thou mighty warrior, help!" " O Father of the two swords, heal us!" and so on to the end of the calendar. (I may remark in passing that the " Father of the two swords" is the saint who has under his special care the votaries of Venice.) Such a scene of blind superstition as that room constantly presented I never before witnessed.

When we reached the convent we found only

thirty or forty tents. They mostly belonged to
tradesmen, who, like ourselves, had come early
to secure a position. The number of those who
had brought their barrels of wine and great
demijohns of arrack, and had already so tempt-
ingly arranged their many-colored bottles in their
booths, gave promise of lively times. Within
the court of the convent were a few choice shops,
and we found we were in time for just the one
we wished beside the church door, the price of
which had been too high for those who preceded
us. Awid, however, with his usual business
tact, secured possession for four dollars, which
he insisted was sufficient hire for the week,
though our friend Makar insisted as stoutly that
it was only the pledge to nail the bargain, and
that the full rent must be forthcoming at the
end of the week. Awid, however, carried his
point; for he maintained that, in selling Bibles
and religious books, we were doing the work of
the Church, which they should do, and therefore
they should give us the shop free. And truly
four dollars seemed enough for a little open stall
three feet by four, which could boast of nothing
but its position; for there every person who
visited the Sitt or entered the church must pass,
and almost step over us and our books. But
this bargain was only a specimen of the system
of gouging which was there carried on. Six
piastres for a water-jar, and eleven for a small

tent mat, of which hundreds were needed by the
visitors, and other things in proportion; the full
price of the article charged for its hire for a week,
and this year after year! One would think they
would be satisfied with the thousands which
come in as regular fees for priestly services
done, and votive offerings, and that they would
exercise the famous Egyptian hospitality in these
smaller matters. But this is a great money-
making institution, and it must be worked to
the utmost.

This piece of business finished, we returned to
our tent for the evening, where we found Barsum, a friend of Awid, from Mansoura, who had
at last year's Mulid bravely stood by Awid in a
hard-fought battle about the truth of the phantoms in the chamber of imagery, in which Awid's
infidelity cost him a sound beating. Barsum is
a noble, intelligent and pious man—one of the
princes who should "come out of Egypt." He
stuck to us through our three days' battle, and
each evening he invited us to dine and spend the
evening with him, where we enjoyed the opportunity of speaking the Word to many of his circle
of acquaintance.

The next morning we commenced work in
our little shop, and as the crowds were now
coming in we were kept busy enough. As I
usually find that the more I have to work the
less I write, my notes of these three days of

hard work are very scanty, and I must fill up
the brief outline chiefly from memory. My plan
was to spend the forenoon and part of the afternoon at the shop, helping Awid. Then, when
the reclining sun gave me a shady spot beside
our tent, I went down, and, spreading our mats,
a small audience of passers-by, of whom Barsum
and his friends usually formed the nucleus, gathered together, and I spent an hour reading and
talking to them, and then in the evening in Barsum's large tent. Occasionally, too, I would
retire from the sultry heat and exciting discussions of the shop to the seething suffocation of
the phantom-room to witness what was going
on there, and then to the church, whose high
arches furnished a delightfully cool retreat, where
I would sit awhile on a mat and refresh myself
while viewing the doings of those who came
there to pay their vows and offer their devotions
to the Sitt. I will try to convey some idea of
what was going on at each of these places.

First, at the book-shop. We were almost
constantly surrounded by a circle, who were
purchasing or reading our books. The Copts,
before buying, usually wish to dip here and there
pretty deeply into a book to see if it is orthodox
doctrine. This, when one is in a hurry, is a great
vexation; for they are never in a hurry, and will
not be pressed. When one has time enough it
is profitable; for these readings often bring up

passages which call for explanation and lead to discussions, and thus there is never any lack of a text and a subject. One never need come to these encounters with any set speech, for it cannot be foreseen what direction the discussion will take. A warm heart, a ready tongue, an intimate acquaintance with the prejudices and notions of those addressed, and a fund of Scripture proofs always at hand—these are the requisites for success in this work. We had two of our men from the boat with us. One of these we left at the tent to guard the stuff and make provision for our bodily wants, and the other we sent around among the tents with a bag of books, and he had good success in selling to those who did not come up to the church, or did not wish to purchase there.

Let us go in for a while to see what is doing in the chamber of imagery, the camera obscura, where the miraculous phantoms pass and repass on the wall. It is crowded, and the close air and stench from so many dirty, sweaty bodies is almost insufferable. During the intervals of the apparitions a man, who seemed to have this department in charge, chanted in a low and not unmusical voice the praises of the Virgin and the Sitt; and then, when the shadow comes, he and all, with uplifted hands or outstretched necks, scream out the ejaculations and prayers. When these shadows flitted over the wall the people below put me in mind of a nest of young birds, with outstretched necks, open bills, and chattering throats, awaiting the mother bird hovering over them. Once, when the interval was longer than usual, the man who chanted entertained the astonished group, by relating how, early that morning, he came there alone, and the Virgin and St. George came and stood there more than an hour. He said they looked down upon him as if they would speak to him, but they did not, and he did not dare to speak to them, but stood fixed in his place and affrighted.

Several times, when the people saw that I had no petitions to offer, and made no demonstrations when the shadows passed (there may, too, have been something of incredulity, perhaps of sarcasm, in my countenance), they came to me and privately asked what I had to say of this. I plainly told them that the shadows were produced by people walking on the roof before the aperture, and I also constantly told the truth to the people whom we met, especially in the tent of Barsum; but Awid and I had agreed that we would reserve our full exposure upon the house-tops of this great imposture till the last great day of the feast, when our books should all have been sold. Otherwise we knew our work would be stopped in the very midst, and we thought a little of the wisdom of the serpent in place here.

One day a deranged girl was brought in to have the devil cast out of her. Poor thing! There she sat in the midst of the crowd sweating and gasping for breath, while those around her were constantly vexing her by asking if she felt no better nor different; if the devil was not yet coming out of her, and the like. I am sure if she had had seven devils, or even a legion in her, they would, under such a discipline, have taken their flight for more comfortable quarters. I do not think she was deranged; but whatever may have been her state, this course of treatment must produce some effect. If mad, it might possibly make her sane; if sane, it was enough to craze her. They say that in such cases, when the demon comes out, he leaves a spot of blood on the garment above the place where he makes his exodus. I have heard many strange stories on this subject, but have not yet sufficiently sifted them to expose the cheat.

They said, that not only did the shadows appear by day, but forms of light passed over the wall by night. These, I suppose, were from persons carrying lanterns on the roof. I went up two different evenings, and though the room was crowded with people as by day, we saw nothing; all was darkness. One night some giggling and other demonstrations gave evidence that some Greek lads and lasses, or other interloping Infidels, were forgetting themselves, or rather, were thinking too much of themselves and each other, and forgetting the sanctity of the place, when an old Coptess fell upon them and gave them such a sound cursing that they were glad to retreat.

But we have breathed this stifling atmosphere long enough. Let us go into the church and sit down upon the cool floor awhile, and see what is going on there. The mats are new and clean. The silk curtains before the altars are the gayest and newest of the large store which devotees have brought as votive offerings to the Sitt, and all is in holiday dress, for on the last great day of the feast the Patriarch himself is to perform high mass here; and the picture of the Sitt, surrounded by her forty Virgins, looks less stiff and formal and staring than the stereotype pattern which may be seen in all the Coptic churches throughout the land. Indeed she seems almost smiling upon the worshipers who file along as each of them stops to pay her his devotions. The walls are disfigured by charcoal remembrances, "O Lord, remember thy servant Abdallah!" "O Sitt Damiane, help!" etc., as well as snatches from the Gospel and Psalms.

But here are our friends the priests, plying their money-making trade. Two of them are now sitting before a woman, holding their hands and a beautifully jeweled cross upon her head, while one of them is repeating prayers to cure

34

her of headache. She must be well attended to and thoroughly cured, for she has brought to the Sitt a candle four feet long and two inches thick, which is now burning before her picture. (As soon as the lady left, the candle was put out and set aside; doubtless to be sold to some other devotee of the Sitt wishing to do a nice thing for her, or to be used on some great occasion when all the congregation would say, "See how liberally the priests have provided for their patroness!")

The third priest has a stout young man in hand who has been troubled with a pain in the side. His doting mother stands by, as his side is bared and anointed with holy oil " in the name of the Lord Jesus, and all the saints and Sittna Damiane," and hereafter it will doubtless be well. He has done with him now, and received the fee in cash, and next, pulling down a little open lamp which is burning before the picture, he dips his finger into the oil and addresses himself to the task of crossing with it, upon their foreheads and between their breasts, some ladies who have come to him for the purpose. I trust his heart is in the prayer which in the mean time he is mumbling; but the Copts generally are beginning to whisper among themselves that this is not the business for monks who are under the vow.

This done, he turns to a man who wishes to

buy and devote to the Sitt an oke (two and three-quarters pounds) of candles. The price is twenty piastres (a double charge of course), and the man objects to the imposition, and an angry dispute is the consequence.

This will suffice for a specimen of the doings of the priests. The people are constantly going and coming; and many, tempted like ourselves by the cool shade of these high arches, sit down and smoke and talk. The boys are around playing and fighting and enjoying themselves generally; and to fill out the picture, myself sitting cross-legged upon the mat with my back supported by the reading-desk, and pencil and paper in hand, " A chiel amang them taking notes, and faith he'll prent 'em." On entering, most of the people do the round of the altars and pictures, performing their genuflections and crossings, and blessing themselves by rubbing their faces with the curtains, and touching or kissing the frames of the pictures. One I saw who had a sore eye. He touched the picture repeatedly with his fingers, and then passed it over his eye. I have not heard whether he afterward found that virtue had gone out of the sightless wood to make him see.

I also peeped in in the evenings, when I came to see the bright shadows upon the wall. I found that at night also the church was a favorite resort, as it was not only cool by day but

warmer than the open air by night; small parties were seated here and there upon the floor,
some of them smoking and drinking and playing
cards. I witnessed one act there which was
the most Christian one I saw in all the Mulid.
One of these parties had become rather boister-
ous, and an old woman in the outer department
of the church began to curse them, and ask them
if they were Jews, that they were thus drinking
and going on in church? I think, from her
voice, that it was she who cursed the Greeks for
"cutting up" the night before in the Sitt's room.
When she spoke she did not see who they were;
but she soon learned who one of them was, to
her sorrow; for a young man who, through the
Mulid, had made himself conspicuous by his sil-
ver-wrought girdle **and** fine horse and swagger-
ing gait, sprang out before her like a wild beast,
and asked her what she meant to call the son of
—— a Jew, and dealt her a sounding slap upon
the cheek. Her feathers dropped. She humbly
apologized that she did not know that the son
of —— was there; but she added, "should you
strike an old woman thus?" and turning her
other cheek, she said, "Strike this one also; the
Gospel says we must do so."

And now let us take a stroll among the tents.
They are pitched very closely together and at
random, without plan or regularity, so that one
has to be constantly on his guard lest he be

tripped up by the ropes. By day the men are mostly quiet, sleeping off the effects of last night's debauch. The women and female slaves (and I never before realized that so many of the Copts possessed them) are about, attending to the duties of the kitchen or gossiping from tent to tent. The Bedouins are in the outskirts of the encampment with their flocks of sheep, and, like Israel on the night of the Passover, almost each house, "according to the eating thereof," must daily have its lamb. The servants of the Sitt are carrying up to the convent back-loads of pelts ; for the law of Moses here reigns, and the skins are the perquisite of the priests. Often, too, a choice quarter with the "rump (tail), and the fat thereof," are sent up with the pelts. By night, feasting and drinking are the order of the programme. I have already intimated that Venus is no favorite with the Sitt ; and it is well, or this would be a hell. But **surely** Bacchus must have been her brother-in-law, or some other very near relative, for in all my residence in the East I have not seen so much drinking as during those few days.

But my stay here must be brought abruptly to a close. I undertook this journey, fleeing from the sentence of the doctors that I must go home, and hoping by it to secure a stock of health which would carry me through the hot summer at Cairo. But the labors by day, and

34*

the cold bed upon the ground in the open tent by night, were too much for me, and Wednesday afternoon I concluded to leave the next morning. That night the hospitality **of our new-made friends, made** it necessary for me to feign to eat three dinners, and give offence by declining a fourth. **The** last of the **three was** at our friend Barsum's. **It** was late in the evening, and I was sorry to find him and his friends squatting in a circle in the midst of the **tent** around the arrack cups. I read him a lecture on temper-**ance, or** rather total abstinence, as he had never been free in the use of the article—to all of which he heartily assented. When rising, and extending my hand, I told him that I too was a priest, and had the power of binding and loosing, as well as he who had that day prohibited his brother priest from praying or baptizing, he took my hand, and solemnly pledged his faith that he **would** not again touch the cup **which** was working such havoc around. He had evidently long felt it his duty to take this step; **and** once taken, he felt so joyful over it that he wished **at once to** go **into the** other tent to tell his wife and children.

After dinner, Awid, weary with the labors of the day, went to our tent to sleep, and I went up with Barsum and **two or three of his friends** for a final visit to the **convent. We found** Makar, with his three trusty priests and a few

friends, sitting on the seat without the convent
gate, eating a late supper, after the long toils
of the day. As Barsum, although apparently
convinced of the truth of my explanation of the
day shadows, seemed yet to be staggered with
the report of the night apparitions, I took him
within to the Sitt's room, and we remained some
time, but saw nothing. It was crowded, as usual;
and while there my spirit was so stirred within
me that, notwithstanding the compact Awid and
I had made not to disturb the shadows until the
books were sold, I felt that I could not leave
without at least making an attempt with Makar
and the priests, who had been so kind to us during our stay. On our return we found that they
had finished discussing their dinner and the day's
toils and gains, and were quietly enjoying their
post-prandial pipes and coffee. They bade us
be seated, when, as kindly as I could (and it was
not a put-on kindness, for my heart yearned
over those deluded ones within), I opened the
subject. I told him that he should shut that
orifice in the Sitt's room; that, as he had come
there so recently, we could not yet suppose him
a willing party in the cheat; but that it was
lamentable to see Christ's servants, purchased
with his precious blood, thus worshiping shadows, etc. At first he was much confused, and
pretended not to understand to what I referred;
but he soon recovered himself, and insisted that

the shadows were true miracles, and started off
in the praise of the many virtues and wonders
of the Sitt. I told him, "Very well; if the mir-
acle be true, let us stop up the aperture, and the
shadows will still appear—that the east one
would still be open, and was enough for light
and ventilation." He said, "Do so; stop it up if
you wish;" but at the same time told a story of
a man who one year undertook to stop it with
his coat, and the Sitt burned his coat; I told
him I would risk my coat; and acting on his
permission, I started for the gate, but he called
me back; and then he threw aside the veil, and
stood forth the bold deceiver. He used language
which implied that he knew it was a cheat; but
that it would not answer to stop it up—that the
people would not endure it, etc. In this latter
I have no doubt he was right; that the next day
had the people found that their shadowy gods
had disappeared, there would have been found a
crowd, like that of Ephesus, to cry by the hour,
" Great is Damiane, protectress of the two seas
and the two lands!" and that, were it known
that he and I had spirited away the shadows,
they would have been ready to tear us in pieces.
I told him that I had to leave the next morning; that I had now done my duty in warning
him of this imposture; and that, if he did not
put a stop to it, I could not be held responsible
if I exposed the cheat to the public, and made

his name and that of the Sitt stink in all the land
of Egypt.   He said I should not be responsible,
and so I left him.

When I got down to the tent, and awaked
Awid and told him what I had done, he was
much concerned as to the reception he and his
books would meet with the next day; but I
knew he was, as the Arabs say, "as big as his
position," which, being interpreted, means equal
to any emergency, and that, in case of trouble, he
would have a strong party with him.

Next morning I arose early for the journey,
and found that Barsum had provided a very fine
horse for me.   As I was leaving, I saw that Makar was already up and without the convent
gate.   I rode up to him, and bade him farewell;
but there was an evident coolness in his manner,
and he barely touched with the tips of his fingers
my cordially extended hand, while he for-
mally wished me a safe journey and a happy return
of my visit to the Sitt.   I turned from him,
vowing vengeance in my heart against him and
his Sitt, and planning how I might best execute
it—whether by writing and publishing an exposure of the imposture, or by arranging one of
the rooms in our mission-house at Cairo as a
camera obscura, and inviting the pilgrims, on
their return by way of Cairo to come up and
witness greater miracles than those they had
gone so far to see.   (This I did one year at Al-

exandria, when the pilgrims returned there from
the Mulid, loud in the praise of the Sitt and her
miracles.) **But** what took place there that day,
and **the course pursued** by the Patriarch and
Bishop—the highest authorities in the church—
convinced me that the time for such open war
had not yet arrived. That morning Awid went
up to the shop with just apprehensions as to the
reception he and his books would meet with from
Makar and his friends. He opened and arranged
his wares, but no one came to purchase. He
waited—still no one came. He then shut his shop,
and went directly to the Patriarch and asked
him why he had prohibited the people from buy-
ing books. The Patriarch called God to witness that he had done no such thing; but Awid
insisted that he must have done so, as all the
people had suddenly stopped buying. The
Patriarch then called Makar up, and the matter
was explained, and he said, "Why did not Mr.
L—— speak to me about it, and I would have
suffered him to shut the orifice?" He then
went down and the Bishop with him, and each
of them bought a Bible, and paid the price before
all the people, and then, holding them up, said,
"See we have bought books; come now, all of
you, and buy." There was then a rush for the
book-shop, **and** all its Bibles and Testaments,
and most of the other books, were soon sold.

Barsum's horse took me down to the river be-

fore the sun became hot; and well it was, for I
was hardly in the boat and started, before it
turned to be the hottest day I ever experienced
in Egypt. Indeed, the oldest resident tells nothing of any such day, and had we many such,
Egypt would deserve the epithet usually applied
to it by the Syrians, Gehennem. Not a breath
of wind was stirring. The air was as hot as the
blast of a furnace. A dark, misty haze hung
over the dead waters of the river in which
the cattle and buffaloes were lying, the latter
with only their eyes and nostrils out of water,
which also they occasionally plunged under by
way of driving away the flies, and among them
the men and boys of the villages; the latter, by
their joyous shouts and gambols, furnishing the
only exhibition of life that could be seen, the
cool water counterbalancing with them the
effects of the hot air. The women, too, as they
came down with their water-jars threw them
down, and stripping off their loose robes plunged
in with the rest; and the swallows, quitting
their gay gyrations in the air, were sitting dis-
consolately on the beach, wondering why they,
too, might not bathe. I followed the example
of the rest, and retired to the bath-room and sat
in the cold water as long as I dared; and then,
when I came out, it was but a few minutes until
my mouth and nostrils were again parched, and
my brain as if bursting from heat. The covers

of the books around were twisting and writhing as if in agony; and the flies, attracted by the shade and the scent of the lunch I had brought with me, came in by thousands to vex me with that pertinacious clinging to one which is the peculiarity of the Egyptian fly. The deck was so hot that I could not stand upon it in my stockings; and to crown all, when evening came and I unrolled the lunch which they had given me at the tents—a cooked chicken and some meat and bread—I found it a mass of putridity, and I supped and breakfasted the next morning on a cup of tea without milk or sugar, and a piece of hard tack begged from the sailor; and hard and black enough it was. So much for an Egyptian sirocco. Home and its comforts were eventually reached, and were most welcome; and the sentence was renewed that a more distant home must be sought.

CHAPTER XVII.

CONCLUSION.

By Rev. J. B. Dales, D. D., *Philadelphia.*

WITH all the interest connected with the preceding narrative and statements, it has been urged that a concluding chapter is called for to give a somewhat more extended view of things as they now are in the land of Egypt. And the following is the more cordially furnished, as it is the result of personal observations made during a visit of some length of time in 1862-3, and which extended as far into Upper Egypt as the first cataract and the confines of Nubia, five hundred and seventy-seven miles above Cairo, and seven hundred and eight from the sea at Alexandria.

Deeply interesting as Ancient Egypt has ever been, from its being both in sacred and profane history one of the first clearly-defined and always one of the most eventful countries in the world, yet of scarcely less interest, in all respects, is Modern Egypt to the traveler, the philanthropist and the Christian at the present time. Situated at that peculiar geographical point in which it may serve as the outlet of the great and perhaps best part of Africa, with almost entire com-

35 (409)

mand of the Red Sea and ready access to every
part of the Mediterranean, Egypt is in an admirable position for being yet one of the best commercial countries in the world.   With the Nile
entering its southern border and traversing its
entire length in a broad, rich, deep stream which
averages everywhere half a mile in width, and
fertilizes by its annual overflows and by various
artificial methods, the whole valley, Egypt is thus
provided with a never-failing supply of water
for its population, of fruitfulness for its soil, and
of natural transportation for its productions to
one of the best of markets. The valley of the Nile,
down to a point twelve miles below Cairo, averages about eight miles in width, and is bordered
by the Arabian and Lybian hills that approach its
eastern and western banks respectively, rising
from three hundred to twelve hundred feet high.
Below the city of Cairo the hills and the desert
entirely disappear, the valley widening out into
an apparently limitless plain, and the river divides and finds its way to the sea by eastern and
western branches, which have their mouths
about one hundred and eighty miles apart, forming thus the two sides of a triangle with the
Mediterranean for its base, and giving the term
Delta to the section of country embraced by
them, from its resemblance in shape to the letter
of that name in the Greek alphabet.

The soil and climate of this valley have bountifully fitted it to be one of the most productive portions of the earth. Wheat, barley, beans, flax, clover, hemp, tobacco, cotton, maize, sugar cane, coffee, indigo, madder, etc., etc., grow with almost equal ease and in great luxuriance. Dates, figs, pomegranates, oranges, lemons, apricots, olives, mulberries and bananas are supplied with almost unfailing abundance. Indeed, every thing indicates that under the influence of the proper Christian education and civilization of its people, a well-directed spirit of enterprise, and a thorough and well-arranged cultivation of the soil, Egypt might, in a comparatively short period, rise to one of the very first positions among the nations.

Hitherto, however, almost every thing has been against the effecting of any great or desirable change in its condition or prospects. More particularly—

First. The civil government has been fearfully in the way. For many years now, since the celebrated Mohammed Ali threw off alike the annoying and threatening power of the Mamelukes at home and the oppressive yoke of the Turkish Government abroad, Egypt has been only a nominal viceroyship of Turkey. Customarily, every new Viceroy, on assuming the government, makes a visit to Constantinople, and is nominally invested with the right to exercise his office, but really Egypt is independent of foreign control.

This, however, in no way relieves or improves the condition of the people. All Egypt is in the hands and subject to the order, and even the demands, of the Viceroy. He may exhaust at his will the finances of the Government in projects for his own personal aggrandisement, or to perform the most liberal and oftentimes ill-judged and extravagant acts of munificence. He may lay any town or village under tribute to furnish a given number of men for public work, or amount of money or grain for carrying out his whims or plans, and no man may obtain remuneration or redress. Every person, therefore, and every thing is under arbitrary and unreasoning and unreasonable authority, and scarcely a single incentive is left to any man to make any personal or really earnest effort to improve his condition. Besides this,

Secondly. The character or nationalities of the population tend to prevent any healthful change. The actual population of Egypt it is exceedingly difficult to ascertain. The last census taken by the Government five years ago (1859) set it down at 5,125,000, but this is generally believed to be far above the real number of inhabitants. Sir Gardner Wilkinson, after residing some time in the country, placed it as low as 1,800,000. This, undoubtedly, is far below the truth. Probably from 3,000,000 to 4,000,000 is a much nearer estimate. But the vast mass of the peo-

ple have many things to keep up separate interests among themselves, and to cause that there should be no common ground upon which they might seek individual and universal improvement. Over 2,000,000 or 2,500,000 of the people are Egyptians of more or less modern date and of a bigoted Moslem faith. There are probably from 300,000 to 500,000 who are Arabs, dwelling in the deserts, and who are more or less of the wild, untamable Bedouin character. There are also nearly the same number probably of Copts, who are understood to be the lineal descendants of the ancient Egyptians, a fine-appearing race, handsome in their features, courteous in their manners, and almost invariably employed by the Government as accountants and in the various departments of business, a position for which they seem to have a remarkable aptitude. Besides these there are 20,000 or 30,000 Turks filling the various civil offices, and then there are smaller numbers of Jews, and especially in the larger cities persons from the various countries of Southern Europe and Western Asia. Now, between all these different classes there is scarcely any thing in common. The very cities of Cairo and Alexandria are divided into different quarters or sections in which the different nationalities have their homes. The Turks having the form of power on their side, lord it over the others. Moslems assume from the su-

35*

periority of their numbers and the exclusiveness of their faith, their right to be separate, and, in some sense, over all others. The Copts, from long custom as the employees and dependents of others, seem to feel that they have no special ground on which they may ever assert, or in any effective way seek independence or even elevation. The Jews here, as in all countries, appear to regard themselves as little else than sojourners; and the great mass of the Franks, as all Europeans and Americans are termed, being attracted here usually by motives of gain, are interested only in whatever will promote their object. All these classes have different schools and studies, different pursuits, and in many cases different customs and languages, and different aspirations and desires, and thus can never, as things now are, have any mutual concern for any great or important changes.

Thirdly. The religious sympathies and habits of the people have greatly interfered with any successful efforts at promoting the general welfare. The Moslem religion, which is the faith of at least two-thirds of all the people, is widespread, exclusive, and, as far as it in any sense dare, is rigidly intolerant. The public institutions are under its influence, and as there are no written laws outside of the Koran, which is in reality the great statute book of the land, the interpretation of all law is in Moslem hands and of course is in favor of the Moslem faith. The Copts are about one-fifteenth, it is estimated, of the entire population, and religiously supposing themselves to be the descendants of the great mass of the people of Egypt who early after the Christian era embraced the Christian faith, they sacredly hold fast the name of their Christian profession, but under exceedingly corrupt and superstitious forms and practices. They require the Scriptures to be read in the public services of their churches, but it is in the old Coptic tongue which scarcely any of the people understand. They render sacred homage to pictures and insist upon priestly confessions and absolutions, upon fastings and penances, and a vast round of good works by which they literally "go about to establish their own righteousness rather than submit themselves to the righteousness of God." Besides Mahommedans and Copts, there are also Roman Catholics, Greeks and Jews in small numbers indeed, but helped as far as necessary from abroad, and being zealously engaged in seeking to draw others into their embrace, they are bitterly opposed to whatever would break in upon surrounding things if it did not tend to advance the interests of their particular systems.

Such in all modern years has been the state of Egypt, and under the influence of all these and other things, little or nothing could be effectively done for real and permanent improvement. But

under the orderings of the Providence of Him
who, while, ages since, He declared Egypt
should be the basest of kingdoms, yet caused
glorious things to be spoken of her, when Princes
should come out of her and He would Himself say, " Egypt, my people," the elements of
great and eventful changes are now unquestion-
ably at work.

First. In a temporal point of view, a spirit of
individual and national enterprise hitherto unknown is rapidly developing itself.   Intercourse
with   European   nations,   especially   with   the
French and English, has led the later Viceroys
to be eagerly disposed to introduce railroads,
vastly improved methods of irrigating the country and cultivating the soil, and various institutions by which far higher attainments shall be
made in general education than at any previous
time.   The tendency of all this, though in many
things tinctured sadly with infidelity, and in almost every respect far from what it ought to be,
is nevertheless towards a gradual undermining
of long-established and ruinous, because ever par-
alysing, customs, and to excite and bring into active exercise a spirit of enterprise and a sense of
individual responsibility, which, when rightly
developed, can never fail to be sooner or later
productive of great and most desirable results.
The late Viceroy, Said Pasha, who died early
on the morning of January 18th, 1863, and

the present Viceroy, Ismail Pasha, who came into power during the forenoon of the same day, have each shown much of this spirit. The opening of the Suez Canal, to connect the Mediterranean and the Red Seas with a good ship channel (a work commenced April 25, 1859, and now in a promising way of completion) ; the building of railroads, already in operation 131 miles between Alexandria and Cairo and 91 between Cairo and Suez; and the projecting of other railways up the valley of the Nile, with steamers on its waters and telegraphic lines on its banks;—all these, with the increasing flow of enterprising foreigners into its bounds to help develop its resources, though it be for their own aggrandisement, tend directly and powerfully to change the long-existing state of things in Egypt and pave the way for a far more promising and eventful future to the whole country.

A striking illustration of all this has lately been given by the Rev. John Hogg, an intelligent missionary of the United Presbyterian Church, residing for several years past in Alexandria and Cairo. In a communication to the General Assembly of the United Presbyterian Church at its late meeting in Philadelphia, he says :

" A great change has passed over this country (Egypt) during the last three years. We refer of course to the present and prospective influence on its civilization of the recent impulse given to cotton trade within its bounds, and of the large increase of wealth which has flowed into its exchequer since its granaries were transformed into cotton gins and the merchant princes of the west became commission agents to the turbaned landowners of the Delta and Nile Valley. Thirty-five millions of dollars were shipped in *specie* into Egypt from England during 1862 in receipt for cotton exported from the Egyptian market. The receipts for the last year must have greatly exceeded that amount,* for almost every *fellah* (peasant) in the country has planted two-thirds of his acres in cotton, while the Viceroy and other pashas scarcely planted any thing else throughout their vast estates. The effect has been almost electric. The whole country is now in a state of transition. The Viceroy and Pashas are amassing immense fortunes. Poor *fellahs* who had never handled a gold coin in their lives are now hoarding them in handfuls. Workmen's wages have been doubled and tripled in the course of a few months. The small coins which formerly constituted the principal currency are now nearly out of use, and even the smallest transaction must be made in silver.

"Beneath the stream of wealth now flowing

* A recent number of the London *Times* states the amount at 12,000,000*l* (about $60,000,000).

into Egypt, irrigating and enriching the upper stratum of society, there is an under current which holds in solution elements whose successive depositions seem destined to raise the whole surface of society to a higher level. We refer to the influx of new ideas and new habits of thought and feeling engendered by so much intercourse with the civilized nations of the west and the stimulus given to the native mind by the importation of the latest productions of the mechanical genius of the age, and their application to the purposes of irrigation and agriculture by nearly all the rich landed proprietors throughout the country. The death by murrain of half a million head of cattle has necessitated the introduction of pumping engines and steam-plowing machinery on an immense scale. The revolution has been rapid and complete. Time-worn and stereotyped implements and processes have become antiquated in one year. The *shadoof* and *sakia* have been supplanted by the steam-engine; the primitive wooden plow of the ancients has given place to steam-plowing machinery of the costliest kind that England can produce; a second track of rails is being laid down between Cairo and Alexandria; another has been measured off from Cairo to Ginneh, in Upper Egypt; branch lines are being increased, the telegraph is almost everywhere, and thus a spirit of active enterprise is being diffused throughout the whole mass of society, which may soon raise 'the basest of kingdoms' to an honorable position among civilized nations, and place it eventually on a sure footing of permanent prosperity." All this is very marked and significant. But

Secondly. Our chief hope of changes that will be for good in the best of all senses, lies in the introduction of the Bible and an Evangelical Christianity to all parts of the country. Nor are we without encouraging tokens of this consummation so devoutly to be desired drawing on. Repeatedly within the last thirty years attempts have been made to establish Protestant missions within its bounds, sometimes in reference to the Jews, sometimes the Copts, and sometimes with an enlarged view of reaching all of every name to whom by any means the gospel might be borne. With few exceptions these efforts have not had any permanent or wide-spread influence, and indeed in most instances have been virtually abandoned. Still the work goes on.

In the fall of 1853, Dr. J. G. Paulding, medical missionary of the mission of the Associate Reformed Church at that time in Damascus, Syria, visited Egypt, with a view of ascertaining whether a mission might be successfully commenced in that country. His impressions were decidedly favorable to the undertaking; and, accordingly, late in the following year (1854), Rev. Thomas M'Cague and wife sailed for this country to inaugurate there a mission for the above church. Not long afterwards, Mr. M'Cague was joined by the Rev. James Barnett, from the mission in Damascus, and at length they established themselves in Cairo. Here they early opened schools, visited from house to house, read the Holy Scriptures, and held discussions with the people in reference to the one only system that sets forth a Saviour for the ruined and the lost of mankind. Their progress was slow, but it was encouraging and sure.

Two years afterward, Rev. Gulian Lansing, also from the mission at Damascus, entered upon the work, and was located at first in Alexandria. Here he opened a place for preaching the gospel, founded a book depot, whence the Scriptures might be circulated, organized schools, and ere long was assisted by Mr. John Hogg, of Scotland, in taking charge of the boys' school, and by Miss Sarah B. Dales, also of Damascus, for the girls' school. All these enterprises were well received, and in various ways they have already been productive of good. In many instances attention was thoroughly roused, and as the Scriptures were read and the instructions in the schools were given in the native tongues of the people, Arabic, Italian, French, English, etc., etc., many were made to hear, for the first time, the way of life, and in several cases were led to rejoice in it, while, in the immediate and entire change that was seen in their lives, and habits, and aims, there was a powerful recommendation of the evangelical faith that they had received.

At length, there came to be felt a most painful want of enlarged mission premises for carrying forward the great work begun. Just at that time, through the munificent generosity of the late Viceroy of Egypt, Said Pasha, encouraged by the late excellent William S. Thayer, United States Consul General to Egypt, a grant was made of a large and most valuable property upon the Ezbekeyeh, or central square, in Cairo, to be for ever the property, and used for the purposes of the mission. In a short period the building was thoroughly refitted and adapted to its purpose, regular chapel services were instituted in it, in both the Arabic and English languages; schools, for both boys and girls, under entirely separate teachers and influences, as is required by Eastern customs, were opened. Rev. Messrs. Lansing and Hogg and Miss Dales were removed thither, and a work was begun which, after years of trial, now has been marked with most signal results. Several hundred persons have been taught in these schools. A church, with a numerous and steadily increasing membership, has been well organized. A book depot has been opened, from which, in connection with the one in Alexandria, thousands of copies of the Bible and other evangelical works

have been scattered abroad, and many of these
have already borne precious fruit. Throughout an
increasingly large community the Sabbath is
being more and more sacredly revered, and the
low habits of idleness, vice and sensuality so
common with the vast mass of the people are
being conscientiously laid aside. The customs
that have ever doomed woman to exclusion and
degradation are being gradually invaded, and
prospects are brightening of her being yet elevated to her true place as the companion, the
equal, the one with man. The attendants upon
the mission-schools are becoming proverbial for
their morality, their industry, their purity and
their worth; and in numerous instances, both in
Alexandria and Cairo, and up the valley of the
Nile, parents are expressing desires to have their
sons and daughters brought up under the institutions of the Christian faith rather than their
own, inasmuch as they believe them, in some
way, far better fitted to make those who enjoy
them upright and happy.

Besides the direct work thus carried on by
the ministry of the Word, and by the schools, in
connection with the mission, a great work has
been in progress for some time in circulating
the word of God and other evangelical reading
throughout almost the entire country. A boat
(as described in the preceding work) was procured, and taking boxes of books, as generously

furnished by the British and Foreign Bible Society, the American Bible Society, the American Tract Society, and other channels of Christian benevolence, the missionaries have gone forth in turn literally sowing the good seed. Thousands upon thousands of volumes have thus been scattered abroad. As we, ourselves, again and again saw, scarcely would the boat be tied up at the bank near one of the many hundred villages along the Nile, before men would come, and sitting down cross-legged on the deck, or on the shore, listen with intense interest while the missionary read and expounded in their own tongue the wonderful works of God, often interrupting him with anxious inquiries and with expressions and nods of warm approval and assent.

In this missionary service, now under the direction and sustained by the United Presbyterian Church of this country, there are at Alexandria Rev. Andrew Watson and wife, and Miss Martha J. M'Kown, together with several natives, engaged as helpers in this great work. In Cairo there are now at work, or temporarily absent on account of exhausted health and strength, Rev. Dr. Barnett and Revs. Thomas M'Cague, G. Lansing, J. Hogg and S. C. Ewing, with their wives, and Misses Sarah B. Dales and Sarah Hart, with several native helpers, both male and female. Thus, there is a well-organized, and steady going forth of those who have that word whose entrance giveth life.

With all these changes introduced, and the good elements for effecting them, more and more thoroughly in operation, there seems, indeed, good ground to have hope for Egypt. With every copy of the word of God there goes a power that is mighty through God. Faithful is He that hath said, "My word shall not return unto me void; it shall accomplish that which I please, and prosper in the thing whereto I sent it." As it tends to deliver all who receive it from the bondage of sin and make them stand forth the freed-men of Christ, so it also tends to lift all such up to appreciate and effectually seek after the rights and the best interests of men, even in this world and in the highest and noblest of all senses. With it, then, finding its way by so many means to the hands and the hearts of the people of Egypt at large, how can we doubt that "because of it," even there, "the wilderness and the solitary place shall be glad, and the desert rejoice and blossom as the rose." Aye, as we ourselves have looked upon the office-bearers in the mission church in Cairo, serious, thoughtful men, of noble frame and more noble mien—men, indeed, that in their devotion of their all to Christ and his cause, show that they are really in earnest in what they do, we could not doubt, that under the providence and

by the word and Holy Spirit of God, the way is
preparing, and the day is coming when, as never
before and in ways that shall not give joy in
heaven, God will have PRINCES COME OUT OF
EGYPT!

THE END.

www.ingramcontent.com/pod-product-compliance
Lightning Source LLC
Chambersburg PA
CBHW020900130726
47900CB00014B/1231